A Manual of
The Theory and Practice of Classical Theatrical Dancing
(*Méthode Cecchetti*)

BY CYRIL W. BEAUMONT AND
STANISLAS IDZIKOWSKI

WITH A PREFACE BY
Maestro Cav. Enrico Cecchetti

AND ILLUSTRATIONS BY
Randolph Schwabe

DOVER PUBLICATIONS, INC.
New York

This Dover edition, first published in 1975, is an unabridged republication of the work originally published by C. W. Beaumont, London, in 1922. This edition is published by special arrangement with Mr. Beaumont.

International Standard Book Number: 0-486-23223-9
Library of Congress Catalog Card Number: 75-17363

Manufactured in the United States of America
Dover Publications, Inc.
180 Varick Street
New York, N.Y. 10014

À M.M. C. W. BEAUMONT
ET S. IDZIKOWSKI.

C'est avec plaisir que j'ai salué l'apparition de votre beau volume sur l'art de la danse et je vous sais gré de l'avoir dédié à mon nom.

Composé par vous, qui cultivez cet art non pas avec le froid esprit professionnel, mais avec amour et le sentiment d'un artiste, ce travail ne pouvait que réussir. Comme par moi, il sera bien accueilli par tous ceux qui s'intéressent au développement de cet art, car même dans le but modeste qu'il s'était imposé, il a su réunir, et résumer avec une synthèse claire et exacte tout ce qu'une école, qui s'est affinée à travers l'expérience de trois splendides générations d'artistes, a su créer de parfait.

Non seulement je loue le mérite de votre travail, mais je souhaite ardemment qu'il soit imité et suivi par des ouvrages plus vastes, et que l'art de la danse attend depuis longtemps.

On ose parfois taxer de vain cet art et parler de décadence. Mais de tels jugements ne peuvent être que la réverbération de la profane étroitesse d'esprit de ceux qui ne conçoivent rien de ce qui s'élève au dessus des plus humbles formes d'activité de la vie quotidienne.

Vain n'est pas cet art, qui montre et développe la beauté merveilleuse du corps humain, telle que nous la montre la sculpture dans le marbre, la peinture sur la toile. La danse est un art superbement beau, non moins antique, noble et digne que les deux autres.

Au point de vue pratique elle est aussi la santé et la force, l'élégance et la grâce. C'est bien à tort que la danse est peu considérée par les physiologistes et a disparu de nos programmes d'éducation physique. Fort supérieure sous cet aspect au sport, qui endurcit les membres dans la raideur de l'effort et abrutit l'âme dans une volonté exaspérée de victoire, où il n'y a que de la compétition musculaire et de la tension des nerfs tendus vers le seul but de fouler aux pieds un adversaire ; la danse développe chaque articulation et chaque muscle selon sa fonction la plus naturelle, avec l'harmonie la plus parfaite et l'équilibre le plus constant. En même temps qu'elle élève l'esprit, elle moule les gestes et enchaîne les poses et les mouvements non pas par oisiveté, mais suivant les règles d'une poésie muette et le rythme de la musique.

Encore moins est-elle décadente. Terpsichore, exilée des temples de l'antique Hellade et plus tard passagère dans les salons de la France et sur les théâtres de l'Italie, elle a trouvé de nos jours en Russie ses Templiers, ses Vestales, ses défenseurs les plus dévoués. Ranimée d'un nouveau souffle de vie, elle réjouit encore par sa beauté l'esprit las des humains.

Nulle autre joie ne me touche dans mon automne de vieil artiste que de voir sur de jeunes tiges refleurir éternelle la fleur de cet art.

Hélas ! Pour celui qui ne sait pas et qui n'a jamais vu, cet art paraît peut-être vain et décadent. Il a eu aussi son classicisme et son romantisme. Cet art aura aussi connu l'école du vrai et l'époque bizarre et tourmentée du futurisme; mais il vivra à jamais jeune et immortel, car la beauté est dans le domaine de l'esprit ce qu'est la matière dans l'ordre physique : elle se transforme, mais ne meurt point.

Londres, 1921.

ENRICO CECCHETTI.

CONTENTS

CONTENTS

PREFACE

It is now nearly three years ago since, with the collaboration of M. Stanislas Idzikowski, I attempted to write a little manual which should serve as a simple text-book to those desirous of entering the profession of dancing.

The book is based entirely on those theoretical and practical principles advocated and taught by the *maestro* Enrico Cecchetti. I wish to acknowledge the fact that both my collaborator and myself are under a very considerable debt to him in that he accorded us the fullest permission to describe his famous exercises which have produced so many dancers of international repute. Unfortunately, M. Idzikowski's professional duties called him abroad before our work was completed. With inexhaustible generosity the *maestro* Cecchetti placed me under a further deep obligation by himself affording me every possible assistance, without which it would have been impossible for me to have brought the book to a conclusion.

CYRIL W. BEAUMONT

BOOK ONE

THEORY

Advice to Those Contemplating
the Study of Dancing.

Pause—and think a score, fifty, a hundred times before you devote yourself to the study of the dance.

Do you realise the difficulty of this art, at once so beautiful and so ungrateful? Do you realise how many obstacles must be surmounted before you can become a dancer, even of average ability? Then think of the labour that must be expended, the injustices, intrigues and jealousies that must be supported before you can become an artist of distinction. If you are still undaunted by these disagreeable facts, you have proved yourself to possess enthusiasm and determination, qualities indispensable to success.

Consider your physical, personal and mental qualifications. If you are too young to do this for yourself, let your parents or guardians give their thought to so vital a matter.

Do not imagine that you can become a dancer in six months. Terpsichore is a jealous goddess, and those who seek fame among her votaries must sacrifice at her altar years of patient study and hours of physical labour. Weigh carefully these words, and if after due consideration you still find yourself consumed with a passion for the dance, the first question that arises is the choice of a master.

Now success or failure in all studies depends chiefly on the manner in which they are commenced. It is impossible to devote too much care to the selection of a master, for your career depends to a very great extent upon the qualifications of your instructor. There are hundreds of so-called teachers, few of whom have distinguished themselves in the art they profess to teach. There are some of moderate abilities whose careless manner of instruction tends to develop in the pupil a habit of careless execution which in time becomes so fixed that it is extremely difficult,

15

sometimes impossible, to eradicate. There are others, good theorists, but incapable of practical demonstration. Similarly, there are excellent demonstrators who understand nothing of the theoretical principles of their art. Finally, there is in dancing, as in other professions, a band of imposters and charlatans whose only qualifications are a sprinkling of technical terms of which they do not understand the meaning, a purely superficial acquaintance with the steps of a few easy dances, a grand manner and an unbounded assurance.

Think, therefore, before you entrust yourself to such teachers and thus assist to preserve their existence. Again, do not run to a master because his academy is within easy distance of your abode, because he dazzles your eyes with prospects of social splendours or boasts of aristocratic connections. These can have no bearing on his capabilities as a teacher.

Remember also that a distinguished dancer is not necessarily a good teacher, particularly if he still performs in public, because he may not possess the gift of imparting his knowledge in a clear and simple manner. Again, because he may have neither the time nor the desire to study seriously the good and bad points of his pupils. Lastly, because he may consider his class as a whole and, therefore, is indifferent to the fact that each pupil is constructed differently, both physically and temperamentally, so that each requires adaptations of the lesson in order to supply his own particular needs.

What then are the qualifications of an experienced professor? First, his school—the sources of his own knowledge. Second, his reputation as a teacher and his distinction as a dancer. Third, his personal qualities, he should be conscientious, patient and a good disciplinarian. Fourth, his capacity both as a practical demonstrator and theoretical exponent. Fifth, the distinction achieved by his pupils. Sixth, the number of years he has been teaching. Again, do not select one master in preference to another because his fees are more moderate. A guinea spent on a lesson which results in a guineasworth of knowledge is a profitable investment, but fifteen shillings spent on a lesson which is unproductive is a waste of money.

Having definitely made your choice of a master, give him your whole confidence. Strive diligently to follow his instructions and ponder deeply on the reasons given for the execution of such and such a movement. A knowledge of the *why* and *wherefore* produces confidence and reliability.

If you feel that you are not making progress do not hastily leave your teacher. There is a trite epigram which states that one mediocre master is worth more than three good ones. A mediocre teacher, however limited his knowledge, will teach all he knows. Now let us suppose that you are in the care of teacher A, you are dissatisfied with your progress and pass to the care of teacher B. Now there is nothing upon which a good teacher prides himself so much, as the superiority of his own method. The first question you will be asked is, " From whom did you receive your previous training ? " You will naturally reply " A." Your reply will immediately arouse his animosity towards A, and he will tell you that A's method is of no value, and that the sooner you forget his principles the better it will be for your knowledge of your art. But in course of time you may find that even with B you do not make the progress expected. Again you change your mind and pass to the care of C. In a very short time you will be so confused with the new method of C and the lingering remnants of the teaching of A and B, that you will know nothing of either the methods of A, B or C.

It may be asked, " What is the most advisable age for a pupil to commence the study of dancing ? " This depends on the nationality of the pupil and the country in which the lessons are received. In northern countries like Great Britain and Russia, children develop slowly ; while in southern countries like Italy and Spain, development is so rapid that at the age of eighteen a girl is already a woman. Such an authority as Maestro Cecchetti considers that in northern countries the advisable age for beginners is from nine to twelve years, but in southern countries, from eight to ten years. He is opposed to the practice of training a child before the age of eight for he does not consider the limbs strong enough to bear the by no means slight exertions of the first exercises at the bar.

In your work you will be ever confronted with difficulties, but do not despair, every obstacle can be surmounted by perseverance and assiduous practice. Remember the painter's advice to his pupils. *Nulla dies sine linea*—No day without a line. Nothing is of greater importance than constant practice. It is necessary even to teachers, therefore, indispensable to pupils. No other art demands so strict an attention in this respect, it is only by practice that one may attain proficiency, and it is only by practice that one may preserve it. A brief period of idleness or indifference regarding this essential of dancing causes the pupil to lose what it has cost him so much labour to acquire—his equilibrium becomes faulty, his muscles hard, his joints stiff and his 'springs' lose their elasticity. To repair a week's indifference requires a month's labour, whereas by daily practice the pupil acquires and maintains that nice poise, facility of movement and elasticity of spring which are a joy to the eye. On the other hand do not work to excess, for then the muscles become strained, the joints weakened so that you can hardly stand. Concentration of thought and diligent careful practice, tempered with moderation, are the foundations of success.

Be sure that you thoroughly understand a movement before you proceed to its execution, for the limbs are the servants of the mind.

In conclusion, as your experience increases, you may with advantage study the sister arts of mime, music, painting, drawing and sculpture.

The first will enable you to compose your features in accordance with the sentiments expressed in your dance. The second will train your ear to distinguish the rhythm and cadence of the accompaniment so that your movements will be in strict harmony with the measure. The third, fourth and fifth will acquaint you with the style and manners of an epoch and will reveal to you the beauty of line, form and composition.

Visit the famous art galleries of the world. If this is not possible, study any of the innumerable books which contain reproductions of those works which have inspired the admiration of all peoples of all ages. Seek to discover why these works afford you pleasure. Thus you will learn what is meant by grace and beauty. Endeavour to apply these same principles to your own art.

THE
ESSENTIAL THEORETICAL PRINCIPLES
OF CLASSICAL THEATRICAL DANCING.

I. THE POSITIONS OF THE FEET.

There are **five** positions of the feet :—

- (a) *First* Position (see Fig. 1).
- (b) *Second* Position (see Fig. 2a).
- (c) *Third* Position (see Fig. 3).
- (d) *Fourth* Position (see Fig. 4).
- (e) *Fifth* Position (see Fig. 5a).

Note that in the *second* and *fourth* positions, the feet are separated by the distance of *one* foot.[1] Note also that in the *fifth* position the first joint of the big toe projects beyond either heel. It is a fault for the toe to coincide with the heel, for there is then visible an unsightly space between the two feet (see Fig 5b).

These positions are subject to many variations. The principal of these are qualified by the terms **à terre** (that is, *on the ground*), **pointe tendue** (that is, *with the toe stretched*), **en l'air** (that is, *in the air*), and **en l'air, demi-position.**

When the entire base of the foot touches the ground, the foot is said to be *à terre*. If we speak simply of the *second* position, *third* position, etc., it is understood that the position is *à terre*, that is, with both feet *flat on the ground*. Similarly, if we say open the *right* foot to the *second* position, it is understood that the pupil will slide his *right* foot along the ground to the *second* position, and then lower the heel to the ground (see Fig. 2a).

If, however, we say open the *right* foot to the *second* position, **pointe tendue**, the pupil will slide the *right* foot to the *second* position, keeping the knee straight and forcing

1 When a foot is placed in, or opened to, the second or fourth positions, it is a fault for the feet to be separated by *less* than the distance of *one* foot. But it should be noted that in some movements (for example, *Glissade, Echappé, Sauté à la seconde*, etc.) it is necessary to increase slightly the distance of *one* foot, in order to facilitate execution.

the instep well outwards, so that the sole is raised to such a degree that only the tips of the toes rest on the floor. The foot is then said to be in the *second* position, *pointe tendue* (see Fig. 2b).

Again, if the foot is maintained, for example, in the *second* position, *pointe tendue*, and then slowly raised until the foot is at right angles to the hip, the foot is said to be in the *second* position, **en l'air** (see Fig. 2c), because, though raised in the air, the foot is still in the *second* position.

Finally, if the foot be in the *second* position, *pointe tendue*, and is then slowly raised until the foot is **halfway** between the *second* position, *pointe tendue* and the *second* position *en l'air*, the foot is said to be in the *second* position, *en l'air* **(demi-position)** (see Fig. 2d). Similarly, the foot may be placed in the *fourth* position, *pointe tendue*, *fourth* position, *en l'air*, and *fourth* position, *en l'air* (*demi-position*). The foot may be extended to the *fourth* position **front** or the *fourth* position **back**.

In order to ascertain the position of a foot, it should be noted that the supporting foot is always in the *first* position, hence it is only the free or active foot that may pass to either of the five positions. These positions can be taken by either the *right* or the *left* foot, accordingly as the *left* or *right* foot is maintained in the *first* position.

II. THE MOVEMENTS OF THE FOOT.

There are **ten** movements of the foot :—

(a) *Pied à terre*, or the foot flat on the ground (see Fig. 6).

(b) *Pied à quart*, or with the heel slightly raised from the ground (see Fig. 7).

(c) *Pied à demi*, also termed *sur la demi-pointe*, or with the heel raised from the ground so that the foot is supported on the ball of the toes (see Fig. 8).

(d) *Pied à trois quarts*, or with the heel raised considerably from the ground (see Fig. 9).

(e) *Pied à pointe*, also termed *sur la pointe*, the foot supported on the extremity of the toes (see Fig. 10).

(f) The foot raised in the air and extended as much as possible, with the instep forced well outward and the *pointe* forced well downward (see Fig. 11).

(g) The foot raised in the air and extended as much as possible, with the instep forced well outward and the *pointe* forced well downward and backward, so that the heel is brought well forward (see Fig. 12).

(h), (i) and (j) (see Figs. 13, 14 and 15), are common faults.

Fig. 13 shows the wrong execution of (*f*) where instead of forcing the point downward and the instep well outward, the pupil clenches the toes under the sole of the foot.

Fig. 14 shows the wrong execution of (*g*) where the pupil forces the foot inward instead of outward, thus the *pointe* is forward and the heel backward, which is a fault.

Fig. 15 is a position of the foot that occurs in Russian national dances, but which is opposed to the laws of classical theatrical dancing. In certain exercises Fig. 9 is a fault, above all in the execution of *pirouettes and pliés*.

III. THE STUDY OF THE LEGS.

In the management of your legs, your chief concern must be to acquire a facility of turning them well **outwards.** Therefore your hips must be free so that your thighs move with ease and your knees turn well outwards. By this means the openings of your legs are rendered easy and graceful.

Pay great attention to your insteps. Do not let them relax either in strength or elasticity. The principal use of the instep is to raise or lower the heel. For this reason in your *battements tendus, battements dégagés, battements relevés, battements frappés sur le cou de pied* and *petits battements sur le cou de pied*, press strongly on the *pointe* so that the instep is forced well outwards.

In forcing out your instep, keep the *pointe* extended (see Fig. 11). Do not clench the toes inwards (see Fig. 13), or force the *pointe* forward (see Fig. 14). These are **grave** faults. **Remember that the heel should be pressed forward and the pointe forced backward** (see Fig. 12). Strive to make your instep easy and strong, for the whole equilibrium of the body depends upon it. Again, as you come to the ground in your *pas sautés* (jumping steps), it is the instep which sustains your weight and by a rapid movement permits you to alight on your toes.

The movement of the knee is inseparable from that of the instep and differs from it in being perfect only when the leg is extended and the *pointe* low as in *ronds de jambe.*

Lastly, never try to make your limbs supple by taking them in your hands and bending, twisting and turning them in all directions. There is no need for you to suffer such martyrdom. It may be necessary for acrobats but not for dancers. **The only manner in which to render the limbs and muscles supple is by diligent and careful practice of the exercises described in Book Two.**

IV. THE STUDY OF THE HAND.

There are **three** principal positions of the hand :—

(*a*) The manner of holding the hand in the *Exercises at the Bar* and *Centre Practice* (see Fig. 16). The fingers are grouped together so that the first and fourth are straight while the second and third are slightly rounded. The thumb rests on the first joint of the second finger and presses against the first joint of the first finger. Notice that the wrist is very slightly bent. By holding the hand in this manner during the first exercises, the pupil acquires a facility of rounding the fingers so that they do not point in all directions, a fault, which if persisted in, soon becomes very difficult to eradicate.

(*b*) The manner of holding the hand in *Adagio* and *Allegro* exercises (see Fig. 17). The position is similar to that of Fig. 16. except that the fingers are more open. Do not permit the fingers to become separated, this is a fault.

(*c*) The manner of holding the hand in *arabesques* (see Fig. 18a). This position is similar to that of Fig. 17, except that the wrist is bent a little more. Thus, by keeping the hand in the same position and turning it on the pivot of the wrist until it is palm downwards, the hand arrives in the position for *arabesque* (see Fig. 18b). Note, therefore, that when the hand is extended *en arabesque*, it is always turned slightly outwards and never turned inwards or extended in a straight horizontal line with the arm.

V. THE POSITIONS OF THE ARMS.

There are **five** principal positions of the arms :—

(*a*) 1*st Position*.—See Fig. 19.
(*b*) 2*nd Position*.—See Fig. 20.
(*c*) 3*rd Position*.—See Fig. 21. Similarly, if the left arm is placed in the fifth position, and the right arm placed at a slight distance from the left side, the arms are also in the third position.
(*d*) 4*th Position*.—See Fig. 22a. Similarly, if the right arm is placed in the second position, and the left arm raised above the head, the arms are also in the fourth position.
(*e*) 5*th Position*.—See Fig. 23a.

Note that in the *first* position, the hands are held at the sides with the finger tips just touching the seam of the knickers.

In the *second* position the arms must not pass beyond the line of the shoulders.

Whenever an arm is rounded in front of the body, as in the *third*, *fourth* or *fifth* positions, it should be extended as much as possible (always preserving a rounded appearance), be in a line with the fork of the ribs, and it must **not pass beyond an imaginary line drawn down the centre of the body.** Again when one or both arms are rounded above the head, the arm or arms should be rounded so that the point of the elbow is imperceptible ; and if the eyes are raised, the finger tips of the hand or hands should be just within the range of vision. Finally, when both arms are rounded above the head or in front of the body, the finger-tips should be separated by a distance of four [1] inches and neither hand should pass **beyond an imaginary line drawn down the centre of the body.**

There is only one *first* position, one *second* position and one *third* position, but there is a derivative of the *fourth* position and two derivatives of the *fifth* position (see Figs. 22b, 23b, 23c). In order to distinguish the *fourth* position shown in Fig 22a from that shown in Fig. 22b, these positions are qualified respectively with the terms *en haut*, that is, *high* ; and *en avant*, that is, *forward*. Again, if the left arm is rounded in front of the body and the *right* arm is in the *second* position, the arms are also in the *fourth* position *en avant*.

The three variants of the *fifth* position as shown in Figs. 23a, 23b and 23c are distinguished respectively by the terms *en avant*, *en haut* and *en bas*, that is, *low*.

Fig. 24 shows a very useful position of the arms for *pas sautés*. It is termed *demi-seconde* position. It will be noticed that it is situated between the *first* and *second* positions.

Fig. 25 shows the arms *en arabesque*. If we consider

1 The distance of **four** inches is not laid down as a fixed arbitrary rule, but merely as an indication of what in general should be the space between the finger-tips. There are some pupils whose arms are abnormally short, when the distance may with advantage be increased. On the other hand, there are pupils whose arms are abnormally long, when it may even be necessary to cross the hands. There can be no better example of this defect than the celebrated *première danseuse*, Maria Taglioni (1809-1884), the length of whose arms was so out of proportion to her body that her father, a famous teacher of dancing, taught her to cross her hands. Here, owing to the grace and skill of the dancer, a defect became an additional charm. How beautiful such poses can be will be easily understood by reference to the many prints which exist of the *danseuse* in her numerous *rôles*.

the arms separately, the left arm is said to be extended to the *fourth* position *back*, and the right is said to be extended to the *fourth* position *front*.[1]

Finally there is another position of the arms termed *en attitude*, see Fig. 26. Similarly, if the left arm is raised above the head and the right arm in the *demi-seconde* position, the arms are also *en attitude*.

We have now to consider the principal positions that can be assumed by a *single* arm. At first sight it would seem that the theory of *port de bras* (see Section VI., page 25) prevents consideration of a single arm.

Secondly, it may seem unnecessary to consider the position of a single arm when the designation of a position is applied to a pose in which both arms participate. But there are occasions in the passage of the body from one pose to another, when one arm remains stationary while the other passes through a series of positions in order to take up a new pose.

In the teaching of dancing by practical demonstration the need for a series of fixed positions of a single arm does not arise, for a pupil can easily be taught the pose an arm should take, or the path it should describe. But for the vital purpose of clear and accurate description it is necessary to state the principal positions that can be assumed by a single arm.

There are **five** principal positions of the single arm.

(*a*) 1*st Position*, which corresponds to the position of *either* arm shown in Fig. 19.

(*b*) 2*nd Position*, which corresponds to the position of *either* arm shown in Fig. 20.

(*c*) 3*rd Position*, which corresponds to the position of the *left* arm shown in Fig. 21.

(*d*) 4*th Position*.

(i) *Fourth* position *en avant*, which corresponds to the position of *either* arm shown in Fig. 23a.

(ii) *Fourth* position *en haut*, which corresponds to the position of *either* arm shown in Fig. 23b. An arm can also be placed in the *fourth* position *en avant* and fully extended, as shown in Fig. 25. In this case the arm is said to be **extended** in the *fourth* position **front** or *fourth* position **back**, accordingly as the arm is extended to the *front* or *rear* of the body.

---

1 See Grands Battements à la quatrième en avant and à la quatriméè en arrière.

(*e*) *5th Position,* which corresponds to the position of *either* arm shown in Fig. 23c.

Note that the positions that can be taken by an arm correspond to those that can be taken by a foot, which gives rise to a very important rule, that is (in general), the arms should be placed in the same position as the feet. Hence, if the feet are placed in the *fifth* position, the arms are placed in the *fifth* position, and so on.

It will be noticed that although a position is assigned to a single arm, it is not correct to assume that by placing both arms in that pose the same position is maintained. Consider the *third* and *fourth* positions of the single arm. If both arms are placed in the *fourth* position *en avant,* the pose becomes that of the *fifth* position of the arms. Why? Because as far back as Noverre (1727-1810) it has been a fixed rule that when both arms form a *rond* or circular pose, they are in the *fifth* position. The difference between the *third* position of the arms and both arms each placed in the *third* position is explained by the necessity of having a pose at once harmonious and pleasing to the eye.

VI.   THE THEORY OF PORT DE BRAS.[1]

The position, opposition and carriage of the arms are the three most difficult things in dancing, and therefore demand the most serious study and attention.

It is a common error of beginners to imagine that the sole aim of the dancer's art is to acquire a brilliancy of execution in the legs ; hence they disdain the study of the arms.   [2] Blasis makes an apt remark regarding this subject which we cannot do better than reproduce : " When the arms accompany each movement of the body with exactitude, they may be compared to the frame that sets off a picture. But if the frame is so constructed as not to suit the painting, however well executed the latter may be, its whole effect is unquestionably destroyed. So it is with the dancer ; for whatever gracefulness he may display in the performance of his steps, unless his arms be lithesome and in strict harmony with his legs, his dance can have no spirit nor liveliness and he presents the same insipid appearance as a painting out of its frame or in one not at all adapted to it."

1   *Port de Bras,* literally the *Carriage of the Arms.*

2   Blasis (Carlo) Code de Terpsichore.

The theory of *port de bras* can be understood best by comparing the body to a stick B D held in a vertical position, and the arms to another stick A C placed in equilibrium across the apex B. If then we depress or elevate A B, B C will rise or fall. Again, suppose A C to be pivoted at B, then the nearer we move A B towards us, the farther away B C will recede.[1] (See Figs. 27 and 28).

Similarly the arms must always move in the same straight line.

Endeavour always to make your arms so nicely curved that the points of the elbows are imperceptible. **Beauty of line** is one of the dancer's greatest assets, and want of attention in this respect is productive of a series of angularities that not only mar whatever other capabilities he may possess, but also provoke the indignation and displeasure of the spectator.

VII. THE POSITIONS OF THE HEAD.

There are **five** principal positions of the head :—

(*a*)   Head erect (see Fig. 29).
(*b*)   Head inclined to one side (see Fig. 30).
(*c*)   Head turned to one side (see Fig. 31).
(*d*)   Head raised (see Fig. 32).
(*e*)   Head lowered (see Fig. 33).

VIII. THE MOVEMENT OF THE HEAD.

In advancing across the stage, the head should incline slightly on the side of the foot that makes the step forward. That is to say, if the *right foot is advanced, the head must be inclined slightly towards the right shoulder, and vice versa.*

In retiring across the stage, the head should incline slightly on the side opposite to the foot that makes the step backward. That is to say, if the *right foot is withdrawn, the head must be inclined slightly towards the left shoulder, and vice versa.*

It should be understood that the rules for the movement of the head when the dancer advances or retires across the stage obtain only during the execution of a *pas*. In walking across the stage, whether advancing or retiring, the head should be held erect.

When the dancer faces the audience and with one foot describes a *rond de jambe à terre en dehors*, so that the foot describes on the ground a semi-circle from *front* to *back*, the

---

[1]   This theory owes its inception to Carlo Blasis.

head should be inclined to the side opposite to the foot that makes the movement. That is to say, if the *right foot describes a rond de jambe à terre en dehors, the head is inclined towards the left shoulder*, and *vice versa*.

When the dancer faces the audience and with one foot describes a *rond de jambe à terre en dedans*, so that the foot describes on the ground a semi-circle from *back* to *front*, the head should be inclined to the same side as the foot that makes the movement. That is to say, if the *right foot describes a rond de jambe à terre en dedans, the head should be inclined towards the right shoulder*, and *vice versa*.

When the dancer faces the audience and turns his body to right or left away from the audience, the *head must be inclined towards the side to which he turns*.

In movements where the body executes a revolution as in *pirouettes, the head should be the last to move as the body turns away from the spectator*, and *the head should be the first to move as the body returns towards the spectator* (see Figs. 34a, 34b).

IX.   THE STUDY OF THE BODY.

Keep your body poised erect and perpendicular on your legs, except in *attitudes* when it should lean slightly *backward* or *forward*, or in *arabesques*, when it should lean *forward*.

Throw out your chest, but keep in your waist. Two faults common to pupils are (i) throwing out their waist at the same time as they throw out their chest, (ii.) throwing out their posteriors when required to keep in their waist.

Let your shoulders be *low, well opened* and forced *well backwards*. Your head should be slightly raised with the features animated and expressive. Your head and shoulders should be supported and adorned by your arms and be disposed in harmony with their movements.

In the execution of your steps, let the body be *quiet, firm* and *free* from *jerkiness*.

X.   ATTITUDES.

There are an infinite number of *attitudes*, so that they depend on the taste of the professor or *chorégraphe*. The pose is derived from the celebrated statue of Mercury by Jean de Bologne.

The celebrated dancer and professor Carlo Blasis was struck with admiration on seeing this beautiful statue, and when he undertook the *rôle* of *Mercury* in his ballet, *The Festival of Bacchus*, he introduced a *pirouette* which concluded with this pose. In dancing, this *pirouette* is known as **pirouette en attitude.**

In general, the *attitude* is a pose in which the body is supported on one foot while the other is raised with the knee bent, the arms rounded and the body curved backward, sideways or forward (see Fig. 35).

XI. ARABESQUES.

These are very charming poses which doubtless owe their inspiration to antique painting and sculpture. The name *arabesque* applied to the flowing ornament of Moorish invention is exactly suited to express those graceful lines which are their counterpart in the art of dancing.

An *arabesque* is made by supporting the body on one foot which can be straight or *demi-plié*, while the other foot is extended in a straight line at right angles to it. The arms are disposed in harmony with the lines made by the legs.

There are **five** principal *arabesques*.

First Arabesque (see Fig. 36).
Second Arabesque (see Fig. 37).
Third Arabesque (see Fig. 38).
Fourth Arabesque (see Fig. 39).
Fifth Arabesque (see Fig. 40).

Note that the extremity of the hand extended to the *fourth* position *front* must always be in a line with the centre of the space between the eyes. The arm extended to the *fourth* position *back* is disposed in the same line, according to the theory of Port de Bras.

The arms are always *en arabesque* as long as they are maintained in the same relative position. Consider, for example, the *third arabesque* (see Fig. 38). Here the arms are extended to the *left* side, but as long as they preserve the same relative position they may be moved to either side, face the audience, be raised or lowered, and still remain in the *third arabesque*.

It is obvious that such positions are capable of infinite variation for the slightest displacement of either foot or either arm at once produces a new pose. Choreographically considered, *arabesques* are generally introduced to conclude a phrase of steps both in the slow movements entitled *adagio* and the sparkling, vivacious movements grouped under *allegro*.

XII.   MOVEMENTS IN DANCING.

There are **seven** movements in dancing—

1. Plier, *to bend.* **2. Etendre,** *to stretch.* **3. Relever,** *to raise.* **4. Glisser,** *to side.* **5. Sauter,** *to jump.* **6. Elancer,** *to dart.* **7. Tourner,** *to turn round.*

XIII.   THE DIRECTIONS OF THE BODY.

There are **eight** directions of the body :—

(*a*)   **Encroisé en avant.** (see Fig. 41).

(*b*)   **A la quatrième en avant** (see Fig. 42).

(*c*)   **Ecarté** (see Fig. 43).

(*d*)   **Effacé** (see Fig. 44).

(*e*)   **A la seconde** (see Fig. 45).

(*f*)   **Epaulé** (see Fig. 46).

(*g*)   **A la quatrième en arrière** (see Fig. 47).

(*h*)   **Encroisé en arrière** (see Fig. 48).

Plate I.

Fig. 1. *First* position of the feet.

,, 2a. *Second* position of the feet.

,, 3. *Third* position of the feet.

,, 4. *Fourth* position of the feet (side view).

Plate I.

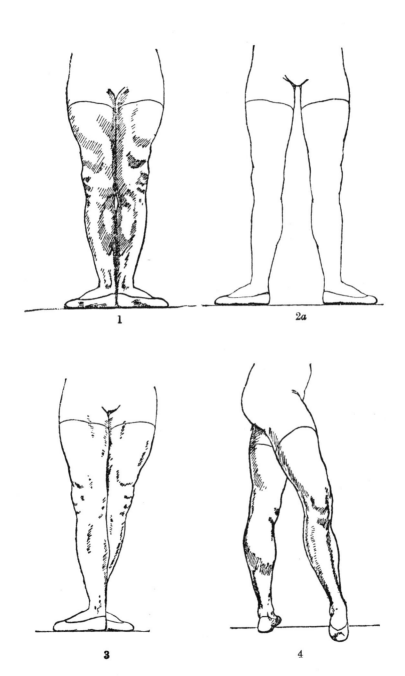

1

2a

3

4

PLATE II.

Fig. 2b. *Right* foot opened to the *second* position, *pointe tendue*.

„ 2c. *Right* foot opened to the *second* position, *en l'air*.

„ 2d. *Right* foot opened to the *second* position, *en l'air* (*demi-position*).

„ 5a. *Fifth* position of the feet.

„ 5b Defective *fifth* position of the feet.

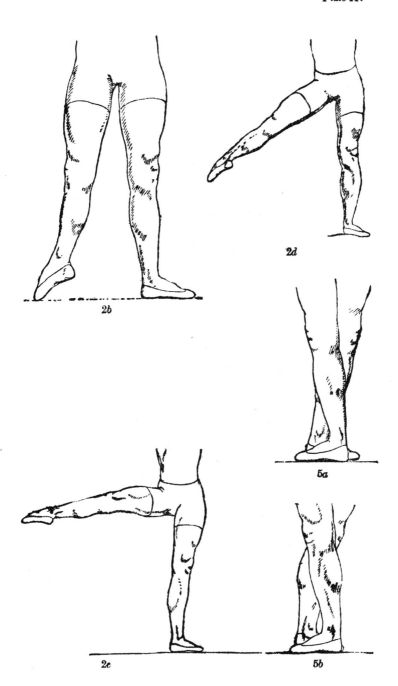

Plate II.

2b

2d

5a

2c

5b

PLATE III.

Fig. 6   *Pied à terre.*

,,   7   *Pied à quart.*

,,   8   *Pied à demi*, also termed *sur la demi-pointe.*

,,   9   *Pied à trois quarts.*

,, 10   *Pied à pointe*, also termed *sur la pointe.*

,, 11   Showing the foot raised in the air and extended as much as possible, with the instep forced well outward and the *pointe* forced well downward.

,, 12   Showing the foot raised in the air and extended as much as possible, with the instep forced well outward and the *pointe* forced well downward and backward, so that the heel is brought well forward.

,, 13   Shows the incorrect execution of Fig. 11.

,, 14   Shows the incorrect execution of Fig. 12.

,, 15   Shows a position of the foot that occurs in Russian and Chinese national dances, but which is opposed to the laws of classical theatrical dancing.

Plate III.

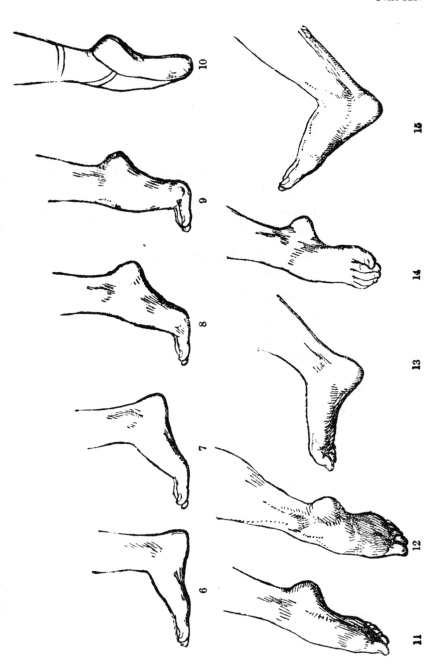

Plate IV.

Plate IV.

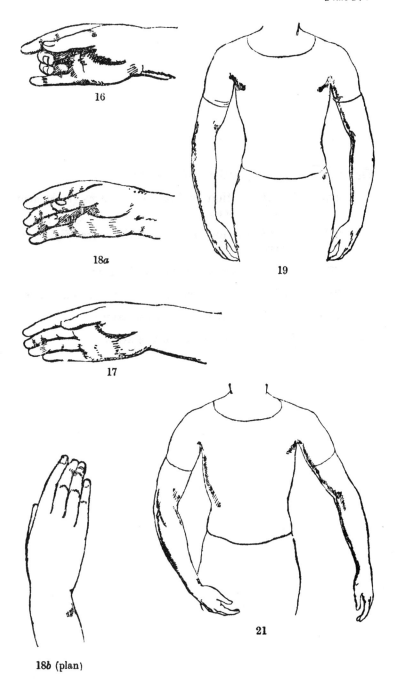

16

18*a*

19

17

18*b* (plan)

21

PLATE V.

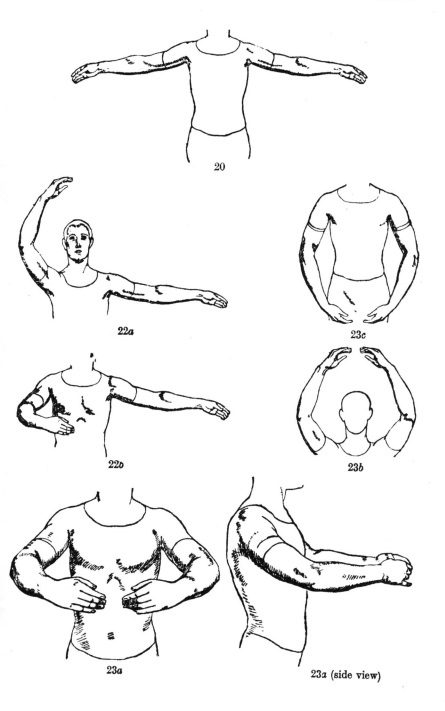

Plate V.

20

22a

22b

23c

23b

23a

23a (side view)

PLATE VI. .

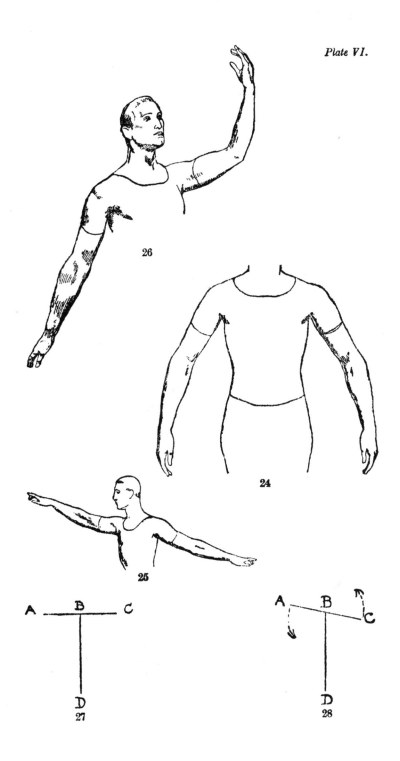

Plate VI.

26

24

25

A _____ B _____ C

D

27

A _____ B _____ C

D

28

PLATE VII.

Plate *VII*

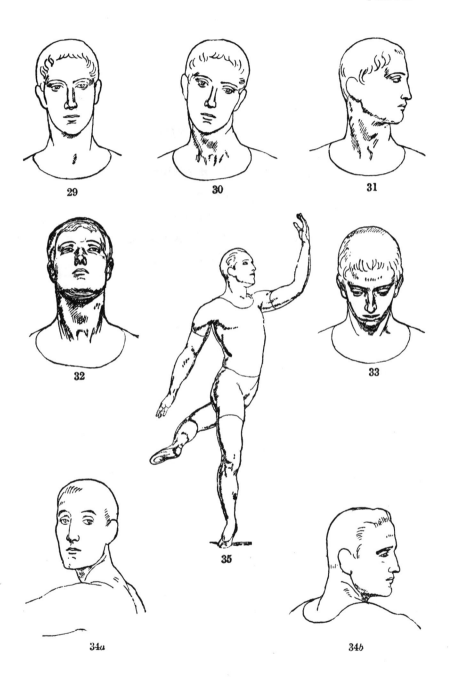

29

30

31

32

33

34a

35

34b

Plate VIII.

Plate VIII.

36   37

38

39   40

PLATE IX.

Fig. 41   Position of the dancer in the direction of the body termed *encroisé en avant*.

„   42   Position of the dancer in the direction of the body termed *à la quatrième en avant*.

„   43   Position of the body in the direction of the body termed *ecarté*.

„   44   Position of the body in the direction of the body termed *effacé*.

Plate IX.

41

42

43

44

Plate X.

45

46

47

48

BOOK TWO

PRACTICE

PART I.

EXERCISES AT THE BAR

These are a group of exercises in which the pupil derives assistance in the support of his body and the maintenance of his equilibrium by clasping a bar with one hand. Generally the bar is of wood, and is fixed to the walls of the practice room in a horizontal position at a distance of about three feet six inches from the floor. In some schools there are two or three such bars set horizontally at different distances from the floor, in order to accommodate the varying heights of the pupils.

The *Exercises at the Bar* can be simple or varied to an infinite degree. In general, they include the following movements, which are mentioned in their order of execution :—

(a) *Plier in the Five Positions of the Feet.*

(b) *Grands Battements à la Quatrième en avant, en l'air.*
    à la Seconde, en l'air.
    à la Quatrième en arrière, en l'air.

(c) *Battements Tendus.*

(d) *Battements Dégagés.*

(e) *Battements Relevés.*

(f) *Ronds de Jambe à Terre en Dehors et en Dedans.*

(g) *Battements Frappés sur le cou de pied.*

(h) *Petits Battements sur le cou de pied.*

(i) *Ronds de Jambe en l'air en Dehors et en Dedans.*

Of what use are these exercises ? *Pliés* perfect the equilibrium and render the joints and muscles soft and pliable. If you were to pass to the execution of *grands battements* without first executing *pliés*, your muscles would be stiff and hard, so that the sudden stretching of the leg would produce a strain, and perhaps even cause you still more serious injury.

A Manual of Classical Dancing

Grands Battements serve to make the hips free and easy.

Battements Tendus serve to stretch and strengthen the muscles, to force the insteps well outwards, and to enable you to slide out and return your foot in the same straight line.

Battements Dégagés serve to render supple the insteps, to strengthen the toes, and to strengthen and render elastic the muscles so that you may attain a good *elevation*, that is, the power to jump high in the air.

Battements Relevés serve to render supple the insteps.

Ronds de Jambe à Terre serve to enable you to turn your leg well outwards, to keep the point of the toe well back and the heel well forward.

Battements Frappés sur le cou de pied serve to strengthen the insteps, to strengthen the toes, and to strengthen and render elastic the muscles, so that you may attain a good *elevation*.

Petits Battements sur le cou de pied serve to render facile and brilliant your *entrechats* and those movements comprised in *batterie*.

Ronds de Jambe en l'air serve to make the knees easy and supple.

Thus, having explained the individual use of each exercise, it will be seen that the *Exercises at the Bar* and *Centre Practice*—which is the same series of exercises performed without the aid of the bar—are to the dancer what scales and arpeggios are to the musician. The professional musician devotes every day one, two, or more hours to the practising of scales and arpeggios. You must practise your exercises in the same manner, but take care that you execute them conscientiously and with precision, for it is these qualities which ennoble your labours and at the same time fit you to dance with ease and grace. Remember always that it is of far greater importance to execute ten movements correctly than to execute a hundred in a careless or slovenly manner.

Do not hurry through the first exercises under the false impression that any mistakes may be corrected later. It is far easier at first to execute properly a movement, than to attempt to correct it later, when the muscles have become accustomed to lax and careless movements.

It will be noticed that we have carefully avoided stating how many times an exercise should be performed. In many schools there exists a curriculum, followed to the letter, by which every day the members of the class perform so many of this step, so many of that movement, without any regard to the individual age, construction, and disposition of the pupils. Nothing could be worse or better calculated to spoil a pupil's career.

A good professor, immediately on receiving a new pupil, will take care to make himself thoroughly acquainted with his or her physical construction and natural disposition.

Very few persons possess entirely straight legs, and consequently very few find it easy to hold them straight. Such persons may be divided into two classes—(*a*) those who, when they stand in the *first* position, find that their knee joints touch or nearly touch, their calves closely touch, and their heels are separated. Such a formation of the legs is termed **jarreté** (literally, *gartered*). (*b*) Those who, when they stand in the *first* position, find that though their heels touch, there is a space between their knee joints. Such a condition of the legs is termed **arqué** (literally, *arched*). Pupils of the first class have generally strongly built frames, and must therefore exercise their knees, their hips, and their insteps scores of times in order to render them easy and supple. Pupils of the second class have generally slightly built frames and a tendency towards " bow-leggedness," and are consequently so weak in the knees that half-a-dozen movements so exhaust them that they are hardly able to stand.

A new pupil may be compared to a sick person. Before the doctor can prescribe, he must understand his patient's constitution ; thus, for one he will prescribe six pills, for another a single pill will suffice. So it is with dancing. A good professor will decide how many *pliés, battements,* etc., the pupil shall execute daily, according to his knowledge of the physical merits and defects of the pupil.

Finally, when you commence your *Exercises at the Bar,* and throughout all your lessons, we counsel you never to make use of a mirror in order to ascertain your appearance. It is impossible to see yourself in a mirror except when you are exactly facing it, and if your head is upright, as it should be, it is possible to see only the reflection of your features and a portion of the upper part of your body. If you try to see the reflection of the lower part of your body, your head must be inclined downwards, which is a fault. Again, if you turn your head or body ever so slightly to right or left, you will be unable to see yourself, therefore you must twist your head, and incidentally your body, in order to see your reflection. If you continue in this habit, you will develop a tendency to execute all your movements to one side. Therefore, take heed and avoid the use of mirrors.

Do not look at your feet during the execution of a movement. Having once grasped the details of a movement, let your sense of touch inform you whether the position of your feet is correct or at fault.

Take care that you exercise each leg equally, for, as Blasis remarks, "a dancer who can only dance with one leg may be compared to a pianist who can only play with one hand."

PLIER IN THE FIVE POSITIONS OF THE FEET.

First Position.

Stand erect with the head upright and the knees straight. Place the feet heel to heel with the toes turned completely outwards in a straight, horizontal line.

The feet are now in the **first** position (see Fig. 1)

Plier in the First Position of the Feet.

Retain the same position, and allow the right arm, slightly rounded, to fall in the *fifth* position (see Fig. 49). With the *left* hand lightly clasp the bar, taking care that the arm is **fully extended.**[1]

Keep the body erect, the heels pressed well together, and slowly bend the knees so that they descend in a line with the toe. As the knees bend allow the heels to gradually rise from the ground so that the body is balanced on the ball of the toes, or, as it is termed technically, *sur les demi-pointes.* Slowly rise, until the body is again erect and the heels firm on the ground.

This action of bending the knees is termed *plier*, meaning to fold or to bend.

---

[1] Pupils who perform these exercises for the first time are advised to place the right arm on their breast with the fingers grouped as shown in Fig. 16. By this means they will avoid the tendency to twist and turn the passive arm and hand. When the pupil is familiar with the *Exercises at the Bar* and *Centre Practice* he may hold the right arm in the *fifth* position, the fingers grouped as shown in Fig. 16.

Later, when he has passed through the exercises on *Adagio*, the right arm may be held in the *fifth* position with the fingers grouped as shown in Fig. 17.

In some schools it is the custom, during the execution of a *plié*, to move the right arm in a circular direction so that it passes from the *fifth* position—*fourth* position *en avant*—*second* position—*fifth* position. This is a fault, for then this simple exercise becomes an *adagio*.

The **plié**, or bend, may be small (*plié à quart*), see Fig. 50 ; medium (*plié à demi* or *demi-plié*), see Fig. 51 ; or large (*grand plié*), see Fig. 52a, accordingly as the knees are bent in a lesser or greater degree. When the pupil is instructed ' **pliez**,' *grand plié* is understood. If only a half-bend is desired, **demi-pliez** is the term employed.

To be of value, this exercise must be performed with the greatest care. **Keep the heels as long as possible on the ground.** The knees should be **at least half-bent**, before the heels are permitted to rise. And when the heels rise from the ground, **they must not be raised higher than sur les demi-pointes.** Take care that the body rises at the same speed at which it descends, and that the knees are maintained in the **same horizontal line.**

Six principal faults common to pupils consist in :—

(i) Rising immediately *sur les demi-pointes* before bending the knees.

(ii) Raising the heels *à trois quarts* (see Fig. 52b).

(iii) Turning the toes too far backwards. It is better to err on the side of too little rather than too much.

(iv) Not keeping the foot flat on the ground prior to the *demi-plié*, so that the portion of the sole nearest the big toe rests on the ground, while that portion of the sole nearest the little toe is raised off the ground. Consequently, the pupil has a tendency to fall forward.

(v) Straightening the knees quicker than they are bent, and *vice versa*. Take care that the body **always rises at exactly the same speed at which it descends.**

(vi) Keeping the feet *sur les demi-pointes* while straightening the knees, and then lowering the heels to the ground.

Second Position.

Remain in the same position as at the end of the last exercise. That is, the body should be erect, the head upright, the knees straight, the *left* arm extended with the hand clasping the bar, the *right* arm in the *fifth* position, and the feet in the *first* position. Keep both knees straight and *slide* the *right* foot out sideways, along the ground, to a distance of twelve inches, so that the right heel is maintained in a straight line with the back of the left heel. Since the knees must be kept straight, it will be noticed that the foot must of necessity gradually rise to the position *pointe tendue*. Lower the heel to the ground.

The feet are now in the **second** position (see Fig. 2a).

Plier in the Second Position of the Feet.

Keep the body erect and *pliez* slowly. This time the heels must *not* rise and fall with the bending and straightening of the knees, but be kept firmly planted on the ground during the execution of the exercise. Take care that the knees are forced well backwards and are always maintained in the same horizontal line.

Third Position.

Remain in the same position as at the end of the last exercise. That is, the body should be erect, the head upright, the knees straight, the *left* arm extended, with the hand clasping the bar, the *right* arm in the *fifth* position, and the feet in the *second* position. Keep both knees straight, raise the heel of the *right* foot so that it is now *pointe tendue*, and draw it back along the ground at a slight angle so as to bring it in front of the left foot. Continue the movement until the *heel* of the *right* foot coincides with the *centre* or *hollow* of the *left* foot. Since the knees must be kept straight, it will be noticed that as the right foot is withdrawn, the heel gradually falls to the ground. The feet are now in the **third** position (see Fig. 3).

Plier in the Third Position of the Feet.

Keep the body erect and *pliez* slowly, allowing the heels gradually to rise and fall with the bending and straightening of the knees. As the body descends and rises, keep the heels pressed firmly one against the other and force them well outwards.

Take care that the knees are forced well backwards and are always maintained in the same horizontal line.

Fourth Position.

Remain in the same position as at the end of the last exercise. That is, the body should be erect, the head upright, the knees straight, the *left* arm extended, with the hand clasping the bar, the *right* arm in the *fifth* position, and the feet in the *third* position.

Keep both knees straight and slide the *right* foot forward to the distance of *one foot*—with the heel turned well outwards—so that the two feet are now in the same parallel line, but separated by a distance of one foot. Since the knees must be kept straight, it will be noticed that the right foot gradually rises *pointe tendue*. Lower the heel to the ground.

The feet are now in the **fourth** position (see Fig. 4).

Exercises at the Bar

Plier in the Fourth Position of the Feet.

Keep the body erect and *pliez* slowly, allowing the heels gradually to rise and fall with the bending and straightening of the knees.

Take care that the knees are forced well backwards and are always maintained in the same horizontal line.

Fifth Position.

Remain in the same position as at the end of the last exercise. That is, the body should be erect, the head upright, the knees straight, the *left* arm extended, with the hand clasping the bar, the *right* arm in the *fifth* position, and the feet in the *fourth* position.

Keep both knees straight, raise the heel of the *right* foot so that it is *pointe tendue*, and draw it back along the ground towards the left foot so that the *heel* and *toe* of the *right* foot nearly coincides with the *toe* and *heel* of the *left* foot. The first joint of the big toe should project beyond either heel.

Since the knees must be kept straight, it will be noticed that the heel of the right foot gradually falls to the ground.

The feet are now in the **fifth** position (see Fig. 5a).

Plier in the Fifth Position of the Feet.

. Keep the body erect and *pliez* slowly, allowing the heels gradually to rise and fall with the bending and straightening of the knees.

As the body descends and rises, keep the heels pressed firmly one against the other, and force them well outwards.

Take care that the knees are forced well backwards and are always maintained in the same horizontal line.

Exercise of the Left Foot in the Five Positions of the Feet.

You have now completed the exercises on the five positions of the feet, in which the *left* hand clasps the bar and the preparatory movements are made by the *right* foot.

Turn round so that you face in the opposite direction, stand erect with the head upright, clasp the bar with the *right* hand and allow the *left* arm, slightly rounded, to fall in the *fifth* position. Repeat the same series of exercises, making the preparatory movements with the *left* foot.

A NOTE ON PLIÉS.

Remember that whenever a *plié* is executed in either the *first, third, fourth,* or *fifth* position, **the heels always rise off the ground** to be lowered again as the knees are straightened.

Take care that the knees are at least half-bent before the heels are permitted to rise. And when the heels rise from the ground, they must not be raised higher than *sur les demi-pointes.*

In the execution of a *plié* in the *second* position, the heels do **not** rise off the ground.

NOTES ON THE FIVE POSITIONS OF THE FEET.

You have learnt that the feet can be placed in **five** positions. In the first series of exercises the *right* foot was placed in front of the *left* foot, in the second series of exercises, their position was reversed. The feet can be placed in only one *first* position and only one *second* position, but there are two positions to each of the *third, fourth* and *fifth* positions.

Place the feet in the *third* position, *right* foot in *front*, now place the feet in the same position with the *left* foot in *front*. In both cases the feet are correctly placed in the *third* position. To distinguish between the two, the position is qualified with the terms **front** or **back**. Thus if the feet are in the *third* position, *right* foot in *front*, the **right** foot is said to be in the **third position front**, while the **left** foot is said to be in the **third position back**. Similarly, the right foot may be placed in the *fourth position front, fourth position back, fifth position front, fifth position back*, accordingly as the right foot is *in front* of, or *behind* the *left* foot when the feet are placed in these positions.

OPEN AND CLOSED POSITIONS.

All positions in which the feet touch one another are called **closed** positions. All positions in which the feet are separated are termed **open** positions.

Therefore, the *first, third,* and *fifth* positions of the feet are termed **closed** positions, and the *second* and *fourth* positions of the feet are termed **open** positions.

Exercises at the Bar

OBSERVATIONS ON THE EXERCISE OF THE FEET IN THE FIVE POSITIONS.

During the execution of these exercises pay great attention to the movements and position of your insteps ; do not let them relax either in strength or elasticity. The principal use of the instep consists in *the raising and lowering of the heels*. Endeavour to make the instep easy and strong, for upon this depends the equilibrium of the whole body.

In the execution of *pliés*, allow the knees to bend and straighten in a manner, perfectly gradual, regular and free from jerks. Take care that one ankle is not higher than the other.

The movements of the arms should be soft, rounded, easy and free from stiffness.

The *fourth* position is the most difficult in which to *plier* well ; the body must neither shake nor sway backwards and forwards, the toes and the knees must be turned well outwards, while the foot at the rear and above all the knee, must move perpendicularly and not forward as it has a marked tendency to do.

In the exercises on the *second* and *fourth* positions, the weight of the body must fall exactly in the centre of the space occupied by the two feet.

Finally, carefully study each position with the aid of the text and diagrams before you proceed to its execution ; and on no account pass from one position to another without feeling assured that you are thoroughly conversant with its every detail.

GRANDS BATTEMENTS.

Grand Battement [1] *à la Quatrième en Avant en l' Air.* [2]

Place the feet in the **fifth** position, *right* foot in front. Stand erect, with the head upright, clasp the bar with the *left* hand, and allow the *right* arm, slightly rounded, to fall as shown in Fig. 49. Raise the right arm to the *fourth* position *en avant*, and open it to the *second* position (see Fig. 20).

Keep the right arm extended, both knees straight, and open the *right* foot to the *fourth* position *front*. Keep the foot *pointe tendue*, and slowly raise it into the air until it is at right angles to the hip.

During this movement the foot and the leg must remain perfectly straight and be extended to the utmost.

The present raised position of the foot is termed *à la quatrième en avant en l'air*, literally *to the fourth in front in the air*, because the foot, though raised, is in the *fourth* position *front* (see Fig. 42).

Gradually lower the foot to the ground until it is in the *fourth* position *front, pointe tendue*, then slide it into the *fitfh* position *front*. The action of raising and lowering the foot in the manner described is termed *grand battement*. Hence the action of raising and lowering the foot in a line perpendicular to the *fourth* position *front*, is termed **grand battement à la quatrième en avant en l'air.**

For the sake of explanation the movement may be divided into four parts :—

1. Open the right foot to the *fourth* position *front, pointe tendue.*

2. Raise the foot in the air to the height of the hip.

3. Lower the foot to the *fourth* position *front, pointe tendue.*

4. Slide the foot back to the *fifth* position *front.*

Now the details are clear, it must be understood that the whole is to be performed in **one sweeping movement.**

Note.—On no account should the foot be raised higher than at right angles to the hip, for then the exercise tends to become an essay in acrobatics, which is opposed to the laws of the dance.

---

1 From *battre,* meaning to *beat* ; therefore, *grand battement* is literally *large beating.*

2 The fact that the foot executes a **grand** *battement* implies that the foot is raised to a position *en l'air,* but to avoid confusion we have thought it better to employ the verbose but more complete appellation.

Moreover, in the case of very young pupils, such a feat enfeebles the hip, which occasions a loss of strength and equilibrium, apart from the possibility of producing a grave physical injury. In the execution of *grands battements* take care that the body does not twist or turn, or the heel rise from the ground during the raising and lowering of the active foot to or from the *fourth* position *front, en l'air.*

Execute several *grands battements à la quatrième en avant en l'air.*

Exercise of the Left Foot.

Face about, keep the body erect, the head upright, the knees straight, clasp the bar with the *right* hand, and allow the *left* arm, slightly rounded, to fall in the *fifth* position. Place the feet in the *fifth* position, *left* foot in front.

Raise the *left* arm—in the circular movement described—until it is extended in the *second* position, then execute several *grands battements à la quatrième en avant en l'air* with the *left* foot.

Grand Battement à la Seconde en l'Air.

Place the feet in the **fifth** position, *right* foot in front. Stand erect, with the head upright and clasp the bar with the *left* hand. Allow the *right* arm, slightly rounded, to fall as shown in Fig. 49. Raise the right arm to the *fourth* position *en avant* and open it to the *second* position.

Keep the right arm extended, both knees straight and open the *right* foot to the *second* position. Keep the foot *pointe tendue*, and slowly raise it sideways into the air until it is at right angles to the hip. During this movement the foot and the leg must remain perfectly straight and be extended to the utmost.

The present raised position of the foot is termed *à la seconde, en l'air*, because the foot, though raised, is in the *second position* (see Fig. 45).

Gradually lower the foot to the ground until it is in the *second* position, *pointe tendue*, then slide it back to the *fifth* position *front*. The action of raising and lowering the foot in a line perpendicular to the *second* position is termed **grand battement à la seconde, en l'air.**

For the sake of explanation the movement may be divided into four parts :—

1. Open the right foot to the *second* position keeping it *pointe tendue*.

2. Raise the foot in the air to the height of the hip.

3. Lower the foot to the *second* position, keeping it *pointe tendue*.

4. Slide the foot back to the *fifth* position *front*.

Now the details are clear it must be understood that the whole is to be performed in **one sweeping movement.**[1]

Execute several *grands battements à la seconde, en l'air.*

You have seen that the feet are placed in the fifth position, right foot in front. Open the foot to the second position, raise it in the air, lower it to the second position and return it to the fifth position *back*. The **second** time the exercise is performed, open the foot from the fifth position back to the second position, raise it in the air, lower it to the second position and return it to the fifth position *front*. The **third** time, open the foot from the fifth position front and return it to the fifth position *back*, and so on, changing **each** time.

Exercise of the Left Foot.

Face about, stand erect, with the head upright, the knees straight, clasp the bar with the *right* hand, and allow the left arm, slightly rounded, to fall in the *fifth* position. Place the feet in the *fifth* position, *left* foot in front.

Raise the *left* arm in the circular movement described, until it is extended in the *second* position, then execute several *grands battements à la seconde, en l'air*, with the *left* foot.

Grand Battement à la Quatrième en Arrière, en l' Air.

Place the feet in the **fifth** position, *left* foot in front. Stand erect, with the head upright, clasp the bar with the *left* hand and allow the *right* arm, slightly rounded, to fall as shown in Fig. 49. Raise the *right* arm to the *fourth* position *en avant* and open it to the *second* position.

Keep the right arm extended, both knees straight and open the *right* foot to the *fourth* position *back*. Keep the foot *pointe tendue*, and slowly raise it into the air until it is at right angles to the hip. During this movement the foot and the leg must remain perfectly straight and be extended to the utmost.

The present raised position of the foot is termed *à la quatrième en arrière, en l'air*, literally *to the fourth back, in the air*, because the foot, though raised, is in the *fourth* position *back* (see Fig. 47).

[1] In the execution of *grands battements à la seconde, en l'air*, the active foot passes behind the arm opened to the *second* position.

Gradually lower the foot to the ground until it is in the *fourth* position *back, pointe tendue,* then slide it into the *fifth* position *back.*

The action of raising and lowering the foot in a line perpendicular to the *fourth* position *back* is termed **grand battement à la quatrième en arrière, en l'air.**

For the sake of explanation the movement may be divided into four parts :—

1. Open the foot to the *fourth* position *back,* keeping it *pointe tendue.*
2. Raise the foot in the air to the height of the hip.
3. Lower the foot to the *fourth* position *back,* keeping it *pointe tendue.*
4. Slide the foot to the *fifth* position *back.*

Now the details are clear it must be understood that the whole is to be performed in **one sweeping movement.**

Duration of Exercise.

Execute several *grands battements à la quatrième en arrière, en l'air.*

Exercise of the Left Foot.

Face about, keep the body erect, the head upright, the knees straight, clasp the bar with the *right* hand, and allow the left arm, slightly rounded, to fall in the *fifth* position. Place the feet in the *fifth* position, *right* foot in front.

Raise the *left* arm in the circular movement described until it is extended in the *second* position. Execute several *grands battements à la quatrième en arrière, en l'air,* with the *left* foot.

BATTEMENTS TENDUS.[1]

Place the feet in the **fifth** position, *right* foot in front. Stand erect, with the head upright, clasp the bar with the *left* hand, and allow the *right* arm, slightly rounded, to fall in the *fifth* position. Keep both knees straight, and open the *right* foot to the *second* position, *pointe tendue.* Notice that, since the knees must be kept straight, the foot gradually rises *sur la demi-pointe,* then *pointe tendue.* Slide the foot to the *fifth* position *back.*

Execute several *battements tendus,* in the following manner. The **first** time, open the right foot to the *second* position *pointe tendue,* return it to *fifth* position *back.* The **second** time, open the foot from the *fifth* position *back* to the *second*

---

1 *Tendu*—stretched. Therefore, *battements tendus,* literally *stretched beatings.*

position and return it to the *fifth* position *front*. The **third** time, open the foot from the *fifth* position *front* and return it to the *fifth* position *back*, and so on, changing **each** time.

Observations.

This exercise must be performed very slowly and very carefully. Keep the knees straight and **press strongly sur la pointe**, so that the instep is forced well outwards. The accent of the stroke is when the foot is **pointe tendue** in the *second* position.

As the foot passes from, or returns to, the *fifth* position, press the heels firmly one against the other and force them well outwards.

If we consider the movement as being composed of **four** measures, the rhythm may be expressed as follows :—

Count 1, as you pass the foot from the *fifth* position *front* to the *second* position, *pointe tendue.*

Count 2, 3, as you force the instep outwards and press strongly on the *pointe tendue.*

Count 4, as you return the foot to the *fifth* position *back.*

Take care that the foot is always returned completely to the *fifth* position and not halfway as in the *third* position.

The rhythm may be expressed in musical notation thus :—

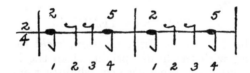

The top numbers refer to the position of the feet at the moment of the beat. The lower numbers correspond to the count.

Exercise of the Left Foot.

Face about, keep the body erect, the head upright, the knees straight and clasp the bar with the *right* hand. Place the feet in the *fifth* position, *left* foot in front. Allow the *right* arm to fall in the *fifth* position. Now perform several *battements tendus* in the same manner as described for the *right* foot.

Exercises at the Bar

BATTEMENTS DÉGAGÉS.[1]

Place the feet in the *fifth* position, *right* foot in front. Stand erect with the head upright, clasp the bar with the *left* hand, and allow the *right* arm, slightly rounded, to fall in the *fifth* position.

Keep both knees straight and open the right foot to the *second* position, *pointe tendue*. Carry the foot out a little further—keeping the toe pointed well downwards—so that since the body must remain erect, it now rises about *four* inches above the ground. Lower it to the *second* position, *pointe tendue*, and return it to the *fifth* position *back*. The **second** time, open the foot from the *fifth* position *back* to the *second* position, *pointe tendue*, and return it to the *fifth* position *front*, and so on, changing **each** time.

Take care that the foot is always returned **completely to the fifth position** and not halfway as in the *third* position.

Execute several *battements dégagés*, passing the foot alternately to the *fifth* position *back* and *fifth* position *front*.

Observations.

The *battement dégagé* is similar to the *battement tendu*, but is executed at twice the speed. As the foot passes from or returns to the *fifth* position, press the heels firmly one against the other and force them well outwards.

If we consider the movement as being composed of four measures, the rhythm may be expressed as follows :—

> Count 1, as you pass the foot from the *fifth* position *front* to the *second* position, *pointe tendue*, and release it from the ground.
>
> Count 2, as you lower the foot to the *second* position, *pointe tendue*, and return it to the *fifth* position *back*.
>
> Count 3. See movement as you count 1.
>
> Count 4. See movement as you count 2.

The rhythm may be expressed in musical notation thus ·—

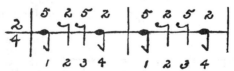

The top numbers refer to the position of the feet at the moment of the beat. The lower numbers correspond to the count.

1 *Battements dégagés*—literally, *disengaged beatings*.

Exercise of the Left Foot.

Face about, keep the body erect, the head upright, the knees straight, and clasp the bar with the *right* hand. Place the feet in the *fifth* position, *left* foot in front. Allow the *right* arm to fall in the *fifth* position. Execute several *battements dégagés* in the same manner as described for the *right* foot.

BATTEMENTS RELEVÉS. [1]

Place the feet in the *fifth* position, *right* foot in *front*. Stand erect with the head upright, clasp the bar with the *left* hand, and allow the *right* arm, slightly rounded, to fall in the *fifth* position.

Keep both knees straight, and open the *right* foot to the *second* position, *pointe tendue*. Lower the *right* heel to the ground, raise the foot again to *pointe tendue* in the *second* position, and return it to the *fifth* position *back*. The **second** time, open the foot from the *fifth* position *back* to the *second* position, *pointe tendue*. Lower the *right* heel to the ground, raise the foot again to *pointe tendue* in the *second* position, and return it to the *fifth* position *front*, and so on, changing each time.

Execute several *battements relevés*, passing the foot alternately to the *fifth* position *back* and *fifth* position *front*.

Observations.

As the foot passes from, or returns to, the *fifth* position, press the heels firmly one against the other, and force them well outwards.

If we consider the movement as being composed of four measures, the rhythm may be expressed as follows :—

> Count 1, as you pass the foot from the *fifth* position *front* to the *second* position, *pointe tendue.*
> Count 2, as you lower the heel to the ground.
> Count 3, as you raise the foot *pointe tendue* in the *second* position.
> Count 4, as you return the foot to the *fifth* position *back.*

The rhythm may be expressed in musical notation thus :—

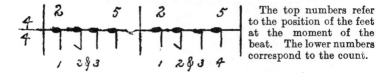

The top numbers refer to the position of the feet at the moment of the beat. The lower numbers correspond to the count.

---

[1] Literally, *raised beatings.*

Exercises at the Bar

Exercise of the Left Foot.

Face about, keep the body erect, the head upright, the knees straight, and clasp the bar with the *right* hand. Place the feet in the *fifth* position, *left* foot in *front*. Allow the *right* arm to fall in the *fifth* position.

Execute several *battements relevés* in the same manner as described for the *right* foot.

RONDS DE JAMBE À TERRE.[1]

Ronds de Jambe à Terre en Dehors.

Stand erect, with the head upright, the knees straight, clasp the bar with the *left* hand, and allow the *right* arm to fall in the *fifth* position. Place the feet in the *fifth* position, *right* foot in *front*.

Demi-pliez on both feet, keeping the heels firmly on the ground. Open the *right* foot to the *fourth* position *front*, *pointe tendue*. Gradually raise the *right* arm to the *fourth* position *en avant*. Since the *right* foot is extended, notice that the knee gradually straightens, but keep the *left* knee bent. Now sweep the *right* foot outwards along the ground so that it falls in the *second* position, *pointe tendue*. At the same time gradually straighten the *left* knee and open the *right* arm to the *second* position. The *right* arm should pass gradually to the *second* position, so that it follows the direction of the moving foot.

Slide the foot to the *first* position; notice that the heel gradually falls to the ground. This is the end of preparation for *rond de jambe à terre en dehors*.

Keep both knees straight, and open the *right* foot to the *fourth* position *front*, *pointe tendue*. Keep the foot *pointe tendue*, and sweep it **outwards** along the ground so that it passes to the *second* position, *pointe tendue*, then to *fourth* position *back*, *pointe tendue*; finally slide it forward to the *first* position.

The complete half-moon traced by the **outward** sweep of the foot, commencing from *first* position to *fourth* position *front pointe tendue*, to *second* position, *pointe tendue*, to *fourth* position *back*, *pointe tendue*, to *first* position, is termed **rond de jambe à terre en dehors** (see Fig. 53a).

Execute several *ronds de jambe à terre en dehors*, but at the last time do not finish in the *first* position, but open the foot to the *fourth* position *front*, *pointe tendue*. Now the foot is placed ready for the execution of *ronds de jambe à terre en dedans*.

1 See the Movement of the Head, pages 26, 27.

A Manual of Classical Dancing

Ronds de Jambe à Terre en Dedans.

Remain in the same position as at the end of the last exercise. That is, the body should be erect, the head upright, the knees straight, the *left* hand clasping the bar, the *right* arm extended in the *second* position, and the *right* foot opened to the *fourth* position *front, pointe tendue.* Describe the same movement as for *ronds de jambe à terre en dehors,* but in the **reverse** manner. That is, withdraw the *right* foot to the *first* position, slide it to the *fourth* position *back, pointe tendue,* and sweep it **inwards** along the ground so that it passes to the *second* position, *pointe tendue,* then to the *fourth* position *front, pointe tendue;* withdraw it to the *first* position. The complete half-moon traced by the **inward** sweep of the foot, as it passes from the *first* position to *fourth* position *back, pointe tendue,* to *second* position, *pointe tendue,* to *fourth* position *front, pointe tendue,* to *first* position, is termed **rond de jambe à terre en dedans** (see Fig. 53b).

Execute several *ronds de jambe à terre en dedans,* but at the last time finish in the *fifth* position *front* and lower the *right* arm to the *fifth* position. To complete the exercise, *demi-pliez* on both feet, keeping the heels firmly on the ground. Open the *right* foot to the *fourth* position *front, pointe tendue;* notice that, since the foot is extended, the knee gradually straightens. Gradually raise the arm to the *fourth* position *en avant.* Keep the *left* knee bent, and sweep the *right* foot outwards along the ground until it falls in the *second* position, *pointe tendue.* At the same time open the *right* arm to the *second* position. The *right* arm should pass gradually to the *second* position, so that it follows the direction of the moving foot. Keep the *left* knee bent and the *right* arm extended, and, continuing the semi-circular sweep along the ground, move the foot to the *fourth* position *back, pointe tendue.* Now reverse the movement, so that the foot passes to the *second* position, *pointe tendue,* then to the *fourth* position *front, pointe tendue.* Withdraw the *right* foot to the *fifth* position *front,* at the same time gradually straighten the *left* knee, and lower the *right* arm to the *fifth* position.

Exercise of the Left Foot.

Face about, keep the body erect, the head upright, the knees straight, and clasp the bar with the *right* hand. Place the feet in the *fifth* position, *left* foot in *front.* Allow the *right* arm to fall in the *fifth* position.

Execute several *ronds de jambe à terre en dehors* and *en dedans* in the manner described for the *right* foot.

Exercises at the Bar

BATTEMENTS FRAPPÉS SUR LE COU DE PIED.[1]

Stand erect, with the head upright, the knees straight, clasp the bar with the *left* hand, and allow the *right* arm, slightly rounded, to fall in the *fifth* position. Place the feet in the position shown (Fig. 54a), *right* foot in front. Notice that the *right* knee is bent and the foot supported *sur la demi-pointe*. Notice also that the side of the *right* heel is pressed against the *left* leg at a point just above the ankle.

That part of the foot that lies between the ankle and the base of the calf is termed the **cou de pied**, or, literally, the neck of the foot. The relation of the *cou de pied* to the leg is similar to that of the wrist to the arm. The *right* foot in Fig. 54a is placed *sur le cou de pied* in *front* of the *left* leg. It can also be placed in the same position *behind* the *left* leg. To distinguish between the two positions, the *right* foot is said to be respectively *sur le cou de pied* **en avant** or *sur le cou de pied* **en arrière**.

Keep the left knee straight, and, without moving the right thigh and pressing firmly *sur la demi-pointe*, slide the foot as if to the *second* position, and then further, so that it rises about *four* inches above the ground (*dégagé*). As the foot rises off the ground, point the toe well downwards so that the instep is forced outwards. Return the foot—in the reverse of the manner in which it was raised—to its original position, but so that it slides *behind* the left leg. The action of sweeping the foot forward and backward in the manner described is termed **battement frappé**.

Execute several *battements frappés*, but in the following manner. The **first** time, the right foot slides from the *front* of the left leg and returns *behind* the left; the **second** time the foot slides from *behind* the left leg and returns in *front* of the left; the **third** time, the foot slides from the *front* of the left leg and returns *behind* the left leg, and so on, changing **each** time.

1 The *battement frappé*, termed *battement frappé sur le cou de pied*, is capable of erroneous interpretation as to the manner of its correct execution. The phrase '*frappé sur le cou de pied*' seems to imply that the active foot strikes the *cou de pied* of the passive or supporting foot. This is incorrect. The accent of the beat is when the active foot strikes the ground, which thereby strengthens the ankle, *pointe*, and muscles of the calf. The striking of the ankle is a waste of effort.

This exercise can also be executed with the supporting foot raised *sur la demi-pointe*. In *this* case the accent of the beat is when the active foot returns *sur le cou de pied* of the supporting foot.

A Manual of Classical Dancing

Observations.

The action of the foot in *battements frappés* is very similar to that of the foot in *battements tendus,* performed quickly, except that instead of the whole leg swinging on the pivot of the hip, it is only that part of the leg from the *knee to the foot* that moves, and it is pivoted at the *knee.* (Fig. 54b).

The *demi-pointe* of the foot strikes the ground firmly as it rises into the air, and returns *sur le cou de pied en arrière* without touching the ground. Take care that the *right* foot does not strike the base of the calf when returned from the *dégagé* position either *sur le cou de pied en avant* or *en arrière.* This is a waste of effort. The foot should be returned quickly but quietly.

If we consider the movement as being composed of four measures, the rhythm may be expressed thus :—

> Count 1, as you pass the foot from the *cou de pied en avant* to the *second* position, *pointe tendue,* and release it from the ground.
>
> Count 2, as you return the foot *sur le cou de pied en arrière.*
>
> Count 3. See movement as you count 1.
>
> Count 4. See movement as you count 2.

The rhythm may be expressed in musical notation thus :—

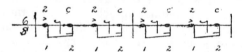

The top numbers refer to the position of the feet at the moment of the beat. C—*cou de pied.* The lower numbers correspond to the count.

Exercise of the Left Foot.

Face about, keep the body erect, the head upright, the knees straight, clasp the bar with the *right* hand, and allow the *left* arm to fall in the *fifth* position. Place the feet in the position shown (Fig. 54a), with the left foot in front. Perform several *battements frappés sur le cou de pied.*

PETITS BATTEMENTS SUR LE COU DE PIED.

Stand erect, with the head upright, the knees straight, clasp the bar with the *left* hand, and allow the *right* arm, slightly rounded, to fall in the *fifth* position. Place the feet in position shown in Fig. 54a. Keep the *right* foot *sur la demi-pointe* and pass it behind the left leg so that it is *sur le cou de pied en arrière.* Now in the reverse manner, keeping the right foot *sur la demi-pointe,* pass it in front of the left leg so that it is again in the position shown in Fig. 54a. The *right* foot should not be moved **more than is sufficient to pass the heel behind.**

Execute several *petits battements sur le cou de pied,* the action of striking the side of the right heel against the **rear** and front of the left leg counting as one. The accent of the beat is when the side of the right heel strikes the **front** of the left leg. The continuous movement may be represented thus :—

1, ti-**tah** ; 2, ti-**tah** ;   .   .   .

ti representing the side of the right heel striking the *rear* of the left leg, *tah* representing the side of the right heel striking the *front* of the left leg.

Observations.

This exercise must be executed with care and as often as possible in order that the pupil may acquire facility and speed of execution. *Petits battements sur le cou de pied* are a valuable preparation for the steps comprised in *batterie.*

Exercise of the Left Foot.

Face about, keep the body erect, the head upright, the knees straight, clasp the bar with the *right* hand, and allow the *left* arm to fall in the *fifth* position. Place the feet in the position shown in Fig. 54a, but with the *left* foot placed *sur le cou de pied en avant.* Perform several *petits battements sur le cou de pied* with the *left* foot.

RONDS DE JAMBE EN L'AIR.[1]

Ronds de Jambe en l'Air en Dehors.[2]

Stand erect, with the head upright, the knees straight, clasp the bar with the *left* hand, and allow the *right* arm, slightly rounded, to fall in the *fifth* position. Place the feet in the **fifth** position, *right* foot in *front.* Open the *right* foot to the *second* position, *en l'air,* at the same time

---

[1] The celebrated dancers Gardel and Vestris are credited with the invention of the *rond de jambe en l'air.* (*Vide Svetlov* (*V.*) *Le Ballet Contemporain,* page 27.)

[2] *Circular movements of the leg in the air*—**outwards.**

raise the *right* arm to the *fourth* position *en avant* and open it to the *second* position.

This is the **preparation** for *ronds de jambe en l'air.* Now, allowing the right knee to bend, and **without moving the position of the thigh,** sweep the *pointe* of the right foot towards and just behind the left leg so that the *pointe* touches the rear of the left calf ; then by a slight movement of the heel bring the *pointe* just in front of the left leg. Now sweep the *pointe* sideways and away from the *left* leg, gradually straightening the knee so that the foot is again extended in the *second* position, *en l'air.* Note that the path described by the *pointe* of the right foot resembles in form an isosceles triangle, having an acute angle at its apex.

The movement made by the foot in the manner described when it traces such a triangle is termed **rond de jambe en l'air en dehors.**

Take care that the raised foot always describes a triangle, and does not—either from carelessness or slovenly execution—swing backwards and forwards in a straight line.

Execute several *ronds de jambe en l'air en dehors,* finish with the foot in the **second** position, *en l'air.*

Observations.

Here, as in *battements frappés,* it is only that part of the leg from *the foot to the knee* that moves, the *knee* acting as the pivot. The accent of the beat is when the foot is in the *second* position, *en l'air.*

Ronds de Jambe en l'Air en Dedans.[1]

Remain as at the end of the last exercise. That is, the body should be erect, the head upright, the knees straight, the *left* hand clasping the bar, the *right* arm extended in the *second* position, the *left* leg supporting the weight of the body, and the *right* leg extended in the *second* position, *en l'air.*

Move the foot in the **reverse** manner of execution of *ronds de jambe en l'air en dehors.* That is, sweep the *pointe* of the *right* foot towards and just in front of the *left* leg until the *pointe* touches the *left* calf, then by a slight movement of the heel bring the *pointe* behind the *left* leg. Now sweep the *pointe* sideways and away from the *left* leg, gradually straightening the knee so that the foot is again extended in the *second* position, *en l'air.*

---

[1] *Circular movements of the leg in the air—***inwards.**

Exercises at the Bar

Execute several *ronds de jambe en l'air en dedans*. Lower the right foot to the *fifth* position *front,* lower the *right* arm to the *fifth* position.

Exercise of the Left Foot.

Face about, keep the body erect, the head upright, the knees straight, clasp the bar with the *right* hand and allow the *left* arm to fall in the *fifth* position. Place the feet in the *fifth* position, *left* foot in *front.* Open the *left* foot to the *second* position, *en l'air,* at the same time open the *left* arm to the *second* position. Execute several *ronds de jambe en l'air en dehors,* finishing with the foot in the *second* position *en l'air.*

Remain in the same position as at the end of the last exercise. Execute several *ronds de jambe en l'air en dedans* and lower the foot to the *fifth* position *front.* Lower the left arm to the *fifth* position.

PART II.

PORT DE BRAS.

In your *Exercises at the Bar* you have learnt the five positions of the feet and those elementary movements of the legs, the varied and skilful combination of which provides the framework for every dance and ballet.

Port de Bras deals with the positions and movements of the arms. Since both arms are active, you will now stand in the **centre** of the practice room, or at a convenient distance from the walls, so that your movements may be free and unimpeded. Now, in order to fix the precise direction in which the head should turn, or the arms be moved, we must consider the walls of the practice room as having **eight imaginary fixed points.** These are the four corners of the room and the centre of each wall. For the purposes of explanation these are numbered respectively 1—4 and 5—8 (see Fig. 55). Hence, if you stand at the point of intersection of imaginary diagonals drawn from corner to opposite corner, the body will face the centre of one wall; while, by standing in the **same** position and aligning the feet on one of the diagonals, the body will face one of the four corners. These positions must be studied with the utmost care.

It is to the Maestro Cecchetti that we owe the invention of this device for assigning to any room a series of fixed points. Just as the circle of a clock face is divided into twelve equal parts which serve to mark the hours, so these imaginary fixed points in the room enable the pupil to execute a dance in a horizontal or diagonal line with a very confident sense of direction. It also enables the pupil to complete a *pirouette* at the point from which it was begun. And when the pupil emerges from the studies of the practice room to display his skill in public, the same system may be applied to the stage. No. 5 is represented by the centre of the audience, Nos. 1 and 2 are the right and left-hand corners of the proscenium frame, No. 7 is the centre of the backcloth, and so on.

To return to the exercises on *Port de Bras*. It should be noticed that in the raising of the arms from one position to another, the *fifth* position *en avant* is all important. It is familiarly termed the ' door,' because just as a door is the proper mode of entrance into a room, or in passing from one room to another, so the *fifth* position *en avant* is the pose through which the arms must pass when raised from one position to another.

Exercises on *Port de Bras* can, of course, be varied *ad infinitum*, and depend on the taste of the professor and the needs of the pupil.

EXERCISES ON PORT DE BRAS.

Exercise I.—Stand erect in the centre of the room and face 2, with the head inclined to 3, the feet in the **fifth** position, *right* foot in front, and the arms in the *fifth* position *en bas*. The direction of the body is *encroisé* (see Fig. 56).

1. [1] Raise the arms to the *fifth* position *en avant* so that they face 2.
2. Open the arms to the *second* position, so that the *right* arm points to 1 and the *left* arm points to 3, **at the same time—**
   Gradually incline the head towards 1 (see Fig. 57).
3. Lower the arms to the *first* position, and pass them to the *fifth* position *en bas*, so that they face 1.
4. Incline the head to 3, and carry the arms—in the same pose—towards 2 (see Fig. 56).

Exercise II.—Remain in the same position as at the end of the last exercise.

The direction of the body is *encroisé*.

1. Raise the arms to the *fifth* position *en avant* so that they face 2.
2. Raise the *left* arm above the head so that it faces 2, **at the same time—**
   Move the *right* arm to the *demi-seconde* position, so that it points to 4.
   (The arms are *en attitude*.)

[1] For the sake of explanation this exercise is divided into parts, but it must be understood that the same is to be performed in **one continuous movement.** Each group of movements is to be **executed simultaneously.**

Bring the head upright and look towards the *left* hand (see Fig. 58).

3. Move the *left* arm downwards and backwards, so that it is extended in the *fourth* position *back*, pointing to 4, **at the same time—**
Move the *right* arm forward[1] so that it is extended in the *fourth* position *front*, pointing to 2.
Incline the head towards 1.
[The arms are *en deuxième arabesque (epaulée)*.]

4. Lower the *left* arm to the first position, pass it to the *fifth* position *en bas*, and then raise it to the *fourth* position *en avant*.
The arms meet in the *fifth* position *en avant*.

5. Repeat 2.

Exercise III.—Stand erect in the centre of the room and face 2, with the head inclined to 3, the feet in the *fifth* position, *right* foot in *front*, and the arms in the *fifth* position *en bas*.

The direction of the body is *encroisé*.

1. Raise the arms to the *fifth* position *en avant* and then to the *fifth* position *en haut*.

2. Incline the head and' arms—in the same pose—towards 1 (see Fig. 59).

3. Open the arms to the *second* position, so that the *left* arm points to 3 and the *right* arm points to 1 (see Fig. 57).

4. Lower the arms to the *first* position, pass them to the *fifth* position *en bas*, and carry them towards 2, **at the same time—**
Incline the head towards 3 (see Fig. 56).

Exercise IV.—Remain in the same position as at the end of the last exercise.

The direction of the body is *encroisé*.

1. Raise the arms to the *fifth* position *en avant*, and—
Raise the *right* arm above the head so that it faces 2, **at the same time—**

Move the *left* arm to the *demi-seconde* position so that it points to 3.
[The arms are *en attitude (encroisée)*] (see Fig. 60).

---

1 The arms must be moved in such a manner that as the *left* arm is lowered the *right* arm is raised in proportion.

2. Raise the *left* arm above the head so that it faces 2, **at the same time**—
Move the right arm to the *demi-seconde* position so that it points to 1.
Incline the head towards 1.
(The arms are *en attitude*) (see Fig. 61).

3. Bring the arms to the *fifth* position *en bas* towards 1.

4. Incline the head to 3 and carry the arms—in the same pose—towards 2 (see Fig. 56).

Exercise V.—Remain in the same position as at the end of the last exercise. The direction of the body is *encroisé*.

1. *Demi-pliez* on both feet and slide the *right* foot to the *fourth* position *front*, **at the same time**—
Raise the arms to the *fifth* position *en avant*.

2. Bring the head erect, **at the same time**—
Straighten both knees and raise the *left* foot, *pointe tendue*—extending the leg to the utmost—so that the weight of the body falls on the *right* foot.
Raise the *left* arm above the head so that it faces 2.
Move the *right* arm downwards and backwards so that it is extended in the *fourth* position *back*, pointing to 4.
Look towards the left hand.
[The pose is *en attitude* (*encroisée*).]

3. *Demi-pliez* in the *fourth* position, straighten the knees and raise the *right* foot *pointe tendue*, so that the weight of the body is transferred to the *left* foot, **at the same time**—
Move the *right* arm forward[1] so that it is extended in the *fourth* position *front*, pointing to 2.
Move the *left* arm downwards and backwards so that it is extended in the *fourth* position *back*, pointing to 4.
Incline the head towards 1.
[The arms are *en deuxième arabesque* (*epaulée*).]

4. *Demi-pliez* in the *fourth* position, **at the same time**—
Bring the arms to the *fifth* position *en avant*.
Bring the head erect so that it faces 2.

5. Repeat No. 2.

---

1 The arms must be moved in such a manner that as the *left* arm is lowered the *right* arm is raised in proportion.

A Manual of Classical Dancing

Exercise V I.—Stand erect in the centre of the room and face 2, with the head inclined to 3, the feet in the *fifth* position, *right* foot in *front*, and the arms in the *fifth* position *en bas*.

The direction of the body is *encroisé*.

1. *Demi-pliez* on both feet and slide the *right* foot to the *fourth* position *front* to 2, at the same time—
Raise the arms to the *fifth* position *en avant*.

2. Straighten both knees and raise the *left* foot *pointe tendue*—extending the leg to the utmost—so that the weight of the body falls on the *right* foot, at the same time—
Raise the *left* arm above the head so that it faces 2.
Move the *right* arm downwards and backwards so that it is extended in the *fourth* position *back*, pointing to 4.
Look towards the *left* hand.
[The pose is *en attitude* (*encroisée*).]

3. *Demi-pliez* in the *fourth* position, at the same time—
Bring the arms to the *fifth* position *en avant*.
Bring the head erect, facing 2.

4. Straighten both knees and raise the *right* foot *pointe tendue*—extending the leg to the utmost—so that the weight of the body falls on the *left* foot, at the same time—
Raise the *right* arm above the head.
Move the *left* arm downwards and backwards so that it is extended in the *fourth* position *back*, pointing to 4.
Incline the head and body—from the waist—to 1 (see Fig. 62).

5. *Demi-pliez* in the *fourth* position, at the same time—
Bring the arms to the *fifth* position *en avant*.
Bring the head and body erect.

6. Repeat No. 2.

Exercise V I I.—Stand erect in the centre of the room and face 2, with the head inclined to 3, the feet in the *fifth* position, *right* foot in *front* and the arms in the *fifth* position *en bas*.

The direction of the body is *encroisé*.

1. *Demi-pliez* on both feet and slide the *right* foot to the *fourth* position *front* to 2, at the same time—
Raise the arms to the *fifth* position *en avant*.

2. Straighten both knees and raise the *left* foot *pointe tendue*—extending the leg to the utmost—so that the weight of the body falls on the *right* foot, **at the same time**—
Raise the arms *en attitude, left* arm up.

3. *Demi-pliez* in the *fourth* position, **at the same time**—
Bring the arms to the *second* position, lower them to the *first* position, pass them to the *fifth* position *en bas* so that they face 2.
Look downwards at the hands.

4. Straighten both knees and raise the *right* foot, *pointe tendue*—extending the leg to the utmost—so that the weight of the body is transferred to the *left* foot, **at the same time**—
Raise the arms to the *fifth* position *en avant*, then to the *fifth* position *en haut*.
Carry the head and arms towards 1. (See Fig. 63.)

5. Repeat No. 3.

6. Straighten both knees and raise the *left* foot *pointe tendue*—extending the leg to the utmost—so that the weight of the body is transferred to the *right* foot, **at the same time**—
Raise the arms to the *fifth* position *en avant*, then to the *fifth* position *en haut*.
Incline the head and carry the arms towards 3.
[The pose is *en attitude* (*encroisée*).]

Exercise V I I I.—Stand erect in the centre of the room and face 2, with the head inclined to 3, the feet in the *fifth* position, *right* foot in *front*, and the arms in the *fifth* position *en bas*. The direction of the body is *encroisé*.

1. *Pliez* on the *right* foot, **at the same time**—
Slide the *left* foot backwards towards 4, until it is in the position shown in Fig. 64.[1]

2. Incline the head and arms towards 3.

3. Raise the right arm above the head towards 3, **at the same time**—
Raise the *left* arm to the *demi-seconde* position so that it points to 3.
Look towards the *right* hand.

4. Raise the *left* arm above the head towards 1, **at the same time**—
Lower the *right* arm to the *demi-seconde* position so that it points to 1.

[1] Refers to position of leg only.

61

Turn the head and body—from the waist—to 1 (see Fig. 64.)

5. Bring the arms to the *fifth* position *en bas*, and look downwards at the arms.

6. Carry the arms, head, and body—from the waist—towards 3.

Repeat Nos. 3, 4, 5 and 6.

Repeat Nos. 3, 4, 5 and 6.

Repeat Nos. 3, 4, 5 and 6.

7. Straighten the knees and raise the *left* foot *pointe tendue*—extending the leg to the utmost—so that the weight of the body is transferred to the *right* foot, **at the same time—**
Raise the *left* arm above the head, facing 2.
Move the *right* arm downwards and backwards so that it is extended in the *fourth* position *back*, pointing to 4.
(The arms are *en attitude*.)

8. Lower the *left* arm to the *fourth* position *en avant* and extend it so that it points to 2, **at the same time—**
Raise the *left* foot to the *fourth* position *back, en l'air*.
Bring the head erect.
(The pose is *en deuxième arabesque*.)

9. Lower the *left* foot to the *fifth* position *back*, **at the same time—**
Bring the arms to the *fifth* position *en bas*.

PART III.

CENTRE PRACTICE.

The Exercises at the Bar have developed your muscles and rendered your limbs soft and pliant, but in the former exercises you have derived great assistance in the maintenance of your balance by the clasping of a bar.

Centre-practice is a group of similar exercises which are performed **without the support of the bar.** Hence you will stand in the centre of the practice-room, or at a convenient distance from the walls, so that your movements may be free and unimpeded. By this means you will acquire uprightness and equilibrium, qualities indispensable to a good dancer.

Turn to *Book II., Part I.,* and repeat all the *Exercises at the Bar,* but, as we have stated already, without the aid of the bar, while where, as in the execution of *ronds de jambe à terre,* the *right* arm was raised to the *second* position, now *both* arms will be raised to that position.

Lastly, do not fail to perform your exercises **daily,** and strive always to polish and perfect each movement, for the greatest artist can find need for improvement in his execution of the simplest step.

PART IV.

ADAGIO.

If you have performed diligently and assiduously the Exercises at the Bar, the Exercises on Port de Bras, and Centre Practice ; which in the art of the dance correspond to scales and arpeggios in music, you have prepared yourself for the execution of those movements collectively entitled *adagio*.

These are slow and very graceful movements, which may be simple, or of the most complex character, yet are so replete with beauty and delicate shades of expression that the manner in which each combination of steps reveals its charms may be likened to the opening of a flower.

The principal use of the exercises in *Adagio* is to develop a sense of equilibrium in the body when it is supported on one foot.

We must now consider the *pas*, or step, which falls naturally into *four* classes :—

    1.   The sliding step, example *glissade.*
    2.   The beating step, example *battement.*
    3.   The turning step, example *pirouette.*
    4.   The jumping step, example *pas élancés* or *pas élevés.*

Each *pas* is composed of a number of *temps*, or single movements, so that the relation of the former to the latter is that of a word to a syllable.   A *pas* must effect a transfer of weight from one foot to the other, subject to this definition it is sometimes possible that a *temps* may be a *pas*.

As we have already remarked, *adagio* is a collection of slow and very graceful movements.   Some of these are *tours,* or slow turning round movements, in which the body revolves slowly on the *demi-pointe* of one foot while the other assumes a variety of positions.   Now and again these *tours* are brought into sharp relief by the introduction of a *pirouette* in which movements are made again by the raised foot during the spinning round of the body on the supporting foot. In order to fix the precise moments at which the raised foot should change its position we must again consider the walls of the practice-room as having *eight* imaginary fixed points.

Each exercise is divided into a series of complete movements, which are numbered in their order of sequence. Included in the same number will be found directions for the movements of the arms, the feet, the body and head, which are to be **simultaneously begun, continued, and concluded.** Again, when once an arm or foot has been placed in the position named **it must not be moved until so instructed.** Suppose, for example, that you are standing on the *left* foot with the *right* foot raised to the *second* position *en l'air*, the arms in the *second* position. You are instructed to execute the following movement :—

1. Without bending the knee, lower the *right* foot to the *second* position and slide it to the *fifth* position *front*.

Gradually lower the arms to the *fifth* position *en bas*.

These movements are grouped under the same number, and therefore must be executed simultaneously. The *right* foot is lowered to the *second* position and the arms move downward in a line with the sides. But if the arms are lowered at the same rate as the foot, they would be the first to complete their movement, since the foot has a relatively greater distance to travel. Hence the arms must be lowered at a slower rate than the foot in order that all the movements may be concluded at the same time

The great value of these exercises lies not only in the grace, skill and facility with which they are executed, but in the sequence in which they are performed. The celebrated *maestro* Cecchetti has drawn up a series of exercises designed for each day of the week, and as soon as the pupil is able to execute correctly the following exercises, he should perform them strictly in the order stated. The table of exercises will be found on page 201.

In conclusion, it must be stated that though by careful study of the text and diagrams you should be able to execute each exercise correctly, it is advisable that at this point your studies be supplemented by the services of a master of repute in order that he may direct and control the varying speed at which each movement should be performed.

These exercises are for the use of pupils of both sexes, with the sole exception that in the case of female pupils —in some exercises—they will rise *sur la pointe* instead of *sur la demi-pointe*.

TROIS RELEVÉS [1]

Stand erect in the centre of the room and face 2, with the head inclined towards 3, the feet in the **fifth** position, **right** foot in *front*, and the arms in the *fifth* position *en bas*. The direction of the body is *encroisé*.

1. *Pliez* in the *fifth* position, then straighten both knees.

2. *Demi-pliez* on both feet [2] and rise *sur les demi-pointes*.

3. Lower the *left* heel to the ground, **at the same time**—
Raise the *right* foot *sur le cou de pied en avant*.
Slightly turn to the *right* so that the body faces 5.

4. Execute a **Developpé à la quatrième en avant en l'air.** That is :—

   (*a*) Raise the *right* foot as high as possible—keeping the toe pointed well downward—so that the toe is in a line with the *left* knee and the thigh raised to the *second* position, *en l'air* (see Fig. 66a), **at the same time**—
   Raise the arms to the *fifth* position *en avant*.

   (*b*) Extend the *right* foot to the *fourth* position *front, en l'air*, **at the same time**—
   Open the arms to the *second* position.

5. Rise on the *left demi-pointe* to preserve the equilibrium.

6. Lower the *left* heel to the ground, **at the same time**—
Without bending the knee, lower the *right* foot to the *fourth* position *front, pointe tendue.*
The arms remain in the *second* position.

---

[1] *Relevé* : from *relever*, to raise.

[2] When the pupil is instructed to *pliez* or *demi-pliez* on both feet and rise *sur les demi-pointes*, the movement must be executed in the following manner. *Demi-pliez* or *pliez*, and as the knees gradually straighten and the body becomes erect, rise **immediately** *sur les demi-pointes*. There must be **no break** between the bringing erect of the body and the rising *sur les demi-pointes*.

In order to bring the feet from the *fifth* position *à terre* to the same position *sur les demi-pointes* or *sur les pointes*, it is imperative to employ a slight spring in order to raise the heels. As the feet fall into the position desired, straighten the knees (see Fig. 65A).

If the heels are raised **slowly**, without a ' spring,' the feet have a tendency to open to the *third* or *second* position (see Fig. 65B), and furthermore, the movement greatly enfeebles and pains the toes.

7. Bring the *right* foot *sur le cou de pied en avant*, **at the same time—**
Rise on the *left demi-pointe*.
Gradually lower the arms to the *fifth* position *en bas*.
When the foot returns *sur le cou de pied en avant*, lower the *left* heel to the ground.
Repeat Nos. 4—7.

8. Execute a **Developpé à la seconde en l'air.** That is :—
(*a*) Raise the *right* foot as high as possible—keeping the toe pointed well downwards—so that the toe is in a line with the *left* knee and the thigh raised to the *second* position, *en l'air*, **at the same time—**
Raise the arms to the *fifth* position *en avant*.
(*b*) Extend the *right* foot to the *second* position, *en l'air*, **at the same time—**
Open the arms to the *second* position.

9. Rise on the *left demi-pointe* to preserve the equilibrium.

10. Lower the *left* heel to the ground, **at the same time—**
Without bending the knee, lower the *right* foot to the *second* position, *pointe tendue*.

11. Bring the *right* foot *sur le cou de pied en avant,* **at the same time—**
Rise on the *left demi-pointe*.
Gradually lower the arms to the *fifth* position *en bas*.
When the foot returns *sur le cou de pied en avant,* lower the *left* heel to the ground.
Repeat Nos. 8—11, except that in No. 11 the *right* foot is withdrawn *sur le cou de pied* **en arrière** instead of **en avant.**

12. Execute a **Developpé à la quatrième en arrière en l'air.** That is :—
(*a*) Raise the *right* foot as high as possible—keeping the toe pointed well downwards—so that the toe is in a line with the *left* knee and the thigh raised to the *second* position, *en l'air*, **at the same time—**
Raise the arms to the *fifth* position *en avant*.
(*b*) Extend the *right* foot to the *fourth* position **back** *en l'air*, **at the same time—**
Open the arms to the *second* position.

13. Rise on the *left demi-pointe* to preserve the equilibrium.

14. Lower the *left* heel to the ground, **at the same time**—
Without bending the knee, lower the *right* foot to the *fourth* position *back, pointe tendue.*

15. Bring the *right* foot *sur le cou de pied en arrière,* **at the same time**—
Rise on the *left demi-pointe.*
Gradually lower the arms to the *fifth* position *en bas.*
When the foot returns *sur le cou de pied en arrière,* lower the *left* heel to the ground.

    Repeat Nos. 12—14.

16. Slide the *right* foot to the *fifth* position *back,* **at the same time**—
Gradually lower the arms to the *fifth* position *en bas.*

Exercise of the Left Foot in Trois Relevés.

Remain as at the end of the last exercise.

Turn slightly to the *right* and face 1 with the head inclined to 4, feet in the **fifth** position, **left** foot in *front,* and the arms in the *fifth* position *en bas.*

The direction of the body is *encroisé.*

Repeat the whole of the last exercise, reading **left for right,** and *vice versa.*

Adagio

GRAND ROND DE JAMBE EN DEHORS ET EN DEDANS.

Stand erect in the centre of the room and face 2, with the head inclined towards 3, the feet in the **fifth** position, **right** foot in front, and the arms in the *fifth* position *en bas*. The direction of the body is *encroisé*.

1. *Pliez* in the *fifth* position, then straighten both knees.

2. *Demi-pliez* on both feet, and rise *sur les demi-pointes*.

3. Lower the *left* heel to the ground, **at the same time**—
Raise the *right* foot *sur le cou de pied en avant*, slightly turn to the *right* on the *left* foot so that the body faces 5.
(The direction of the body is *en face*.)

4. Execute a *Developpé à la quatrième en avant en l'air*. That is :—
Raise the *right* foot as high as possible—keeping the toe pointed well downward—so that the toe is in a line with the *left* knee and the thigh raised to the *second* position, *en l'air* ; then extend the foot to the *fourth* position *front, en l'air*, **at the same time**—
Gradually raise the arms to the *fifth* position *en avant*.

5. Execute a **grand rond de jambe en l'air en dehors.**
That is, keep the right foot extended, and **the** knee straight, and move the leg from *fourth* position *front, en l'air—second* position, *en l'air—fourth* position *back, en l'air*.[1]
As the foot moves from *fourth* position *front, en l'air—second* position, *en l'air*, open the arms to the *second* position.[2] Keep the arms extended, as the foot moves from *second* position, *en l'air—fourth* position *back, en l'air*.

6. *Demi-pliez* on the *left* foot.

7. Execute a **Jeté en arrière.**[3] That is :—
Spring backwards so that the *right* foot falls in the

---

[1] *Grand rond de jambe en l'air* **en dedans** is executed by moving the foot in the reverse direction.

[2] The arms should be opened gradually so that they move simultaneously with the foot.

[3] From *Jeter,* to throw—*Jeté en arrière* is a *throwing step made backwards.*

fourth position *back*. **At the same time** bring the *left* foot *sur le cou de pied en avant* and lower the arms to the *fifth* position *en bas*. Now execute with the *left* foot a *petit battement sur le cou de pied*.[1]

8. Execute a *Developpé à la quatrième en arrière en l'air*. That is :—
Raise the *left* foot as high as possible—keeping the toe pointed well downwards—so that the toe is in a line with the *right* knee and the thigh raised to the *second* position, *en l'air* ; then extend the foot to the *fourth* position *back*, *en l'air*, **at the same time—**
Keep the arms rounded and raise them to the *fifth* position *en avant*.

9. Execute a *grand rond de jambe* **en l'air en dedans.**
As the foot moves from *fourth* position *back*, *en l'air—second* position, *en l'air*, open the arms to the *second* position. Keep the arms extended as the foot moves from *second* position, *en l'air—fourth* position *front*, *en l'air*.

10. Rise on the *right demi-pointe* to preserve the equilibrium, **at the same time—**
Raise the arms to the *fifth* position *en haut*.

11. Lower the *right* heel to the ground, **at the same time—**
Without bending the *left* knee, lower the *left* foot to the *fourth* position *front* and slide it to the *fifth* position *front*.
Gradually lower the arms to the *fifth* position *en bas*.

Exercise of the Left Foot in Grand Rond de Jambe en Dehors et en Dedans.

Turn slightly to the *right* and face 1, with the head inclined to 4, the feet in the **fifth** position, **left** foot in front, and the arms in the *fifth* position *en bas*.
The direction of the body is *encroisé*.
Repeat the whole of the last exercise, reading **left** for **right**, and *vice versa*.

[1] The foot beats **front** to **back**. This ' *battement* ' is employed in order to bring the *left* foot *sur le cou de pied en arrière* in preparation for the execution of a *Developpé à la quatrième en arrière*.

Adagio

GRAND FOUETTÉ.

Stand erect in the centre of the room and face 2, with the head inclined towards 3, the knees straight, the feet in the **fifth** position, **right** foot in front, and the arms in the *fifth* position *en bas*.

The direction of the body is *encroisé*.

Part I.—*Grand Fouetté en face.*

1. *Demi-pliez* on both feet and rise *sur les demi-pointes*.
2. Raise the arms *en attitude* (*left* arm up).
3. Execute Second Exercise on *Port de Bras*. That is :
   (*a*) Move the *left* arm so that it is extended to the *fourth* position *back*, pointing to 4, **at the same time—**
   Move the *right* arm forward so that it is extended to the *fourth* position *front*, pointing to 2.
   Incline the head towards 1.
   (*b*) Lower the *left* arm to the *first* position, pass it to the *fifth* position and raise it to the *fourth* position *en avant*. Bring the head erect facing 2.
   The arms are now in the *fifth* position *en avant*.
   (*c*) Repeat No. 2.
   Look towards the left hand.
4. Lower the *left* heel to the ground, **at the same time—**
   Raise the *right* foot *sur le cou de pied en avant*.
   Lower both arms to the *fifth* position *en bas*. Turn on the *left* foot to the **right** so that the body faces 1. (The direction of the body is *effacé*.)
5. Execute a *Developpé à la quatrième en avant en l'air*. That is :—
   Extend the *right* foot to the *fourth* position *front*, *en l'air*, **at the same time—**
   Raise the arms to the *fourth* position *en avant* (*left* arm across the body).
   Incline the head towards 2.
6. *Demi-pliez* on the *left* foot (see Fig. 67).
7. In **one sweeping movement** slightly turn to the **left**, so that the body faces 5, **at the same time—**
   Straighten the *left* knee and rise *sur la demi-pointe*.
   Move the right foot to the *second* position, *en l'air*.
   Move the left arm in a semi-circle so that it passes above the head (see **Fig. 68**), and then to the *second* position.

Raise the *right* arm above the head, as shown in Fig. 69.

Raise the head erect, facing 5.

When the *right* foot has passed to the *second* position, *en l'air*, lower the *left* heel to the ground.

(The direction of the body is *en face*.)

8. Execute with the right foot a *demi-grand rond de jambe en l'air en dehors*, and bend the *right* knee so that the foot passes *à l'attitude*, at the same time—
Slightly turn the body to the **right** so that it faces 1.
The pose is *en attitude* (*encroisé*).

9. Lower the *right* arm to the *fourth* position *en avant*, at the same time—
Bring the head erect, facing 1.

10. *Demi-pliez* on the *left* foot, at the same time—
Slightly lower the *right* arm and extend it in a line with and at right angles to the shoulder so that it points to 1.
Move the *left* arm in a semi-circle backward and downward so that it points to 3.
Extend the *right* foot—straightening the knee—so that it is in a line parallel with the *left* arm.
The pose is *en quatrième arabesque* (*encroisée*).

11. Execute a *Developpé à la quatrième en avant en l'air* (*effacée*). That is :—
(a) Bend the *right* knee so that the thigh moves gradually to *second* position, *en l'air*, and the flat of the *right* foot—with the heel turned well outward—is in a line with the side of the *left* knee, at the same time—
Straighten the *left* knee.
Lower the arms to the *fifth* position *en bas*, and raise them to *fifth* position *en avant*.
(b) Extend the. *right* foot to *fourth* position *front*, *en l'air*, at the same time—
Open the arms to the *second* position.
Incline the head towards 2.

12. Execute a **Ballotté** (*epaulé*). That is :—
(a) *Demi-pliez* on the *left* foot, at the same time—
Lower the *right* foot to the *fourth* position *front*, *pointe tendue*.
(b) Slide the *right* foot to the *fifth* position *front*, at the same time—
Straighten the *left* knee, then—

Rise *sur les demi-pointes*, **at the same time**—
Lower the arms to the *fifth* position *en bas*.
(*c*) Lower the *right* heel to the ground, **at the same time**—
Raise the *left* foot *sur le cou de pied en arrière*.
(*d*) Raise the *left* foot as high as possible—keeping the toe pointed well downward—until the toe is in a line with the *right* knee and the thigh raised to the *second* position, *en l'air*, **at the same time**—
Raise the arms to the *fifth* position *en avant*.
(*e*) Extend the *left* foot to the *fourth* position **back,** *en l'air*, **at the same time**—
Extend the arms towards 1.
Bring the head erect, facing 1.
The pose is *en cinquième arabesque* (*epaulée*).

13. Execute a *Ballotté* (*effacé*). That is :—
(*a*) *Demi-pliez* on the *right* foot, **at the same time**—
Lower the *left* foot to the *fourth* position **back,** *pointe tendue*.
Open the arms to the *second* position.
(*b*) Slide the *left* foot to the *fifth* position **back, at the same time**—
Straighten the right knee, then—
Rise *sur les demi-pointes*, **at the same time**—
Lower the arms to the *fifth* position *en bas*.
(*c*) Lower the *left* heel to the ground, **at the same time**—
Raise the *right* foot *sur le cou de pied en avant*.
(*d*) Raise the *right* foot as high as possible—keeping the toe pointed well downward—until the toe is in a line with the *left* knee and the thigh raised to the *second position, en l'air*, **at the same time**—
Raise the arms to the *fifth* position *en avant*.
(*e*) Extend the *right* foot to the *fourth* position *front, en l'air*, pointing to 1, **at the same time**—
Open the arms *en attitude* (*left* arm up).
Incline the head towards 2.

14. *Demi-pliez* on the *left* foot, **at the same time**—
Lower the *right* foot to the *fourth* position *front, pointe tendue*.
Bring the arms to the *second* position.

15. Slide the *right* foot to the *fifth* position *front*, **at the same time**—
Straighten the left knee, then—

Rise *sur les demi-pointes,* **at the same time—**
Lower the arms to the *fifth* position *en bas.*
Turn slightly to the **left** so that the body faces 5.
Bring the head erect, facing 5.
The direction of the body is *en face.*

16. Lower both heels to the ground, then
Slide the *left* foot to the *fourth* position *back, pointe tendue,* **at the same time—**
Bend the *right* knee.
Keep the arms rounded, and raise them to the *fourth* position *en avant* (*left* arm across body).
Slightly incline the head to 8.

17. Execute with the *left* foot a *grand rond de jambe à terre en dedans.*
As the *left* foot moves from the *fourth* position *back* to the *second* position, open the *left* arm to the *second* position, pointing to 6. Bring the head erect.
As the foot moves from the *second* position to the *fourth* position *front,* sweep the *right* arm in a semi-circle forward and inward so that it is in the *fourth* position *en avant,* **at the same time—**
Slightly turn the body to the **right** so that it faces 1.
Slightly incline the head to 2.
(The direction of the body is *encroisé.*)

18. Slide the *left* foot to the *fifth* position *front,* allowing the *left* knee to bend, **at the same time—**
Lower the arms to the *fifth* position *en bas.*

19. Bring the body erect and rise *sur les demi-pointes,* **at the same time—**
Raise the *right* arm above the head.
Move the *left* arm in a semi-circle outward and backward so that it points to 3.
The arms are *en attitude.*

Part II.—*Grand Fouetté en Tournant.*

20. Execute Second Exercise on *Port de Bras.* That is :
(*a*) Move the *left* arm in a semi-circle forward and inward until it points to 1, **at the same time—**
Move the *right* arm in a semi-circle outward and backward until it points to 3.
Incline the head to 2.
(*b*) Lower the *right* arm to the *first* position, pass it to the *fifth* position, and then raise it to the *fourth* position *en avant,* **at the same time—**
Bring the head erect.

(*c*)   Raise the *right* arm above the head, **at the same time**—

Move the *left* arm in a semi-circle outward and **backward** so that it points to 3.

Look towards the *right* hand.

The arms are *en attitude*.

21.   Lower the *right* heel to the ground, **at the same time**—

Raise the *left* foot *sur le cou de pied en avant*.

Lower both arms to the *fifth* position *en bas*.

Slightly turn to the **left** so that the body faces 5.

The direction of the body is *en face*.

22.   Execute a *Developpé à la quatrième en avant en l'air*.   That is :—

(*a*)   Raise the *left* foot as high as possible—keeping the toe pointed well downwards—so that the toe is in a line with the *right* knee and the thigh raised to the *second* position, *en l'air*, **at the same time**—

Raise the arms to the *fifth* position *en avant*.

(*b*)   Extend the *left* foot to the *fourth* position *front*, *en l'air*, **at the same time**—

Raise the arms to the *fourth* position *en avant* (*right* arm across the body).

23.   *Demi-pliez* on the *right* foot.

24.   Straighten the *right* knee and rise *sur la demi-pointe*, **at the same time**—

Move the *left* foot from *fourth* position *front*, *en l'air*, to *second* position, *en l'air*.

Raise the *right* arm above the head and lower it to the *second* position.

Gradually raise the *left* arm above the head.

25.   Execute a *demi grand rond de jambe en l'air en dehors*.   That is :—

Move the *left* foot from *second* position, *en l'air*— *fourth* position *back*, *en l'air*, but allow the knee to bend so that the pose is *en attitude*.

26.   (*a*)   Lower the *left* arm to the *fourth* position *en avant*.

(*b*)   Extend the *left* foot to *fourth* position *back*, *en l'air*, **at the same time**—

Extend the *left* arm until it is in a line with and at right angles to the *left* shoulder so that it points to 5.

Move the *right* arm in a semi-circle outward and backward so that it points to 7.

The pose is *en deuxième arabesque*.

(c)   *Demi-pliez* on the *right* foot.

27.   Execute a *Developpé en tournant en dehors à la quatrième en avant en l'air (effacé).*   That is :—
Turn to the **left** on the *right demi-pointe* until the body passes 2 and faces 2 again.[1]
During the pirouette[2]—
(a)   Sweep the *left* arm downward and backward so that it points to 7.
(b)   Straighten the *right* knee and rise *sur la demi-pointe.*
(c)   Bend the *left* knee so that the thigh moves gradually to the *second* position, *en l'air*, and the toe is in a line with the *right* knee, **at the same time**—
Lower the arms to the *fifth* position *en bas* and raise them to the *fifth* position *en avant.*
(d)   When the body faces 2 for the last time
Extend the *left* foot to the *fourth* position *front, en l'air*, so that it points to 2, **at the same time**—
Open the arms to the *second* position.
Incline the head towards 1.
The direction of the body is *effacé.*

28.   *Demi-pliez* on the *right* foot.

29.   Lower the *left* foot to the *fourth* position *front* and—
allowing the *left* knee to bend—slide it to the *fifth* position *front*, **at the same time**—
Lower the arms to the *fifth* position *en bas.*
Bring the body erect, facing 2.

30.   Rise *sur les demi-pointes.*

31.   Execute **sur place, a pas de bourré en tournant en dehors sur les demi-pointes** until the body faces 8. That is :—
Keep the body *sur les demi-pointes* and move to the **left** in a semi-circle by a series of little close steps until the body faces 8.

32.   Lower the *left* heel to the ground, **at the same time**—
Raise the *right* foot *sur le cou de pied en arrière.*

33.   Raise the *right* foot as high as possible—keeping the toe pointed well downwards—until the toe is in a line with the *left* knee and the thigh raised to the *second* position, *en l'air*, **at the same time**—
Raise the arms to the *fifth* position *en avant.*

1   The body moves from 5-2-6-3-7-4-8-1-5-2.

2   (a) is the preparation for the movement, (b) and (c) are to be executed during the *tour.*

Adagio

34. Extend the *right* foot as if to *fourth* position *back, en l'air*, keeping the *right* knee bent, so that it points to 6, **at the same time—**
Raise the *left* arm above the head.
Raise the *right* arm to the *second* position and move it in a semi-circle outward and backward so that it points to 6.

35. *Demi-pliez* on the *left* foot, **at the same time—**
Straighten the *right* knee.
Lower the *left* arm to the *fourth* position *en avant*, then extend it in a line with and at right angles to the shoulder. The pose is *en quatrième arabesque*.

36. Lower the *right* foot to the *fourth* position *back*, and— allowing the knee to bend—slide it to the *fifth* position *back*, **at the same time—**
Lower the arms to the *fifth* position *en bas*.

37. Bring the body erect and rise *sur les demi-pointes*.

38. Execute *sur place*, a *pas de bourré en tournant en dehors sur les demi-pointes* until the body faces 2. That is :—
Keep the body *sur les demi-pointes* and move to the **left** in a semi-circle by a series of little close steps until the body faces 2.

39. Lower the *right* heel to the ground, **at the same time—**
Raise the *left* foot *sur le cou de pied en avant*.

40. Execute a *Developpé à la quatrième en avant en l'air (effacée)*. That is :—
(*a*) Raise the *left* foot as high as possible—keeping the toe pointed well downwards—until the toe is in a line with the *right* knee and the thigh raised to the *second* position, *en l'air*, **at the same time—**
Raise the arms to the *fifth* position *en avant*.
(*b*) Extend the *left* foot to *fourth* position *front, en l'air*, pointing to 2, **at the same time—**
Raise the arms *en attitude* (*right* arm up).
Incline the head towards 1.

41. *Demi-pliez* on the *right* foot, **at the same time—**
Lower the *left* foot to the *fourth* position *front*.

42. Slide the *left* foot to the *fifth* position *front*, allowing both knees to bend, **at the same time—**
Lower the arms to the *fifth* position *en bas*.

43. Bring the body erect and rise *sur les demi-pointes*, **at the same time—**
Bring the head erect, facing 2.

44. Lower the *left* heel to the ground, **at the same time—**
    Raise the *right* foot *sur le cou de pied en arrière*.

45. Raise the *right* foot as high as possible—keeping the toe pointed well downwards—so that the toe is in a line with the *left* knee and the thigh raised to the *second* position, *en l'air*, **at the same time—**
    Raise the arms to the *fifth* position *en avant*.

46. Move the *right* foot *en attitude*, **at the same time—**
    Raise the arms *en attitude* (*right* arm up).

47. Extend the *right* foot to the *fourth* position *front*, *en l'air*, **at the same time—**
    Lower the *right* arm a little above the line of the waist, then extend it in a line with and at right angles to the shoulder. Move the *left* arm in a semicircle outward and backward so that it is in a line parallel to the *right* foot.

48. *Demi-pliez* on the *left* foot.

49. Execute a *Developpé en tournant en dehors à la quatrième en avant en l'air* (*effacée*). That is :—
    Take strength with the *right* arm and turn to the **right** on the *left demi-pointe* until the body passes 1 and faces 1 again.[1]
    During the *pirouette*[2]—
    (*a*) Sweep the *right* arm to the *second* position.
    (*b*) Straighten the *left* knee and rise *sur la demi-pointe*.
    (*c*) Bend the *right* knee so that the thigh moves gradually to the *second* position, *en l'air* and the toe—with the heel turned well outwards—is in a line with the *left* knee, **at the same time—**
    Lower the *arms* to the *fifth* position *en bas*, and raise them to the *fifth* position *en avant*.
    (*d*) When the body faces 1 for the last time—
    Extend the *right* foot to the *fourth* position *front*, *en l'air*, **at the same time—**
    Raise the arms to the *second* position.

50. Rise on the *left demi-pointe*.

51. Execute a *Jeté en avant*. That is :—
    Quickly spring forward on the *right* foot so that it falls in the *fourth* position *front* and faces 1, **at the same time—**

---

1 The body moves from 2-5-1-8-4-7-3-6-2-5-1.

2 (*a*) is the preparation for the movement, (*b*) and (*c*) are to be executed during the *tour*.

Slide the *left* foot to the *fifth* position *back* (allowing both knees to bend).

Lower the arms to the *fifth* position *en bas.*

52. Execute a **Temps levé à** l'arabesque. That is :—

(*a*) Spring lightly upward into the air on the **right** foot.

Raise the *left* foot to the *fourth* position *back, en l'air* (*demi-position*), **at the same time**—

Raise the arms to the *demi-seconde* position.

(*b*) Come to the ground on the *right* foot, **at the same time**—

Slide the *left* foot to the *first* position, allowing both knees to bend.

Lower the arms to the *fifth* position *en bas.*

(*c*) Open the *left* foot to the *fourth* position *front* (*encroisé*), **at the same time**—

Raise the right foot—with the leg well extended—*pointe tendue.*

Open the arms between the *fifth* position *en avant* and the *second* position.

53. (*a*) Open the arms to the *second* position.

(*b*) Lower the *right* arm to the *first* position, pass it to the *fifth* position, then raise it to the *fourth* position *en avant,* and bring it close to the body so that it rests against the breast, **at the same time**—

Move the *left* arm backward so that it points to 3.

Incline the head towards 8 and look downwards at the feet (see Fig. 70).

NOTE.—This exercise is too long and arduous to be executed first with the *right* leg, then with the *left.* Consequently, according to the table of exercises for the week, it is performed with the *right* foot on *Monday,* and with the *left* foot on *Saturday.*

A Manual of Classical Dancing

[1] COUPÉ ET FOUETTÉ, EN AVANT ET EN ARRIÈRE.

Stand erect in the centre of the room and face 2, with the head inclined to 3, the knees straight, the feet in the **fifth** position, **right** foot in front, and the arms in the *fifth* position *en bas*. The direction of the body is *encroisé*.

1. *Demi-pliez* on both feet and rise *sur les demi-pointes*.
2. Lower the *left* heel to the ground, **at the same time**— Raise the *right* foot *sur le cou de pied en avant*.
3. Execute a *Developpé à la quatrième en avant en l'air*. That is :—
   Raise the *right* foot as high as possible—keeping the toe pointed well downwards—until the toe is in a line with the *left* knee and the thigh raised to the *second* position, *en l'air*, then extend the foot to the *fourth* position *front*, *en l'air*, **at the same time**— Keep the arms rounded and raise them to the *fifth* position *en avant*.
4. *Demi-pliez* on the *left* foot.
5. Execute a *Coupé en avant*. That is :—
   Step forward so that the *right* foot falls in the *fourth* position *front*, with the leg well extended, **at the same time**— Raise the *left* foot to the *fourth* position *back*, *en l'air*. Open the arms to the *second* position.
6. Execute a *Developpé à la seconde en l'air*. That is :
   (*a*) Bend the *left* knee so that the thigh moves gradually to the *second* position, *en l'air*, and the toe of the *left* foot—with the heel turned well outward— is in a line with the *right* knee, **at the same time**— Lower the arms to the *fifth* position *en bas*.
   (*b*) Extend the *left* foot to the *second* position *en l'air*, **at the same time**— Gradually raise the arms to the *second* position.
7. Execute with the *left* foot a *double rond de jambe en l'air en dedans*.[2]
8. Execute a **Fouetté** [3] **à terre en dedans**. That is :— Without bending the *left* knee, sweep the *left* foot

[1] This exercise can also be executed *en tournant*, that is to say, the *fouetté à terre* is executed *en tournant* instead of *en face*.

[2] Remember that after the execution of *ronds de jambe en l'air* the foot always remains in the *second* position, *en l'air*.

[3] Fouetté, from *fouetter*, to *whip*. It implies a whipping movement of the raised foot as it passes rapidly in front of or behind the supporting foot.

80

across the ground and bring it *sur le cou de pied en avant*, then quickly pass it *sur le cou de pied en arrière*. The movement is exactly similar to that of *petit battement sur le cou de pied*. **At the same time—**
Lower the arms to the *fifth* position *en bas*.

9. Execute a *Developpé à la seconde en l'air*. That is :
   (*a*) Raise the *left* foot as high as possible—keeping the toe pointed well downwards—until the toe is in a line with the *right* knee and the thigh raised to the *second* position, *en l'air*.
   (*b*) Open the *left* foot to the *second* position, **en l'air, at the same time—**
   Raise the arms to the *second* position.

10. Execute a *Developpé à la quatrième en avant en l'air*. That is :—
    (*a*) Bend the left knee so that the toe—with the toe pointed well downwards—is in a line with the *right* knee and the *left* thigh raised to the *second* position, *en l'air*, **at the same time—**
    Lower the arms to the *fifth* position *en bas*.
    (*b*) Extend the *left* foot to the *fourth* position *front*, *en l'air*, **at the same time—**
    Keep the arms rounded and raise them to the *fifth* position *en avant*.

11. *Demi-pliez* on the *right* foot.

12. Execute a *Coupé en avant*. That is :—
    Step forward so that the *left* foot falls in the *fourth* position *front*, with the leg well extended, **at the same time—**
    Raise the *right* foot to the *fourth* position *back, en l'air*, **at the same time—**
    Open the arms to the *second* position.

13. Execute a *Developpé à la seconde en l'air*. That is :
    (*a*) Bend the *right* knee so that the toe—with the toe pointed well downwards—is in a line with the *left* knee and the *right* thigh raised to the *second* position, *en l'air*, **at the same time—**
    Lower the arms to the *fifth* position *en bas*.
    (*b*) Extend the *right* foot to the *second* position, *en l'air*, **at the same time—**
    Raise the arms to the *second* position.

14. Execute with the *right* foot a *double rond de jambe en l'air en dedans*.

15. Execute a *Fouetté à terre en dedans*. That is :—
Sweep the *right* foot across the ground and bring
it *sur le cou de pied en avant*, then quickly pass it
sur le cou de pied en arrière. The movement is
exactly similar to that of *petit battement sur le cou
de pied.* **At the same time—**
Lower the arms to the *fifth* position *en bas*.

16. Execute a *Developpé à la seconde en l'air*. That is :—
Raise the *right* foot as high as possible—keeping the
toe pointed well downwards—until the toe is in a
line with the *left* knee and the thigh raised to the
second position, *en l'air.*
Raise the arms to the *fifth* position *en avant*.
(*b*) Open the *right* foot to the *second* position, *en
l'air*, **at the same time—**
Open the arms to the *second* position.

17. Execute a *Developpé à la quatrième en arrière en
l'air*. That is :—
(*a*) Bend the *right* knee so that the toe of the *right*
foot—with the heel turned well outward—is in a
line with the *left* knee and the *right* thigh in the
second position, *en l'air*, **at the same time—**
Lower the arms to the *fifth* position *en bas*.
(*b*) Extend the *right* foot to the *fourth* position
front, en l'air, **at the same time—**
Keep the arms rounded and raise them to the *fifth*
position *en avant*.

18. *Demi-pliez* on the *left* foot.

19. Execute a *Coupé en arrière*. That is :—
Step backward so that the *right* foot—with the leg
well extended—falls in the *fourth* position *back*, **at
the same time—**
Raise the *left* foot to the *fourth* position *front en l'air*.
Open the arms to the *second* position.
Repeat No. 6.

20. Execute with the *left* foot a *double rond de jambe
en*[1] *l'air en dehors*.

21. Execute a **Fouetté à terre en dehors.** That is :—
Sweep the *left* foot across the ground and bring it
sur le cou de pied en arrière, then quickly pass it
sur le cou de pied en avant. The movement is exactly

---

[1] Remember that after the execution of *ronds de jambe en l'air*
the foot always remains in the *second* position, *en l'air*.

Adagio

similar to that of *petit battement sur le cou de pied.*
At the same time—
Lower the arms to the *fifth* position *en bas.*

Repeat No. 9.

22. Execute a *Developpé à la quatrième en arrière en l'air.* That is :—
   (a) Bend the *left* knee so that the toe of the *left* foot—with the heel turned well outwards—is in a line with the *right* knee and the *left* thigh is in the *second* position *en l'air*, **at the same time—**
   Lower the arms to the *fifth* position *en bas.*
   (b) Extend the *left* foot to the *fourth* position **back,** *en l'air*, **at the same time—**
   Keep the arms rounded and raise them to the *fifth* position *en avant.*

23. *Demi-pliez* on the *right* foot.

24. Execute a *Coupé en arrière.* That is :—
   Step backward so that the *left* foot—with the leg well extended—falls in the *fourth* position *back.*
   Raise the *right* foot to the *fourth* position *front, en l'air*, **at the same time—**
   Open the arms to the *second* position.

   Repeat No. 13.

25. Execute with the *right* foot a *double rond de jambe en l'air en dehors.*

26. Execute a *Fouetté à terre en dehors.*

   Repeat No. 16.

27. (a) Rise on the *left demi-pointe* to preserve the equilibrium, **at the same time—**
   Slightly turn to the **right** so that the body faces 1.
   Incline the head towards 4.
   (b) Lower the *right* foot to the *fifth* position *front,* **at the same time—**
   Lower the arms to the *fifth* position *en bas.*

QUATRE PIROUETTES EN DEDANS.

Stand erect in the centre of the room and face 2, with the head inclined towards 3, the knees straight, the feet in the **fifth** position, **right** foot in front, and the arms in the *fifth* position *en bas*. The direction of the body is *encroisé*.

1. *Demi-pliez* on both feet.
2. Slide the *right* foot to the *fourth* position *front*, keeping the knees bent.
3. Bring the body erect and raise the *left* foot *pointe tendue*, **at the same time—**
   Raise the arms *en attitude*, *left* arm up.
4. Execute **Grand Preparation pour pirouette en dedans.** That is :—
   (*a*) Rise on the *right demi-pointe*, **at the same time—** Raise the *left* foot as if to the *fourth* position *back*, *en l'air*, allowing the knee to bend.
   The pose is *en attitude* (*encroisée*)
   (*b*) Lower the *right* heel to the ground and *demi-pliez* on the *right* foot, **at the same time—** Straighten the *left* knee.
   Lower both arms to the *fifth* position *en avant* and extend them so that the pose is *en cinquième arabesque* (*encroisée*).
   (*c*) Lower the *left* foot to the *fourth* position *back*, **at the same time—** Straighten the *right* knee.
   Incline the head and body, from the waist, toward 1.
   Raise the *right* arm above the head so that it faces 2. Sweep the *left* arm in a semi-circle outward and backward until it points to 4.
   The arms are *en attitude*.
   (*d*) Execute a *Port de Bras* to the *fourth* position *en avant.* That is :—
   (i) Move both arms to the *second* position, **at the same time—** Bring the head erect, facing 2.
   (ii) Lower the *right* arm to the *first* position, pass it to the *fifth* position, and raise it to the *fourth* position *en avant.*
   (*e*) *Demi-pliez* on both feet.
5. Execute *un tour* **en dedans de pirouette à la seconde,** as follows :—
   Turn round **to the right** on the *right demi-pointe*

so that the body passes 5 and continues in the same direction until it faces 5 again.[1]

Exactly at the commencement of the *pirouette*—

Sweep the *right* arm to the *second* position, **at the same time**—

Sweep the *left* foot to the *second* position, *en l'air.*

Continue in the same pose and direction until the body faces 5.

When the body faces 5—

Lower the *right* heel to the ground.

6. Return the body to the pose *en attitude* (*encroisée*). That is :—

Slightly turn the body to the left so that it **faces 2, at the same time**—

Raise the arms *en attitude, left* arm up.

Execute a *demi grand rond de jambe en l'air en dehors* and pass the *left* foot *à l'attitude.*

Raise the head and look towards the *left* hand.

7. Execute *Grand Preparation pour pirouette en dedans.*

8. Execute *un tour* **en dedans de pirouette en attitude**, as follows :—

Turn round to the **right** on the *right demi-pointe* until the body faces 2.[2]

During the *pirouette*—

Straighten the *right* knee and rise *sur la demi-pointe*, **at the same time**—

Move the *left* foot *à l'attitude.*

Keep both arms rounded and raise them to the *fifth* position *en avant*; continuing the movement, raise the *left* arm above the head and open the *right* arm to the *second* position.

When the body faces 2—

Lower the *right* heel to the ground.

9. Execute *Grand Preparation pour pirouette en dedans.*

10. Execute *un tour* **en dedans de pirouette en arabesque**, as follows :—

Turn round to the **right** on the *right demi-pointe* so that the body passes 8, and continue in the same direction until it faces 8 again.[3]

During the *pirouette*—

---

1 The body moves from 2-5-1-8-4-7-3-6-2-5.

2 The body moves from 2-5-1-8-4-7-3-6-2.

3 The body moves from 2-5-1-8-4-7-3-6-2-5-1-8.

Straighten the *right* knee and rise *sur la demi-pointe*, **at the same time—**
Extend the *left* foot to the *fourth* position *back, en l'air.*
Keep both arms rounded, raise them to the *fifth* position *en avant*, and
Extend the *right* arm in a line with and at right angles to the shoulder.
Sweep the *left* arm in a semi-circle outward and backward until it is parallel to the raised *left* foot.
When the body faces 8 for the last time—
Lower the *right* heel to the ground.
The pose is *en première arabesque.*

11. Turn to the *left* on the flat of the *right* foot until the body faces 2, then—
Slightly bend the *left* knee so that the foot passes *à l'attitude*, **at the same time—**
Bring the arms to the *fifth* position *en avant*, then raise them *en attitude, left* arm up.

12. Execute *Grand Preparation pour pirouette en dedans.*

13. Execute *un tour* **en dedans de pirouette** [1] **sur le cou de pied**, as follows :—
Turn round to the *right* on the *right demi-pointe* so that the body passes 5, and continue in the same direction until it faces 5 again. [2]
(*a*) Exactly at the commencement of the *pirouette—*
Straighten the *right* knee and rise *sur la demi-pointe.*
(*b*) Sweep the *left* foot to the *second* position, *en l'air*, **at the same time—**
Open the *right* arm to the *second* position.
(*c*) Bend the *left* knee so that the toe—with the heel turned well outwards—is in a line with the *right* knee and the thigh raised to the *second* position, *en l'air*, then gradually lower the *left* foot *sur le cou de pied en avant*, **at the same time—**
Lower the arms to the *fifth* position *en bas.*
(*d*) When the body faces 5 for the last time—
Lower the *right* heel to the ground.

---

[1] In the execution of a *tour en dedans de pirouette sur le cou de pied*, the raised foot must not be simply brought *sur le cou de pied.* First, quickly sweep the foot to the *second* position, *en l'air*, then bend the knee so that the toe of the raised foot is in a line with the knee of the supporting foot, then—during the execution of the *pirouette*—gradually lower the raised foot *sur le cou de pied en avant.*

[2] The body moves from 2-5-1-8-4-7-3-6-2-5.

(e) Lower the *left* foot to the *fifth* position *front*, allowing the knee to bend, **at the same time**—
Raise the *right* foot *sur le cou de pied en avant.*
(f) Straighten the *left* knee, pointing to 1.
Slide the*right* foot to the *fourth* position *front*, *pointe tendue*, **at the same time**—
Raise the arms *en attitude* (*left* arm up).
Incline the head and body—from the waist—towards 2.
(The direction of the body is *effacé*.)[1]

Exercise of the Left Foot in Quatre Pirouettes en Dedans.

Stand erect in the centre of the room and face 1, with the head inclined to 4, the knees straight, the feet in the **fifth** position, **left** foot in front, and the arms in the *fifth* position *en bas.*

The direction of the body is *encroisé.*

Repeat the whole of the last exercise, reading **left for right**, and *vice versa* ; while, owing to the reverse direction of the body's turns, the wall numbers stated above will now correspond to those directly opposite—that is : 8—6, 3—4, 4—3, 6—8, 1—2, 7—5, 5—7, 2—1.

---

[1] In the exercise described above the pupil is required to perform only **one each** of the *Quatre Pirouettes en dedans*, but as he gains in knowledge and **facility** of execution, he may perform two or three of each of the *Quatre Pirouettes en dedans.*

ROND DE JAMBE DEVELOPPÉ.

Stand erect in the centre of the room and face 2, with the head inclined to 3, the knees straight, the feet in the **fifth** position, **right** foot in front, and the arms in the *fifth* position, *en bas*. The direction of the body is *encroisé*.

1. *Pliez* on both feet.
   As the heels rise from the ground carry the *left* hand outward so that it is six inches from the knee.

2. Execute *deux tours en dehors developpés à la seconde en l'air*. That is :—
   Turn to the **right** on the *left demi-pointe* so that the body passes 5, and continue in the same direction until it faces 5 again.[1]
   During the execution of the *tour*—
   (*a*) Gradually straighten the *left* knee and rise *sur la demi-pointe*, **at the same time**—
   Bring the *right* foot *sur le cou de pied en avant* and raise the *right* foot as high as possible—keeping the toe pointed well downwards—until the toe is in a line with the *left* knee and the thigh raised to the *second* position, *en l'air*.
   Bring the arms to the *fifth* position *en avant*.
   (*b*) When the body faces 5 for the last time—
   Lower the *left* heel to the ground, **at the same time**—
   Extend the *right* foot to the *second* position, *en l'air*.
   Open the arms to the *second* position.

3. Execute a *Developpé à la quatrième en avant en l'air*. That is :—
   (*a*) Bend the right knee so that the toe of the *right* foot—with the heel turned well outwards—is in a line with the *left* knee and the thigh raised to the *second* position, *en l'air*, **at the same time**—
   Lower the arms to the *fifth* position *en bas*.
   (*b*) Extend the *right* foot to the *fourth* position *front*, *en l'air*, **at the same time**—
   Keep the arms rounded and raise them to the *fifth* position *en avant*.

4. Execute very slowly **one** *grand rond de jambe en l'air en dehors*.
   As the foot moves from *fourth* position *front*, *en l'air*, to the *second* position *en l'air*, open the arms to the *second* position.
   Keep the arms extended as the foot moves **from**

---

1 The body moves 2-5-1-8-4-7-3-6-2-5.

Adagio

second position *en l'air* to *fourth* pos. *back, en l'air.*

5. Execute quickly **one** *grand rond de jambe en l'air en dedans*,[1] then **one** *grand rond de jambe en l'air en dehors.*

   The arms remain in the *second* position.

6. Execute a *Developpé à la seconde*, that is :—

   (*a*) Bend the *right* knee so that the toe of the *right* foot—with the heel turned well outwards—is in a line with the *left* knee and the thigh raised **to** the *second* position, *en l'air*, **at the same time**—
   Lower the arms to the *fifth* position *en bas.*

   (*b*) Extend the *right* foot to the *second* position, *en l'air*, **at the same time**—
   Raise the arms to the *fifth* position *en avant* and open them to *second* position.

7. Execute *un tour en dedans developpé à la seconde en l'air.* That is :—
   Turn to the **left** on the *left demi-pointe* until the body faces 5 again.[2]
   (*a*) Exactly at the commencement of the *pirouette*—
   Rise on the *left demi-pointe*, **at the same time**—
   Bend the *right* knee so that the toe of the *right* foot —with the heel turned well outwards—is in a line with the *left* knee and the thigh raised to the *second* position, *en l'air*, **at the same time**—
   Lower the arms to the *fifth* position *en bas.*
   (*b*) When the body faces 5—
   Lower the *left* heel to the ground, **at the same time**—
   Extend the *right* foot to the *second* position, *en l'air.*
   Raise the arms to the *fifth* position *en avant* and open them to the *second* position.

8. Slowly turn the body to the left until it faces **6.** During this movement, keep the *right* foot—**well** extended—pointing to 8, and execute a **Degagé en dedans.** That is :—
   Allow the *right* leg to turn slowly inwards on the pivot of the hip.
   During the execution of this movement the **arms remain in the same line,**[3] except that the *left* arm

---

1 When the foot executes *quickly* and *successively* one *grand rond de jambe en l'air en dedans*, then one *grand rond de jambe en l'air en dehors*, this movement is termed *rond de jambe balancé.*

2 The body moves from 5-2-6-3-7-4-8-1-5.

3 The hands turn slowly, palms downwards.

is slightly raised, and consequently the *right* arm slightly lowered,[1] so that the pose is *en première arabesque*.[2]

9. Rise on the *left demi-pointe* to preserve the equilibrium.

10. Lower the *left* heel to the ground.
Slightly turn the body to the right so that it faces 5, then—
Lower the *right* foot to the *fifth* position back, at the same time—
Lower the arms to the *fifth* position *en bas*.

Exercise of the Left Foot in Rond de Jambe Developpé.

Stand erect in the centre of the room and face 1, with the head inclined to 4, the knees straight, the feet in the fifth position, left foot in front, and the arms in the *fifth* position *en bas*. The direction of the body is *encroisé*.

Repeat the whole of the last exercise, reading left for right, and *vice versa*; while, owing to the reverse direction of the body's turns, the wall numbers stated above will now correspond to those directly opposite—that is : 8—6, 3—4, 4—3, 6—8, 1—2, 7—5, 5—7, 2—1.

---

[1] The *left* hand points to 6 and the *right* hand to 8.
[2] See *Arabesques*, Fig. 36.

Adagio

DEVELOPPÉ CECCHETTI.

Stand erect in the centre of the room and face 2, with the head inclined to 3, the knees straight, the feet in the fifth position, right foot in front, and the arms in the *fifth* position *en bas*. The direction of the body is *encroisé*.

1. *Pliez* on both feet.
2. As the heels rise from the ground, carry the *left* hand outwards so that it is six inches from the *left* knee.
3. Execute *deux tours en dehors developpés à la seconde en l'air*. That is :—
   Turn to the **right** on the *left demi-pointe* so that the body passes 5 and continue in the same direction until it faces 5 again.[1]
   During the execution of the *tour*—
   (a) Gradually straighten the *left* knee and rise *sur la demi-pointe*, **at the same time**—
   Bring the *right* foot *sur le cou de pied en avant* and raise the foot as high as possible—keeping the toe pointed well downwards—until the toe is in a line with the *left* knee and the thigh raised to the *second* position, *en l'air*.
   (b) When the body faces 5 for the last time—
   Lower the *left* heel to the ground, **at the same time**—
   Extend the *right* foot to the *second* position, *en l'air*.
   Carry the arms to the *second* position.
4. *Demi-pliez* on the *left* foot.
5. Execute a **Jeté de coté**, as follows :—
   Jump sideways on the *right demi-pointe* so that the foot points to 8, **at the same time**—
   Raise the *left* foot to the *second* position, *en l'air*, straightening the *left* knee.
   Lower the *right* heel to the ground.
   The arms remain in the *second* position.
6. *Demi-pliez* on the *right* foot.
7. Execute a **Jeté de coté**, as follows :—
   Jump sideways on the *left demi-pointe* so that the foot points to 6, **at the same time**—
   Raise the *right* foot to the *second* position, *en l'air*, straightening the *right* knee.
   Lower the *left* heel to the ground.
   The arms remain in the *second* position.
8. Rise on the *left demi-pointe*.
9. Lower the *right* foot to the *fifth* position *front*, **at the same time**—

[1] The body moves from 2-5-1-8-4-7-3-6-2-5.

91

A Manual of Classical Dancing

Lower the *left* heel to the ground.
Lower the arms to the *fifth* position *en bas*.
Slightly turn the body to the **left** so that it faces **2.**
Incline the head to 3.

Repeat No. 1.

10. Execute *deux tours en dehors developpés à la quatrième en avant en l'air*. That is :—
Turn to the **right** on the *left demi-pointe* so that the body passes 5, and continue in the same direction until it faces 5 again.

During the execution of the *tour*—
(*a*) Gradually straighten the *left* knee and rise *sur la demi-pointe*, **at the same time**—
Bring the *right* foot *sur le cou de pied en avant* and raise the foot as high as possible—keeping the toe pointed well downwards—until the toe is in a line with the *left* knee and the thigh raised to the *second* position, *en l'air*.
(*b*) Extend the *right* foot to the *fourth* position *front*, *en l'air*, **at the same time**—
Lower the *left* heel to the ground.
Keep the arms rounded and raise them to the *fifth* position *en avant*.

11. *Demi-pliez* on the *left* foot.

12. Execute a *Jeté en avant*. That is :—
Spring forward on the *right demi-pointe* so that the foot points to 5, **at the same time**—
Extend the *left* foot to *fourth* position *back, en l'air*, straightening the *left* knee.
Open the arms to the *second* position.
Lower the *right* heel to the ground.

13. Execute a *Developpé à la seconde en l'air*. That is:—
(*a*) Bend the *left* knee so that the toe of the *left* foot—with the heel turned well outwards—is in a line with the *right* knee and the thigh raised to the *second* position, *en l'air*, **at the same time**—
Lower the arms to the *fifth* position *en bas* and raise them to the *fifth* position *en avant*.
(*b*) Open the *left* foot to the *second* position, *en l'air*, **at the same time**—
Open the arms to the *second* position.

14. Execute a *Rond de jambe en l'air en dedans*.

15. Execute a **Fouetté à terre en tournant en dedans.**
Without bending the *left* knee, sweep the *left* foot

92

across the ground and bring it *sur le cou de pied en avant*, and then quickly pass it *sur le cou de pied en arrière.* The movement is exactly similar to that of *petit battement sur le cou de pied.* **At the same time—**
Lower the arms to the *fifth* position *en bas.*
During the execution of the *fouetté à terre*, rise on the *right demi-pointe* and quickly turn to the **right** until the body faces 5.
When the body faces 5—
Lower the *right* heel to the ground.

Repeat No. 13.

16. Rise on the *right demi-pointe* to preserve the equilibrium.

17. Lower the *right* heel to the ground, **at the same time—**
Lower the *left* foot to the *fifth* position *back.*
Lower the arms to the *fifth* position *en bas.*
Slightly turn the body to the **left** so that it faces 2.
Incline the head **to 3.**

Repeat No. 1.

18. Execute *deux tours en dehors developpés à la quatrième en arrière en l'air.* That is :—
Turn to the **right** on the *left demi-pointe* so that the body passes 5, and continue in the same direction until the body faces 5 again.
During the execution of the *tour—*
(*a*) Gradually straighten the *left* knee and rise *sur la demi-pointe*, **at the same time—**
Bring the *right* foot *sur le cou de pied en avant* and raise the *right* foot as high as possible—keeping the toe pointed well downwards—until the toe is in a line with the *left* knee and the thigh raised to the *second* position, *en l'air.*
Lower the arms to the *fifth* position *en bas.*
(*b*) When the body faces 5 for the last time—
Extend the *right* foot to the *fourth* position *back, en l'air*, **at the same time—**
Raise the arms to the *fifth* position *en avant*, and open them to the *second* position.

19. (*a*) Lower the arms to the *first* position, pass them to the *fifth* position *en bas*, then raise them to the *fifth* position *en avant.*

(*b*)   Slightly turn to the *right* on the flat of the *left* foot, so that the body faces 1, **at the same time—** Move the *right* leg *à l'attitude.*

Raise the *right* arm above the head and sweep the *left* arm in a semi-circle outward and backward so that it points to 3.

The pose is *en attitude* (*encroisé*).

20.   Rise on the *left demi-pointe.*

21.   Lower the *left* heel to the ground and *demi-pliez* on the *left* foot, **at the same time—** Lower the *right* arm and extend it in the *fourth* position *en avant,* pointing to 1.

Lower the *left* arm to the *first* position, pass it to the *fifth* position *en bas,* and extend it in the *fourth* position *en avant,* pointing to 1.

Straighten the *right* knee so that the foot is extended to the *fourth* position *back, en l'air.*

The pose is *en cinquième arabesque.*

22.   Execute a **Pas de bourré renversé en tournant en dehors.**
(*a*)   Straighten the *left* knee and rise *sur la demi-pointe,* **at the same time—**
Lower the *right* foot to the *fifth* position *back* and keep it *sur la demi-pointe.*

Open the arms to the *second* position.

During the execution of these movements turn the body to the *right* until it faces 4.

Incline the head and body—from the waist—towards 1.

(*b*)   Continue to turn the body to the **right** until it faces 2.   During the execution of the *tour—*
(i)   Step on the *left demi-pointe* towards 8.   (Note that the feet are in the second position.)
(ii)   Lower both heels to the ground and *demi-pliez* on both feet, **at the same time—**
Bring the *right* foot to the *fifth* position *front.*

Lower the arms to the *fifth* position *en bas.*

Bring the head erect, facing 2.

(*c*)   Slide the *right* foot to the *fourth* position *front,* **at the same time—**
Raise the arms *en attitude* (*left* arm up).

Raise the *left* foot—with the leg well extended—*pointe tendue.*

23.   Execute *Grand Preparation pour pirouette en dedans.*

24.   Execute the **fourth** *pirouette en dedans.*   That is, *pirouette en dedans sur le cou de pied.*

Adagio

Exercise of the Left Foot in Developpé Cecchetti.

Stand erect in the centre of the room and face 1, **with the** head inclined to 4, the knees straight, the feet in the **fifth** position, **left** foot in front, and the arms in the *fifth* **position** *en bas.* The direction of the body is *encroisé.*

Repeat the whole of the last exercise, reading *left* for *right,* and *vice versa* ; while, owing to the reverse direction of the body's turns, the wall numbers stated above will now correspond to those directly opposite—that is : 8—6, 3—4, 4—3, 6—8, 1—2, 7—5, 5—7, 2—1.

DEVELOPPÉ FOUETTÉ CECCHETTI.

Stand erect in the centre of the room and face 2, with the head inclined to 3, the feet in the **fifth** position, **right** foot in front, and the arms in the *fifth* position *en bas*. The direction of the body is *encroisé*.

1. *Demi-pliez* and rise *sur les demi-pointes*.
2. Lower the *left* heel to the ground, **at the same time**—
   Raise the *right* foot *sur le cou de pied en avant*.
3. Execute a *Developpé à la quatrième en avant en l'air* (*encroisé*). That is :—
   (*a*) Raise the *right* foot as high as possible—keeping the toe pointed well downwards—so that the toe is in a line with the *left* knee and the thigh raised to the *second* position, *en l'air*, **at the same time**—
   Raise the arms to the *fifth* position *en avant*.
   (*b*) Extend the *right* foot to the *fourth* position *front, en l'air*, pointing to 2, **at the same time**—
   Raise the arms *en attitude* (*left* arm up).
   Slightly incline the head and body from the waist towards 1.
4. Rise on the *left demi-pointe* to preserve the equilibrium.
5. Withdraw the *right* foot *sur le cou de pied en avant*, **at the same time**—
   Lower the *left* heel to the ground.
   Gradually lower the arms to the *fifth* position *en bas*.
6. Execute a *Developpé à la quatrième en avant en l'air* (*encroisé*), but this time—
   Raise the arms *en attitude* (*right* arm up), **at the same time**—
   Slightly incline the head and body from the waist towards 3.
7. *Demi-pliez* on the *left* foot.
8. Lower the *right* arm to the *fourth* position *en avant*.
9. Execute *un tour en dehors developpé à la quatrième en avant en l'air* (*encroisé*). That is :—
   (*a*) Execute a *grand rond de jambe en l'air en dehors*.
   As the foot moves from the *fourth* position *front, en l'air*—*second* position, *en l'air*—
   Open the *right* arm to the *second* position.
   As the foot moves from the *second* position, *en l'air*—*fourth* position *back, en l'air*—
   Straighten the *left* knee and rise *sur la demi-pointe*.
   The arms remain in the *second* position.

(*b*)   Bend the *right* knee so that the *right* toe—with the heel turned well outwards—is in a line with the *left* knee and the thigh raised to the *second* position, *en l'air*, **at the same time**—
Lower the arms to the *fifth* position *en bas.*
During these movements, *pirouette* to the *right* so that the body returns facing 2.
When the body faces 2—
Lower the *left* heel to the ground, **at the same time**—
Extend the *right* foot to the *fourth* position *front, en l'air*, pointing to 2.

Repeat No. 3.

11.   *Demi-pliez* on the *left* foot.

12.   Lower the *left* arm to the *fourth* position *en avant.*

13.   Execute a *Fouetté en l'air degagé à la quatrième en arrière en l'air* (*encroisé*) *en tournant en dedans.*
That is :—
(i) Straighten the *left* knee.
(ii) Turn to the **left** on the *left demi-pointe.*
(iii) As the body passes from 2 to 3—
In one semi-circular movement sweep the *left* arm above the head and lower it to the *second* position, **at the same time**—
Gradually raise the *right* arm above the head.
The arms are *en attitude.*
(iv) Continue to turn in the same pose and direction until the body faces 1.
As the body passes from 3 to 1—
Keep the *right* foot in the *second* position, *en l'air* and pointing to 3, so that the body continues to turn, but from the waist only.
When the body faces 1—
(*a*) Lower the *left* heel to the ground, **at the same time**—
Bend the *right* knee so that the foot passes *à l'attitude.*
The pose is *en attitude* (*encroisée*).
(*b*) Lower the *left* arm to the *fifth* position
then raise it to the *fourth* position *en avant.*
(*c*) Gradually turn outward the *left* wrist and extend the arm in the *fourth* position *front*, **at the same time**—
Gradually turn outward the wrist of the *right* hand and extend it in a line with and at right angles to the shoulder.

Extend the *right* foot to the *fourth* position *back*, *en l'air*.

The pose is *en troisième arabesque* (*encroisée*).

14. Slightly turn the body to the *left* so that it faces 5, **at the same time**—

    Lower both arms to *fifth* position *en avant* and open them to the *second* position. To complete the movement, lower the *right* arm to the *fifth* position and raise it to the *fourth* position *en avant*. Slightly incline the head towards 2.

    Bend the *right* knee so that the foot passes *à l'attitude*.

    The pose is *en attitude* (*en face*).

15. Turn the wrists so that the palms are downwards, **at the same time**—

    Extend the *right* foot to the *fourth* position *back*, *en l'air*, pointing to 4.

    Demi-pliez on the *left* foot.

    The pose is *en troisième arabesque* (*epaulée*).

16. Execute *un tour developpé en dedans*. That is :—

    Step backwards on the *right demi-pointe*, towards 4, **at the same time**—

    Lower the arms to the *fifth* position *en bas*.

    Raise the *left* foot as high as possible—keeping the toe pointed well downwards—so that the toe is in a line with the *right* knee and the thigh raised to the *second* position, *en l'air*.

    Then, **without stopping**, *pirouette* to the **right** until the body passes 8 and faces 8 again.

    When the body faces 8 for the last time—

    Lower the *right* heel to the ground.

17. Execute a *Developpé à la première arabesque*. That is :—

    Extend the *left* foot to the *fourth* position *back*, *en l'air*, pointing to 6, **at the same time**—

    Raise the arms to the *fifth* position *en avant*, then—

    Lower the *right* arm and extend it in a line with and at right angles to the shoulder.

    Sweep the *left* arm in a semi-circle outward and backward until it is extended in a line parallel with the *left* foot.

    The pose is *en première arabesque*.

18. Keep the arms extended and, without bending the *right* knee, bend the body downward from the waist until the finger-tips of the *right* hand touch the ground, **at the same time**—

The *left* leg should move naturally upward so that the *right* arm and *left* leg are always in the same straight line.

19. Slowly raise the body from the waist until the pose is again *en première arabesque*.

20. Execute a *Degagé à la seconde en l'air*. That is :—
Keep *right* foot pointing to 6, and turn body—from the waist only—until it faces 5, at the same time—
Turn the *right* wrist inwards.
Raise the *left* arm above the head so that the two arms meet in the *fifth* position *en haut*.
Incline the body as far as possible towards 8. (The arms, head, and body should be in a horizontal line with the raised foot.)

21. Execute a *Fouetté à terre en arrière*. That is :—
Sweep the *left* foot across the ground and bring it *sur le cou de pied en arrière*, at the same time—
Quickly in one sweeping movement bring the arms to the *second* position and lower them to the *fifth* position *en bas*.
Bring the head and body erect, facing 5.

22. Gradually *demi-pliez* on the *right* foot and slightly turn to the left, facing 2, at the same time—
Raise the *left* foot as if to *fourth* position *back, en l'air*, allowing the *left* knee to bend.
Raise the arms to the *fifth* position *en avant* and extend them in the *fourth* position *front*, so that the right arm points to 2, and the left arm to 4.
Straighten the *left* knee so that the foot is extended to the *fourth* position *back, en l'air*.
Incline the head towards 3, and look towards 1.
The pose is *en cinquième arabesque* (*encroisée*).

23. Execute a *Developpé degagé à la quatrième en avant en l'air* (*effacé*). That is :—
(*a*) Straighten the *right* knee, at the same time—
Bring the head erect, facing 5.
Bend the *left* knee so that the toe—with the toe pointed well downwards—is in a line with the right knee and the thigh raised to the *second* position, *en l'air*.
Bring the arms to the *fifth* position *en avant*.
(*b*) Extend the *left* foot to *fourth* position *front, en l'air*, pointing to 2, at the same time—
Raise the arms *en attitude* (*left* arm up).
Incline the head and body towards 8.

24. Rise on the *right demi-pointe*.

25. Execute a *Jeté à la quatrième position* (*effacé*).
That is :—
Spring forward on the *left* foot towards 2.
As the *left* foot touches the ground—
Demi-pliez on the *left* foot and raise the *right* foot
to the *fourth* position *back, en l'air*, pointing to 4,
at the same time—
Gracefully lower the *left* hand so that the finger-
tips touch the lips, then extend the hand [1] in a line
with and at right angles to the *left* shoulder.
The pose is *en quatrième arabesque* (*effacé*).

26. Execute a *Pas de bourré en sussous*. That is :—
(*a*) Straighten the *left* knee and *rise sur la demi-
pointe*, **at the same time**—
Lower the *right* foot to the *fifth* position *back*, and
keep it *sur la demi-pointe*.
Lower the arms to the *fifth* position *en bas*.
(*b*) Open the *left* foot to the *second* position—
keeping it *sur la demi-pointe*, **at the same time**—
Open the arms to the *second* position.
(*c*) Lower the *left* heel to the ground, **at the same
time**—
Slide the *right* foot to the *first* position and lower the
heel to the ground.
(*d*) *Demi-pliez* on both feet, then slide the *right*
foot to the *fifth* position *front* (*encroisé*), **at the same
time**—
Lower the arms to the *fifth* position *en bas*.
(*e*) Straighten both knees, **at the same time**—
Raise the *left* foot *pointe tendue*.
Raise the arms to the *fifth* position *en avant*, palms
upwards.

27. Execute *Grand Preparation pour pirouette en dedans*.

28. Execute *deux tours en dedans de pirouette sur le cou
de pied developpés à la seconde en l'air*.

29. Rise on the *right demi-pointe*, **at the same time**—
Open the *left* foot to the *second* position, *en l'air*,
pointing to 6.
Raise the arms to the *fifth* position *en haut*, then
lower them to the *second* position.
Incline the head and shoulders towards 8.

---

[1] Palm upwards.

Adagio

Exercise of the Left Foot in Developpé Fouetté Cecchetti.

Stand erect in the centre of the room and face 1, with
the head inclined to 4, the knees straight, the feet in the
fifth position, **left** foot in *front*, and the arms in the *fifth*
position *en bas*. The direction of the body is *encroisé*.

Repeat the whole of the last exercise, reading *left* for
right, and *vice versa* ; while, owing to the reverse direction
of the body's turns, the wall numbers stated above will now
correspond to those directly opposite—that is : 8—6, 3—4,
4—3, 6—8, 1—2, 7—5, 5—7, 2—1.

PAS DE CHACONNE CECCHETTI.

Stand erect in the centre of the room and face 2, with the head inclined towards 3, the knees straight, the feet in the *fifth* position, **right** foot in front, and the arms in the *fifth* position *en bas*. The direction of the body is *encroisé*,

1. *Pliez* on both feet.
2. As the heels rise from the ground, carry the arms to the *third* position, *right* arm across the body.
3. Execute *deux tours en dehors developpés à la seconde en l'air*. That is :—
   Turn to the **right** on the *left demi-pointe* so that the body passes 5, and continue in the same direction until it faces 5 again.
   During the execution of the *tour*—
   (*a*) Gradually straighten the *left* knee and rise *sur la demi-pointe*, **at the same time**—
   Bring the *right* foot *sur le cou de pied en avant* and raise the *right* foot as high as possible—keeping the toe pointed well downwards—until the toe is in a line with the *left* knee and the thigh raised to the *second* position, *en l'air*.
   Lower the arms to the *fifth* position *en bas*.
   (*b*) When the body faces 5 for the last time—
   Lower the *left* heel to the ground, **at the same time**—
   Extend the *right* foot to the *second* position, *en l'air*.
   Raise the arms to the *fifth* position *en avant* and open them to the *second* position.
4. *Demi-pliez* on the *left* foot.
5. Execute a *Jeté de coté*, as follows :—
   Jump sideways on the *right demi-pointe* so that the *right* foot points to 8, **at the same time**—
   Raise the *left* foot to the *second* position, *en l'air*, straightening the knee.
   The arms remain in the *second* position.
   Lower the *right* heel to the ground.
6. *Demi-pliez* on the *right* foot.
7. Execute a *Jeté de coté*, as follows :—
   Jump sideways on the *left demi-pointe* so that the *left* foot points to 6, **at the same time**—
   Raise the *right* foot to the *second* position, *en l'air*, straightening the knee.
   The arms remain in the *second* position.
   Lower the *left* heel to the ground.
8. *Demi-pliez* on the *left* foot.

Adagio

9. (*a*) Execute a *Jeté de coté* (see No. 5).
    (*b*) Execute *un tour en dedans developpé à la quatrième en arrière en l'air*. That is :—
    (i) Rise on the *right demi-pointe*, **at the same time**—
    Bend the *left* knee so that the toe of the *left* foot—with the heel turned well outwards—is in a line with the *right* knee and the thigh raised to the *second* position, *en l'air*.
    Lower the arms to the *fifth* position *en bas*.
    During the execution of these movements, *pirouette* **to the right** until the body faces 8.
    (ii) When the body faces 8—
    Lower the *right* heel to the ground, **at the same time**—
    Extend the *left* foot to the *fourth* position *back, en l'air*, pointing to 6.
    Raise the arms to the *fifth* position *en avant*, then—
    Extend the *right* arm in the *fourth* position *front*, pointing to 8.
    Extend the *left* arm in the *fourth* position *back*, pointing to 6.
    The pose is *en première arabesque*.

10. Slightly turn the body to the **left** so that it faces 5, **at the same time**—
    Bring the arms to the *second* position.

11. (*a*) Lower the *left* arm—turning the hand palm downwards—and gracefully pass it to the *first* position, then to the *fifth* position, then raise it to the *fourth* position *en avant*, and carry it near to the breast, **at the same time**—
    Turn the *right* hand—palm downwards—and lower it to the *demi-seconde* position.
    Both arms point to 8.
    The arms are *en troisième arabesque*.
    (*b*) Pass the *left* foot *à l'attitude*, **at the same time**—
    Incline the head and body—from the waist—towards 8.

12. *Demi-pliez* on the *right* foot.

13. Execute a *Jeté en arrière à l'attitude*. That is :—
    (*a*) Spring backwards on the *left demi-pointe*, at **the same time**—
    Raise the arms *en attitude*, *right* arm up.
    Raise the *right* foot to the *fourth* position *back en l'air*, and quickly bend the knee so that the foot passes *à l'attitude*.

During the movement, turn to the **left** so that the body faces 1.

(*b*) When the body faces 1—

Lower the *left* heel to the ground, **at the same time**—

Raise the *left* arm to the *fourth* position *en haut*.

The arms are in the *fifth* position *en haut*.

Incline the head and body—from the waist—to 2.

14. Bring the head and body erect, facing 5, **at the same time**—

Lower the *right* foot to the *fifth* position *back*.

Lower the arms to the *fifth* position *en bas*.

15. Execute **Grand Preparation pour pirouette en dehors.**
That is :—

(*a*) Rise *sur les demi-pointes*, **at the same time**—

Raise the arms to the *fifth* position *en avant*.

(*b*) Lower the *right* heel to the ground, **at the same time**—

Open the *left* foot to the *second* position, and carry it a little further so that the toe is raised about four inches from the ground. The movement is exactly similar to that of *battement degagé*.

Open the arms to the *second* position.

(*c*) Rise on the *right demi-pointe*.

(*d*) Lower the *right* heel to the ground, **at the same time**—

Lower the *left* foot to the *second* position. (Immediately the feet come to the ground, *demi-pliez* on both feet.)

Carry the *left* arm to the *fourth* position *en avant*.

16. Execute *trois tours en dehors de* **pirouette** relevé **à la seconde en l'air.** That is :—

Pirouette to the **right** on the *right demi-pointe*, until the body faces 5.

At the commencement of the pirouette—

Open the *left* foot to the *second* position, *en l'air*, at **the same time**—

Open the *left* arm to the *second* position.

Each time the body returns facing 5—

Lower the *right* heel to the ground with **a** *plié à quart*, and quickly rise *sur la demi-pointe*.

When the body faces 5 for the last time—

Bring the *left* foot *sur le cou de pied en avant*, at **the same time**—

Raise the arms to the *fifth* position *en haut*.

Without stopping—

17. Execute *trois tours en dehors de pirouette sur le cou de pied*, with the arms in the *fifth* position *en haut*.

18. Execute an *Echappé à la quatrième position*, left foot *back*. That is :—

    Lightly spring upwards into the air on the *right* foot.

    Come to the ground with the feet in the *fourth* position, *right* foot in front, **at the same time**—

    Open the arms between the *fifth* position *en avant* and the *second* position.

Exercise of the Left Foot in Pas de Chaconne Cecchetti.

Stand erect in the centre of the room and face 1, with the head inclined to 4, the knees straight, the feet in the *fifth* position, **left** foot in front, and the arms in the *fifth* position *en bas*. The direction of the body is *encroisé*.

Repeat the whole of the last exercise, reading *left* for *right*, and *vice versa*; while, owing to the reverse direction of the body's turns, the wall numbers stated above will now correspond to those directly opposite—that is : 8—6, 3—4, 4—3, 6—8, 1—2, 7—5, 5—7, 2—1.

A Manual of Classical Dancing

TEMPS DE COURANTE.[1]

Stand erect in the centre of the room and face 1, with the head inclined to 2, the knees straight, the feet in the fifth position, **right** foot in *front*, and the arms in the *fifth* position *en bas*.

The direction of the body is *effacé*.

Part I.—*Temps de Courante sur les demi-pointes.*

1. Execute with the *right* foot a *developpé à la quatrième en avant en l'air—demi-position—(effacé).* That is :—
   (a) *Demi-pliez* on both feet.
   (b) Bring the *right* foot *sur le cou de pied en avant.*
   (c) Raise the arms to the *fifth* position *en avant* and open the *right* arm to the *second* position, pointing to 4, **at the same time**—
   Extend the right foot to the *fourth* position *front*, *en l'air*, pointing to 1.

2. Step forward on the *right* foot and keep it *sur la demi-pointe.*
   As the *right* foot touches the ground, *raise* the *left* foot *à l'attitude (demi-position).*

3. Bring the *left* foot to the *fifth* position *back*, keeping it *sur la demi-pointe.*

4. Lower the *right* heel to the ground, **at the same time**—
   Raise the *left* foot *sur le cou de pied en arrière.*
   Lower the arms to the *fifth* position *en bas.*

5. Execute a *Developpé à la quatrième en arrière en l'air—demi-position—(effacé).* That is :—
   (a) *Demi-pliez* on the *right* foot.
   (b) Extend the *left* foot to the *fourth* position *back*, *en l'air (demi-position)*, pointing to 3.

6. Step backward on the *left* foot and keep it *sur la demi-pointe*, **at the same time**—
   Raise the arms *en attitude (left* arm up).
   As the *left* foot touches the ground—
   Raise the *right* foot to the *fourth* position *front*, *en l'air (demi-position).*

1 **Courante**, the name of a dance of the Middle Ages. Louis XIII. excelled in the execution of this dance, and danced it many times with the ladies of his court. Though the name still survives, the present dance has little in common with its predecessor; it is infinitely more animated in its movements.—(**Desrat**, *Dictionnaire de la Danse.*)

Adagio

7. Bring the *right* foot to the *fifth* position *front* and keep it *sur la demi-pointe.*

8. Lower the *right* heel to the ground, **at the same time—**
Bring the *left* foot *sur le cou de pied en arrière.*
Lower the arms to the *fifth* position *en bas.*

9. *Demi-pliez* on the *right* foot, **at the same time—**
Slide the *left* foot to the *fourth* position *back* and keep it *sur la pointe tendue.*
Keep the *left* arm rounded and raise it to the *fourth* position *en avant.*
Open the *right* arm to the *second* position.
Incline the head and body from the waist to 8.

10. Execute a *Grand rond de jambe à terre en dedans.*
(i) As the *left* foot moves from the *fourth* position *back* to the *second* position, open the *left* arm to the *second* position, **at the same time—**
Raise the *right* arm to the *second* position.
Bring the head erect, facing 5.
(ii) As the *left* foot moves from the *second* position to the *fourth* position *front*, sweep the *right* hand in a semi-circle forward and inward so that it is in the *fourth* position *en avant*, **at the same time—**
Lower the *left* arm to the *demi-seconde* position.
Gradually incline the head and body from the waist towards 6.

11. Slide the *left* foot to the *fifth* position front, allowing the *left* knee to bend, **at the same time—**
Lower the arms to the *fifth* position *en bas.*

12. Bring the body erect and rise *sur les demi-pointes*, **at the same time—**
Raise the arms *en attitude* (*right* arm up).
Incline the head and body from the waist to **6.**
Keep the feet *sur les demi-pointes* in the *fifth* position and turn to the **right,** *sur les demi-pointes*, by a series of little close steps, so that the body passes 5, continue in the same manner and direction until it faces 2 again.
As the body passes from 5—8—
Gradually lower the *right* arm to the *second* position, **at the same time—**
Raise the *left* arm to the *second* position.
Bring the head and body erect.
As the body passes from 8—6—

Gradually raise the *left* arm above the head.
Lower the *right* arm to the *demi-seconde* position.
(Thus the arms are *en attitude, left* arm up.)
When the body faces 2—
Incline the head and body—from the waist—towards 1.

13. Lower the *right* heel to the ground, **at the same time**—
Bring the *left* foot *sur le cou de pied en avant.*
Lower the arms to the *fifth* position *en bas.*

14. Execute a *Developpé à la quatrième en avant en l'air* (*demi-position*). That is :—
(a) Raise the *left* foot as high as possible—keeping the toe pointed well downwards—until the toe is in a line with the *right* knee and the thigh raised to the *second* position, *en l'air*, **at the same time**—
Raise the arms to the *fifth* position *en avant.*
(b) Extend the *left* foot to the *fourth* position *front, en l'air* (*demi-position*), pointing to 2, **at the same time**—
Open the *left* arm to the *second* position, pointing to 3.

Repeat Nos. 2 to 12, reading **left** for **right** and *vice versa,* while, owing to the reverse direction of the body's turns, the wall numbers stated above will now correspond to those directly opposite—that is : 8—6, 3—4, 4—3, 6—8, 1—2, 7—5, 5—7.

Part II.—*Temps de Courante* (Sauté).

15. Lower both heels to the ground, **at the same time**—
Lower both arms to the *fifth* position *en bas.*

16. *Demi-pliez* on both feet.

17. Execute with the *right* foot a **Temps levé** *sur le cou de pied en avant.* That is :—
Spring upward into the air on both feet.
While the body is in the air—
Bring the *right* foot *sur le cou de pied en avant,* **at the same time**—
Slightly incline the head and body from the waist to 2.
As the *left* foot comes to the ground—
Allow the *left* knee to bend.

18. Execute a *Developpé à la quatrième en avant en l'air—demi-position—(effacé).*

Adagio

Raise the arms to the *fourth* position *en avant* (*left* arm across the body).

19. Step forward on the *right* foot towards 1 and keep it *sur la demi-pointe*.
As the *right* foot touches the ground—
Raise the *left* foot *à l'attitude* (*demi-position*).

20. Bring the *left* foot to the *fifth* position *back* and—
Demi-pliez on both feet, **at the same time**—
Lower the arms to the *fifth* position *en bas*.

21. Execute with the *left* foot a **Temps levé** *sur le cou de pied en arrière*. That is :—
Spring upward into the air on both feet.
While the body is in the air—
Bring the *left* foot *sur le cou de pied en arrière*.
As the *right* foot comes to the ground—
Allow the *right* knee to bend.

22. Execute a *Developpé à la quatrième en arrière en l'air—demi-position* (*epaulé*).
The *left* foot points to 3.
Raise the arms *en attitude, left* arm up.

23. Step backward on the *left* foot and keep it *sur la demi-pointe*.
As the *left* foot touches the ground—
Raise the *right* foot to the *fourth* position *front, en l'air—demi-position* (*effacé*), pointing to 1.

24. Bring the *right* foot to the *fifth* position *front* **and**—
Demi-pliez on both feet, **at the same time**—
Lower the arms to the *fifth* position *en bas*.

25. Execute an *Emboité en tournant en dedans*. That is :—
(*a*) Execute with the *left* foot a *Temps levé sur le cou de pied en avant*. That is :—
Spring upward into the air on both feet **and come** to the ground on the *right* foot.
While the body is in the air—
Bring the *left* foot *sur le cou de pied en avant*.
Come to the ground on the *right* foot, allowing **the** knee to bend, **at the same time**—
Incline the head towards 1.
During this movement, turn to the **right so that the** body faces 4.
(*b*) Execute with the *right* foot a *Temps levé sur le cou de pied en avant*. That is :—
Spring upward into the air and towards **6**.
While the body **is** in the air—

Bring the *right* foot *sur le cou de pied en avant,* at the same time—
Incline the head towards 2.

(*c*) Execute an *Assemblé coupé en avant.* That is : Spring upward into the air on the *left* foot. Come to the ground, allowing the knees to bend, with the feet in the *fifth* position, *right* foot in *front*, facing 5.

26. Execute **trois petits changements**, finishing in the *fifth* position, *left* foot in *front*.

   Manner of executing *petit changement* :—
   Give a little spring upward into the air, but so small that the toes hardly leave the ground, the two feet then simultaneously interchange (that is, as the *right* foot passes *behind* the *left* foot, the *left* foot passes in *front* of the *right* foot), so that the feet come to the ground—allowing the knees to bend—in the *fifth* position, *left* foot in *front*.

   (*b*) The second *changement* finishes with the feet in the *fifth* position, *right* foot in *front*.

   (*c*) The third *changement* finishes with the feet in the *fifth* position, *left* foot in *front*.

Repeat Nos. 15 to 26, reading **left** for **right,** and *vice versa* ; while, owing to the reverse direction of the body's turns, the wall numbers stated above will now correspond to those directly opposite—that is : 8—6, 3—4, 4—3, 6—8, 1—2, 7—5, 5—7, 2—1.

Adagio

UN TOUR EN DEDANS DE PIROUETTE RENVERSÉ À LA SECONDE, EXECUTÉ EN DIAGONALE.

Stand at the far end of the room near to 3 and facing 1, with the head upright, the feet in the *fifth* position, **right** foot in front, and the arms in the *fifth* position *en bas*. The direction of the body is *effacé*.

1. Execute with the right foot a *Jeté en avant à la quatrième* position.
Spring forward on the *right* foot towards 1.
As the foot touches the ground—
Raise the *left* foot slightly off the ground.

2. (*a*) *Demi-pliez* on both feet and—
Lower the *left* foot to the ground and slide it to the *first* position, then to *fourth* position *front*, and slightly raise it off the ground.
(*b*) Lower the *left* foot to the ground, **at the same time**—
Raise the *right* foot to the *fourth* position *back, en l'air.*
Raise the arms to the *fifth* position *en avant* **and**—
Extend the *left* arm to the *fourth* position *front.*
Extend the *right* arm to the *fourth* position *back.*
The pose is *en première arabesque (encroisée).*

3. Execute *un tour en dedans de pirouette renversé à la seconde.* That is :—
(*a*) Bend the *right* knee so that the toe is in a line with the *left* knee and the thigh raised to the **second** position, *en l'air,* **at the same time**—
Bring the arms between the *fifth* position *en avant* and the *second* position.
(*b*) *Pirouette* on the *left* demi-pointe to the **left** until the body faces 1.
As the body passes from 1—2—
Incline the arms, head, and body—from the waist—to the *right.*
Continue to turn until the body faces 1, **at the same time**—
Gradually bring the head and body erect.
The arms pass to the *fifth* position *en haut.*
When the body faces 1—
In **one very quick movement, simultaneously**—
Open the arms to the *demi-seconde* position.
Incline the head and arms—from the waist—as far as possible to 2.

Open the *right* foot to the *second* position, *en l'air*, pointing to 4.

4. Execute with the *right* foot a *Jeté en avant à la quatrième position.* That is :—
   Spring forward on the *right* foot towards 1.
   As the foot touches the ground—
   Raise the *left* foot slightly off the ground, **at the same time**—
   Bring the body erect.
   Bring the arms to the *fifth* position *en bas*.

5. (*a*) Lower the *left* foot to the ground, *demi-pliez* on both feet and slide the *left* foot to the *first* position, then to *fourth* position *front*, and slightly raise it off the ground.
   (*b*) Lower the *left* foot to the ground, **at the same time**—
   Raise the *right* foot to the *fourth* position *back*, *en l'air*.
   Raise the arms to the *fifth* position *en avant*, and—
   Extend the *left* arm to the *fourth* position *front*.
   Extend the *right* arm to the *fourth* position *back*.
   The pose is *en première arabesque* (*encroisée*).

6. Execute *un tour en dedans de pirouette renversé à la seconde*.

Repeat the whole exercise *ad libitum*, then repeat with the *left* foot, reading *left* for *right*, and *vice versa* ; while, owing to the reverse direction of the body's turns, the wall numbers stated above will now correspond to those directly opposite—that is : 8—6, 3—4, 4—3, 6—8, 1—2, 7—5, 5—7, 2—1.

Adagio

DEUX TOURS EN DEDANS DE PIROUETTE RENVERSÉ À LA SECONDE.

Stand near to 1 and facing 1, with the head upright, the feet in the *fourth* position, **right** foot *back* and *pointe tendue*, the arms in the *fifth* position *en bas*. The direction of the body is *encroisé*.

1. Execute a *Coupé en arrière*. That is :—
   (*a*) Withdraw the *right* foot *sur le cou de pied en arrière*, **at the same time**—
   Demi-pliez on the *left* foot and rise *sur la demi-pointe*.
   (*b*) Place the *right* foot in the position occupied by the *left* foot, and *demi-pliez* on the *right* foot, **at the same time**—
   Raise the *left* foot *sur le cou de pied en avant*.
   Slightly turn the body to the **left** so that it faces 5.

2. Execute a *Petit Fouetté sauté en arrière*. That is :—
   (*a*) Spring upward into the air on the *right* foot, **at the same time**—
   Open the left foot to the *second* position, *en l'air*.
   Open the arms to the *demi-seconde* position.
   (*b*) Come to the ground on the *right* foot, allowing the knee to bend, **at the same time**—
   Bring the *left* foot *sur le cou de pied en arrière*.
   Bring the arms—palms downward—to the *third* position, *left* arm across body.
   Slightly turn the body to the **left** so that it faces 2.
   Incline the head to 1.
   The pose is *en cinquième arabesque (encroisée)*.

3. Execute with the *left* foot a *Jeté en arrière*. That is :—
   Spring backwards on the *left* foot towards 3.
   As the foot touches the ground—
   Raise the *right* foot as high as possible so that the toe is in a line with the left knee and the thigh raised to the *second* position *en l'air*.

4. Execute *un tour en dedans de pirouette sur le cou de pied*.
   Pirouette to the **left** until the body faces 1, and **immediately**—

5. Execute *un tour en dedans de pirouette renversé à la seconde en l'air*. That is :—
   Pirouette on the *left demi-pointe* to the **left** until the body faces 1.

113

As the body passes from 1—2—

Incline the arms, head, and body—from the waist—to the right.

Continue to turn until the body faces 1, at the same time—

Gradually bring the head and body erect.

The arms pass to the *fifth* position *en haut*.

When the body faces 1—

In one very quick movement, simultaneously—

Open the arms to the *demi-seconde* position.

Incline the head and body—from the waist—as far as possible to 2.

Open the *right* foot to the *second* position, *en l'air*, pointing to 4.

6. Execute with the right foot a *Jeté en avant à la quatrième position*.

    Spring forward on the *right* foot towards 1.

    As the foot touches the ground—

    Raise the *left* foot slightly off the ground, at the same time—

    Bring the body erect.

    Bring the arms to the *fifth* position *en bas*.

7. Lower the *left* foot to the ground, *demi-pliez* on both feet, and slide the *left* foot to the *first* position, then to the *fourth* position *front*, at the same time—

    Raise the *right* foot *pointe tendue*.

    Bring the arms to the *fifth* position *en bas*.

Repeat the whole exercise *ad libitum* and then repeat on the *left* foot, reading *left* for *right*, and *vice versa*; while, owing to the reverse direction of the body's turns, the wall numbers stated above will now correspond to those directly opposite—that is: 8—6, 3—4, 4—3, 6—8, 1—2, 7—5, 5—7, 2—1.

Adagio

CINQ RELEVÉS.

Stand erect in the centre of the room and face 2, with the head upright, the feet in the **fifth** position, **right** foot in *front*, and the arms in the *fifth* position *en bas*.

The direction of the body is *encroisé*.

1. *Pliez* in the fifth position, then straighten both knees.
2. *Demi-pliez* on both feet and rise *sur les demi-pointes*.
3. Lower the *left* heel to the ground, **at the same time**—
Raise the *right* foot *sur le cou de pied en avant*.
4. Execute a *Developpé à la quatrième en avant en l'air*. That is :—
(a) Raise the *right* foot as high as possible—keeping the toe pointed well downwards—until the toe is in a line with the *left* knee and the thigh raised to the *second* position, *en l'air*, **at the same time**—
Gradually raise the arms to the *fifth* position *en avant*.
(b) Extend the *right* foot to the *fourth* position *front, en l'air*.
Open the arms to the *second* position.
5. Rise on the *left demi-pointe* to preserve the equilibrium.
6. Lower the *left* heel to the ground, **at the same time**—
Without bending the knee, *lower* the *right* foot to the *fourth* position *front, pointe tendue*.
The arms remain in the *second* position.
7. Withdraw the *right* foot *sur le cou de pied en avant*, **at the same time**—
Raise the *left* foot *sur la demi-pointe*.
Gradually lower the arms to the *fifth* position *en bas*.
(As the right foot returns *sur le cou de pied en avant*, lower the *left* heel to the ground.)
8. Execute a *Developpé à la seconde en l'air*. That is:—
(a) Raise the *right* foot as high as possible—keeping the toe pointed well downwards—until the toe is in a line with the *left* knee and the thigh raised to the *second* position, *en l'air*, **at the same time**—
Gradually raise the arms to the *fifth* position *en avant*.
(b) Extend the *right* foot to the *second* position, *en l'air*, **at the same time**—

Gradually open the arms to the *second* position.

9. Rise on the *left demi-pointe* to preserve the equilibrium.

10. Lower the *left* heel to the ground, **at the same time—** Without bending the knee, lower the *right* foot to the *second* position, *pointe tendue.*

11. Withdraw the *right* foot *sur le cou de pied en arrière*, **at the same time—**
    Raise the *left* foot *sur la demi-pointe.*
    (As the *right* foot returns *sur le cou de pied en arrière*, lower the *left* heel to the ground.)
    Lower the arms to the *fifth* position *en bas.*

12. Execute a *Developpé à la quatrième en arrière en l'air.* That is :—
    (*a*) Raise the *right* foot as high as possible—keeping the toe pointed well downwards—until the toe is in a line with the *left* knee and the thigh is raised to the *second* position, *en l'air*, **at the same time—**
    Gradually raise the arms to the *fifth* position *en avant.*
    (*b*) Extend the *right* foot to the *fourth* position *back, en l'air*, **at the same time—**
    Gradually raise the arms to the *second* position.

13. Rise on the *left demi-pointe* to preserve the equilibrium.

14. Lower the *left* heel to the ground, **at the same time—** Without bending the knee, lower the *right* foot to the *fourth* position *back, pointe tendue.*

    Repeat No. 11.

    Repeat Nos. 8, 9, 10.

    Repeat No. 7.

    Repeat Nos. 4, 5.

15. Without bending the knee, lower the *right* foot to the *fourth* position *front, pointe tendue*, and bring it *sur le cou de pied en avant*, **at the same time—**
    Gradually lower the arms to the *fifth* position *en bas.*
    (As the *right* foot returns *sur le cou de pied en avant*, lower the *left* heel to the ground.)

16. Execute with the *right* foot a *Battement degagé à la seconde sur le cou de pied.* That is :—
    (*a*) Slide the *right* foot to the *second* position **and a** little further so that it rises about four inches from the ground.

Adagio

As the foot rises from the ground, rise on **the left** demi-pointe, **at the same time—**
Incline the head towards 6.
Gradually raise the arms to the *second* position.
(*b*) Lower the *left* heel to the ground and *demi-pliez* on the *left* foot, **at the same time—**
Bring the *right* foot to the *fifth* position *back*, allowing the knee to bend.
Turn the body to the *right* so that it faces 1.
Incline the head to 4.
(*c*) Straighten both knees.

Exercise of the Left Foot in Cinq Relevés.

Remain as at the end of the last exercise and repeat **the** whole of the last exercise, reading **left** for **right**, and *vice versa* ; while, owing to the reverse direction of the body's turns, the wall numbers stated above will now correspond to those directly opposite—that is : 8—6, 3—4, 4—3, 6—8, 1—2, 7—5, 5—7, 2—1.

A Manual of Classical Dancing

PAS DE LA MASCOTTE.[1]

Stand erect in the centre of the room and face 2, with the head inclined to 3, the feet in the *fifth* position, **right** foot in *front*, and the arms in the *fifth* position *en bas*. The direction of the body is *encroisé*.

1. *Pliez* on both feet, then straighten the knees.

2. *Demi-pliez* on both feet and rise *sur les demi-pointes*, **at the same time—**
   Slightly turn to the *right* so that the body faces 5.

3. Lower the *left* heel to the ground, **at the same time—**
   Raise the *right* foot *sur le cou de pied en avant*.

4. Execute a *Developpé à la quatrième en avant en l'air*.
   (*a*) Raise the *right* foot as high as possible—keeping the toe pointed well downwards—so that the toe is in a line with the *left* knee and the thigh raised to the *second* position, *en l'air*.
   (*b*) Extend the *right* foot to the *fourth* position *front*, *en l'air*, **at the same time—**
   Raise the arms to the *fifth* position *en avant*.
   Demi-pliez on the *left* foot.

5. Execute a *Relevé à la seconde en l'air*.   That is :—
   Straighten the *left* knee and rise *sur la demi-pointe*, **at the same time—**
   Move the *right* foot to the *second* position, *en l'air*.
   Open the arms to the *second* position.
   (As the *right* foot reaches the *second* position, *en l'air*, lower the *left* heel to the ground.)

6. Execute a *Developpé à la quatrième en arrière en l'air*.
   (*a*) Bend the *right* knee so that the toe—with the heel turned well outwards—is in a line with the *left* knee and the thigh raised to the *second* position, *en l'air*, **at the same time—**
   Lower the arms to the *fifth* position *en bas*.
   (*b*) Extend the *right* foot to the *fourth* position *back*, *en l'air*, **at the same time—**
   Raise the arms to the *fifth* position *en avant*.
   Demi-pliez on the *left* foot.

7. Execute a *Relevé à la seconde en l'air*.

8. Execute a *Developpé à la quatrième en avant en l'air* (*encroisé*).   That is :—
   (*a*) Bend the *right* knee so that the toe—with the

---

[1] This exercise is entitled *Pas de la Mascotte* because it was composed by the *Maestro Cecchetti* on the occasion of the opening of his *Academie de Danse*, in London.

heel turned well outwards—is in a line with the *left* knee and the thigh raised to the *second* position, *en l'air*, at the same time—
Lower the arms to the *fifth* position *en bas*.
Turn slightly to the **left** so that the body faces 2.
(*b*) Extend the *right* foot to the *fourth* position *front, en l'air* (*encroisé*), pointing to 2, at the same time—
Raise the arms to the *fifth* position *en avant*, then to the *fourth* position *en haut, left* arm up.
Incline the head towards 1.

9. Execute a *Developpé à la quatrième en arrière en l'air*.
(*a*) Bend the *right* knee so that the toe—with the heel turned well outwards—is in a line with the *left* knee and the thigh raised to the *second* position, *en l'air*, at the same time—
Lower the arms to the *fifth* position *en avant*.
Turn to the **left** so that the body faces 6.
(*b*) Extend the *right* foot to the *fourth* position *back, en l'air*, pointing to 8, at the same time—
Extend the *left* arm to the *fourth* position *front*, pointing to 6.
Extend the *right* arm to the *fourth* position *back*, pointing to 8.
The pose is *en première arabesque*.

10. Execute with the *right* foot a *Degagé à la seconde en l'air*. That is :—
Keep the right foot pointing to 8, and allowing the foot to turn on the pivot of the hip, turn the head and body—from the waist only—to the **right**, so that the body faces 5, at the same time—
Turn the *left* wrist inwards.
Raise the *right* arm above the head so that the arms form the *fifth* position *en haut*.
(The arms, head, and body must be in a horizontal line with the *right* foot.)

11. Turn to the **right** on the *left demi-pointe* until the body faces 2.

12. Rise on the *left demi-pointe*.

13. Execute a *Jeté à la quatrième position* (*effacé*). That is :—
Spring forward on the *right demi-pointe* towards 1.
As the *right* foot touches the ground—
Lower the *right* heel to the ground and *demi-pliez*

119

on the *right* foot, **at the same time—**
Raise the *left* foot to the *fourth* position *back, en l'air.*
Gracefully lower the *right* hand so that the finger-tips touch the lips, then extend the hand—palm upwards—to the *fourth* position *front,* pointing to 1.
The pose is *en quatrième arabesque (effacée).*

14. Execute a *Pas de bourré en sussous.* That is :—
   (*a*) Straighten the *right* knee and rise *sur la demi-pointe*, **at the same time—**
   Lower the *left* foot to the *fifth* position *back,* and keep it *sur la demi-pointe.*
   Lower the arms to the *fifth* position *en bas.*
   (*b*) Open the *right* foot to the *second* position, keeping it *sur la demi-pointe*, **at the same time—**
   Open the arms to the *second* position.
   (*c*) Lower the *right* heel to the ground, then—
   Demi-pliez on both feet and slide the *left* foot to the *first* position and lower the *left* heel to the ground.
   (*d*) Slide the *left* foot to the *fifth* position *front,* then to the *fourth* position *front (encroisé),* pointing to 1, **at the same time—**
   Move the arms *en arabesque, left* arm pointing to 1, *right* arm pointing to 3.
   Incline the head to 2.
   The pose is *en deuxième arabesque (epaulée).*

15. Execute *deux tours en dedans de pirouette en attitude.* That is :—
   Straighten the *right* knee, rise *sur la demi-pointe* and turn to the **right** until the body passes 2 and again faces 2.
   During the movement—
   Raise the *left* arm above the head, **at the same time—**
   Raise the *left* foot *à l'attitude.*

16. Execute *Grand Preparation pour pirouette en dedans.*

17. Execute *deux tours en dedans de pirouette à l'attitude renversé.* That is :—
   (*a*) First *tour.*
   Rise on the *right demi-pointe* and *pirouette* to the **right** until the body returns to 2.
   At the commencement of the *pirouette*—
   Sweep the *left* arm to the *fourth* position *en avant,* **at the same time—**
   Raise the *left* foot *à l'attitude.*
   (*b*) Second *tour.*
   Continue to *pirouette* to the **right.**

As the body passes from 2—1—
Incline the arms, head, and body—**from the waist**—
to the *left*.
As the body passes from 1—4—
Gradually bring the head and body erect, **at the same time**—
The arms pass to the *fifth* position *en haut*.
As the body passes from 4—3—
Incline the arms, head, and body—from the waist—
to the *right*.
As the body passes from 3—2—
In one very quick movement, **simultaneously**—
Open the arms to the *second* position.
Incline the head and body—from the waist—as far possible towards 1.
(*c*) Lower the *left* foot to the *fifth* position *back*, **at the same time**—
Bring the head and body erect, facing 5.
Lower the arms to the *fifth* position *en bas*.

18. Execute a *Glissade* with the *left* foot. That is :—
(*a*) *Demi-pliez* on both feet.
(*b*) Slide the *left* foot to the *second* position, keeping it *sur la demi-pointe*, **at the same time**—
Raise the *right* foot off the ground.
Open the arms to the *demi-seconde* position.
(*c*) Lower the *right* foot to the *fifth* position *front* and *demi-pliez* on the *right* foot, **at the same time**—
Lower the arms to the *fifth* position *en bas*. Without stopping—

19. Execute a *Grand assemblé en avant à la seconde en l'air*. That is :—
(*a*) Slide the *left* foot to the *second* position and execute a *grand battement à la seconde en l'air (sauté)*.
Exactly as the foot passes to the *second* position, *en l'air*—
Leap upwards into the air on the *right* foot.
Open the arms to the *second* position.
(*b*) While the body is in the air—
Bend the *left* knee and bring together the soles of the two feet.
Come to the ground—allowing the knees to bend—with the feet in the *fifth* position, *left* foot in *front*, **at the same time**—
Lower the arms to the *fifth* position *en bas*.
(*c*) Straighten both knees.

A Manual of Classical Dancing

Exercise of the Left Foot in Pas de la Mascotte.

Stand erect in the centre of the room and face 1, with the head inclined to 4, the knees straight, the feet in the *fifth* position, *left* foot in *front*, and the arms in the *fifth* position *en bas*. The direction of the body is *encroisé*.

Repeat the whole of the last exercise, reading *left* for *right*, and *vice versa*; while, owing to the reverse direction of the body's turns, the wall numbers stated above will now correspond to those directly opposite—that is : 8—6, 3—4, 4—3, 6—8, 1—2, 7—5, 5—7, 2—1.

Adagio

PAS DE CHACONNE.[1]

Stand erect in the centre of the room and face 5, with the head upright, the feet in the **fifth** position, **right** foot in *front*, and the arms in the *fifth* position *en bas*.

The position of the body is *en face*.

1. *Demi-pliez* on both feet.

2. Slide the *right* foot to the *fourth* position *front*, *pointe tendue*, **at the same time**—
   Keep the arms rounded and raise them to the *fifth* position *en avant*.

3. Execute with the *right* foot a *rond de jambe à terre en dehors*.
   As the foot moves from the *fourth* position *front* to the *second* position—
   Open the arms to the *second* position.
   As the foot moves from the *second* position to the *fourth* position *back*—
   Keep the arms extended, **at the same time**—
   Incline the head towards 6.

4. Slide the *right* foot to the *fifth* position *back*, allowing the *right* knee to bend, **at the same time**—
   Lower the arms to the *fifth* position *en bas*.

5. Bring the body erect and rise *sur les demi-pointes*.

6. Lower the *right* heel to the ground, **at the same time**—
   Bring the *left* foot *sur le cou de pied en avant*.

7. Execute with the *left* foot **eight** *petits battements* [2] *sur le cou de pied*.

8. Rise on the *right demi-pointe*.

9. Change the position of the feet so that the *left* heel is lowered to the ground and the *right* foot raised *sur le cou de pied en avant*.

---

1 **Chaconne.** This name is of frequent occurrence in the art of the dance during the Middle Ages. It seems difficult to allow the etymology of the word given by the various early writers, who attribute its derivation to a ribbon called *chaconne*, which was worn at the neck by the young elegants of the period. This ribbon was attached to the collar of the shirt so that it fell over the chest. Therefore, logically, it would appear that the dance called *chaconne* was greatly in vogue among the youthful nobility of that age. The word appears also in relation to music, because there are records of *chaconnes* which have nothing to do with the dance.—(**Desrat**, *Dictionnaire de la Danse*.)

2 The foot beats *back* to *front*, *back* to *front*, *back* to *front*.

10. Execute a *Developpé à la quatrième en avant en l'air.*
    (*a*) Raise the *right* foot as high as possible—keeping the toe pointed well downwards—until the toe is in a line with the *left* knee and the thigh raised to the *second* position, *en l'air*, **at the same time**—Raise the arms to the *fifth* position *en avant.*
    (*b*) Extend the *right* foot to the *fourth* position *front en l'air*, pointing to 5, **at the same time**—Open the *right* arm to the *second* position.
    Incline the head towards 8.

11. *Demi-pliez* on the *left* foot.

12. Execute a *Jeté en avant.* That is :—
    Spring forward on the *right* foot towards 5.
    As the foot touches the ground—
    Raise the *left* foot to the *fourth* position *back, en l'air.*
    The arms remain in the *fourth* position *en avant.*

13. Execute a *grand rond de jambe en l'air en dedans* (*encroisé*).
    As the foot moves from the *fourth* position *back, en l'air* to the *second* position, *en l'air*—Open the *left* arm to the *second* position, **at the same time**—Bring the head erect.
    As the foot moves from the *second* position, *en l'air* to the *fourth* position *front, en l'air*, pointing to 1, Sweep the *right* arm inward so that it is in the *fourth* position *en avant.*
    Incline the head to 2.

14. Rise on the *right demi-pointe.*
    Lower both heels to the ground, so that the feet are in the *fourth* position.

15. *Demi-pliez* on both **feet, at the same time**—Bring the head erect.

16. Straighten the *left* knee and rise *sur la demi-pointe*, **at the same time**—Raise the *right* foot *à l'attitude.*
    Turn the hands so that the palms are downwards, slightly lower them and carry them to the **left.**
    Slightly incline the head and body from the waist towards 2.
    The pose is *en cinquième arabesque* (*encroisée*).

17. Execute *un tour en dehors developpé à la quatrième en avant en l'air (encroisé)*. That is :—
Turn to the *right* on the flat of the *left* foot until the body faces 2.[1]
As the body passes from 1—4—
Turn the *right* knee so that the toe is in a line with the *left* knee and the thigh raised to the *second* position, *en l'air*, at the same time—
Raise the arms to the *fourth* position *en avant (right* arm across the body).
Bring the body erect.
As the body passes from 4—3—
Gradually incline the head to the *right*, at the same time—
Gradually extend the *right* foot to the *fourth* position *front, en l'air*.
When the body faces 2—
The *right* foot should be fully extended, pointing to 2.
The head and shoulders should be inclined to 1.
The pose is *à la quatrième position en avant en l'air (encroisé)*.

18. *Demi-pliez* on the *left* foot.

19. Execute a *Jeté de coté*, followed by *un tour en dedans de pirouette à la seconde*. That is :—
(a) Spring sideways on the *right demi-pointe* so that it falls in the *second* position.
The arms remain in the *fourth* position *en avant*.
As the foot touches the ground—
Raise the *left* foot to the *second* position, *en l'air*, and immediately—
(b) Execute *un tour en dedans de pirouette à la seconde*.[2] That is :—
Pirouette on the *right demi-pointe* to the right until the body faces 5.
Exactly at the commencement of the *pirouette*—
Open the *right* arm to the *second* position, at the same time—
Bring the body erect.
When the body faces 5—
Lower the *right* heel to the ground.
(The *left* foot remains in the *second* position, *en l'air*.)

---

1 The body moves from 1-8-4-7-3-6-2.
2 The body moves from 2-5-1-8-4-7-3-6-2-5.

20. Execute a *Demi grand rond de jambe en l'air en dedans.* That is :—
Move the *left* foot to the *fourth* position *front, en l'air (encroisé),* at the same time—
Sweep the arms inward so that they are in the *fifth* position *en avant.*
Slightly turn the body to the *right* so that it faces 1.

21. Lower the *left* foot to the *fourth* position *front, pointe tendue,* at the same time—
Lower the arms between the *fifth* position *en avant* and the *fifth* position *en bas.*

22. Bring the *left* foot *sur le cou de pied en avant,* at the same time—
Bring the head erect.

23. Execute a *Developpé à l'attitude (effacé).* That is:—
(*a*) Raise the *left* foot as high as possible until the toe is in a line with the *right* knee and the thigh raised to the *second* position, *en l'air,* at the same time—
Raise the arms to the *fifth* position *en avant.*
(*b*) Raise the *left* foot *à l'attitude,* at the same time—
Raise the arms *en attitude (left* arm up).
The *right* arm points to 4.
The *left* arm faces 1.
Look towards the *left* hand.

24. Extend the *left* foot to the *fourth* position *back, en l'air,* pointing to 3, at the same time—
Lower the *left* arm to the *fourth* position *en avant* and extend it until it is in a line with and at right angles to the *left* shoulder.
Move the *right* arm outward and backward until it is in a line parallel with the *left* foot.
The pose is *en deuxième arabesque (epaulée).*

25. Execute **three** *fouettés à terre.*[1]
(i) Keep the *left* knee straight and sweep the *left* foot across the ground into the air so that it is raised four inches above the ground, pointing to 1.
(ii) In the reverse manner sweep the *left* foot backwards so that it is raised slightly in the air, pointing to 3.
(iii) Repeat (i), but allow the *left* knee to bend slightly

---

[1] This *fouetté* resembles the execution of *grands battements en cloche.* That is, a *grand battement* from the *fourth* position *front, en l'air—fourth* position *back, en l'air,* or *vice versa, degagé en avant et en arrière.*

Adagio

when the foot passes to the *fourth* position *front*, *en l'air* (*demi-position*), **at the same time—**
Open the arms to the *second* position.

26. Lower the *left* foot to the *fifth* position *front* and *demi-pliez* on both feet, **at the same time—**
Lower the arms to the *fifth* position *en bas*.

27. Execute **two** *grands changements*, facing 5. That is :
(*a*) Leap upwards into the air on both feet.
While the body is in the air—
Bend both knees and bring together the flat of the soles, forcing the insteps well outwards.
Come to the ground—allowing the knees to bend— with the feet in the *fifth* position, *right* foot in front.
(*b*) Repeat (*a*), finishing with the feet in the *fifth* position, *left* foot in front.

Exercise of the Left Foot in Pas de Chaconne.

Stand erect in the centre of the room and face 5, with the head upright, the knees straight, the feet in the **fifth** position, **left** foot in *front*, and the arms in the *fifth* position *en bas*. The direction of the body is *en face*.

Repeat the whole of the last exercise, reading **left for right**, and *vice versa*, while, owing to the reverse direction of the body's turns, the wall numbers stated above will now correspond to those directly opposite—that is : 8—6, 3—4, 4—8, 6—8, 1—2, 7—5, 5—7, 2—1.

PREMIÈRE ET SECONDE ARABESQUE.

Stand erect in the centre of the room and face 2, with the head inclined to 3, the feet in the fifth position, right foot in *front*, and the arms in the *fifth* position *en bas*.

The direction of the body is *encroisé*.

1. *Demi-pliez* on both feet.
2. (*a*) Slide the *right* foot to the *fourth* position *front*, straightening both knees.
   (*b*) Raise the *left* foot *pointe tendue* so that the weight of the body falls on the *right* foot, **at the same time—**
   Slightly open the arms between the *fifth* position *en bas* and the *second* position.
   Incline the head to 3.
   The direction of the body is *encroisé en arrière*.
3. Execute a *port de bras*, thus :—
   (*a*) Lower the *left* heel to the ground and *demi-pliez* on both feet, **at the same time—**
   Lower the arms to the *fifth* position *en bas*.
   (*b*) Straighten both knees and raise the *right* foot *pointe tendue* so that the weight of the body is transferred to the *left* foot, **at the same time—**
   Raise the arms to the *fifth* position *en avant*, now open the arms a little more so that their position is halfway between the *fifth en bas* and *second* positions.
   Slightly incline the head towards 1.
   The direction of the body is *encroisé en avant*.
4. Bring the *right* foot *sur le cou de pied en avant*, **at the same time—**
   Lower the arms to the *fifth* position *en bas*.
5. Execute a *Developpé à la première arabesque*. That is:—
   (*a*) Raise the *right* foot as high as possible so that the toe is in a line with the *left* knee and the thigh raised to the *second* position, *en l'air*, **at the same time—**
   Raise the arms to the *fifth* position *en avant*.
   Turn to the left so that the body faces 6.
   (*b*) Slightly raise the *left* arm and extend it in a line with, and at right angles to, the *left* shoulder, pointing to 6, **at the same time—**
   Sweep the *right* hand outward and backward until it is in a line parallel to the *right* calf, pointing to 8.
   Straighten the *right* knee and extend the *right* foot to the *fourth* position *back*, *en l'air*, pointing to 8.
   The pose is *en première arabesque*.

6. Keep the same pose and turn to the *left* on the flat of the *left* foot until the body again faces 6.

7. (*a*) Keep the arms extended and, without bending the *left* knee, bend the body downwards from the waist until the finger-tips of the *left* hand touch the ground, while the *right* leg moves naturally upward so that the *left* arm and the *right* leg are always in the same straight line.
(*b*) Raise the body from the waist until the pose is again *en première arabesque*.

8. Execute a **Grand fouetté en l'air en tournant en dedans.** That is :—
(*a*) Rise on the *left demi-pointe*.
(*b*) Lower the *left* heel to the ground, **at the same time—**
Sweep the *right* foot to the *fourth* position *front, en l'air*, pointing to 6.
Lower the arms to the *fifth* position *en bas*, keep them rounded, and then raise them to the *fifth* position *en avant*.
Incline the head to 5.
(*c*) Now rise on the *left demi-pointe* and turn to the *left* in the same pose until the body faces 8.
Leave the *right* arm and *right* leg pointing to 8, and (allowing the arm and leg to pivot respectively on the shoulder and hip) turn the body to the *left* until the body faces 6, **at the same time—**
Gradually raise the *left* arm to the *fourth* position *en haut*.
When the body faces 6—
Extend the *left* arm to the *fourth* position *front*, pointing to 6.
The pose is again *en première arabesque*.

9. Execute a *Grand fouetté en l'air en tournant en dedans (demi-tour)*. That is :—
(*a*) Rise on the *left demi-pointe*.
(*b*) Lower the *left* heel to the ground, **at the same time—**
Sweep the *right* foot to the *fourth* position *front, en l'air*, pointing to 6.
Lower the arms to the *fifth* position *en bas*, keep them rounded, and raise them to the *fifth* position *en avant*.
(*c*) Now rise on the *left demi-pointe* and turn to the *left* in the same pose until the body faces 7.

When the body faces 7, leave the *right* arm and *right* leg pointing to 7, and (allowing the arm and leg to pivot respectively on the shoulder and hip) turn the body to the *left* until it faces 5.

As the body passes from 7—5—

Raise the *left* arm to the *fourth* position *en haut*.

10. (*a*) Lower the *left* arm to the *fourth* position *en avant* and open the arms to the *second* position.

(*b*) Lower the *right* arm to the *fifth* position and raise it to the *fourth* position *en avant*, **at the same time**—
Incline the head to 6.

(*c*) Turn the hands palm downwards, lower them, and carry them to the *left*.

The pose is *en troisième arabesque* (*effacée*).

11. *Demi-pliez* on the *left* foot, **at the same time**—
Move the *right* foot to the *fourth* position *back*, *en l'air* (*epaulé*), pointing to 4, **at the same time**—
Extend both arms.

The pose is *en cinquième arabesque* (*effacée*).

12. Execute a *Jeté en arrière*, followed by *un tour en dedans de pirouette developpé à la première arabesque*. That is :—

(*a*) Spring on the *right demi-pointe* towards 4.

As the foot touches the ground—

Raise the *left* foot as high as possible so that the toe is in a line with the *right* knee and the thigh raised to the *second* position *en l'air*, **at the same time**—
Lower the arms to the *fifth* position *en bas*.

(*b*) Pirouette on the *right demi-pointe* to the **right**, until the body passes 8 and faces 8 again, **at the same time**—

Gradually raise the arms to the *fifth* position *en avant*.

When the body faces 8 for the last time—

Extend the *left* foot to the *fourth* position *back*, *en l'air*, pointing to 6, **at the same time**—
Extend the *right* arm to the *fourth* position *front*, pointing to 8.

Extend the *left* arm to the *fourth* position *back*, pointing to 6.

The pose is again *en première arabesque*.

13. (*a*) Lower the *left* arm to the *first* position and raise it, **at the same time** slightly lower the *right* arm so that the two meet in the *fifth* position *en avant*.

(b) Sweep the *right* arm backward until it is parallel with the *left* calf, **at the same time**—
Extend the *left* arm in a line with, and at right angles to, the *left* shoulder.
Turn the head to the *left* so that it faces 5.
The pose is *en deuxième arabesque (epaulée)*.

14. Execute a *Developpé degagé à la seconde*. That is:—
Keep the *left* foot pointing to 6, and (allowing the leg to turn on the pivot of the hip), turn the **body from the waist only** to the *left* until it faces 5.
As the body passes from 8—5—
Raise the *left* arm in front of the head, **at the same time**—
Bring the *right* arm to the *fourth* position *en avant*.
Incline the head and body—from the waist—to 8.

15. In the same pose turn to the *left* on the flat of the *right* foot until the body again faces 1, *left* foot pointing to 2.
When the body faces 1—
Rise on the *right demi-pointe*, **at the same time**—
Open the *right* arm to the *second* position.
Slightly lower the *left* hand so that the finger-tips touch the lips.

16. Execute a *Jeté en avant*. That is :—
Spring forward on the *left demi-pointe* towards 2.
Raise the *right* foot to the *fourth* position *back, en l'air*, **at the same time**—
Lower the *left* heel to the ground and *demi-pliez* on the *left* foot.
Gracefully extend the *left* hand [1] in a line with and at right angles to the *left* shoulder, pointing to 2.
Move the *right* arm backwards so that it points **to 4.**

17. Execute a *Pas de bourré en sussous*. That is :—
(a) Straighten the *left* knee and rise *sur la demi-pointe*, **at the same time**—
Lower the *right* foot to the *fifth* position *back* and keep it *sur la demi-pointe*.
Bring the arms to the *fifth* position *en bas*.
(b) Slide the *left* foot to the *second* position, keeping it *sur la demi-pointe*, **at the same time**—
Open the arms to the *demi-seconde* position.
(c) Lower the *left* heel to the ground, **at the same time**—
Slide the *right* foot to the *first* position, lower the

---

[1] Palm upwards.

heel to the ground, and *demi-pliez* on the *right* foot.
Lower the arms to the *fifth* position *en bas*.
(*d*) Slide the *right* foot to the *fifth* position *front*,
then to the *fourth* position *front*, at the same time—
Raise the *left* foot *sur la pointe tendue*.
Raise the arms *en attitude*, *left* arm up.
The pose is *en attitude* (*encroisée*).

18. Execute **Grand** *preparation pour pirouette en dedans*.

19. Execute *un tour en dedans de pirouette sur le cou de
pied*.   That is :—
Pirouette to the *right* on the *right demi-pointe* so that
the body passes 5 and returns to 5.[1]
At the commencement of the *pirouette*—
Bring the *left* foot *sur le cou de pied en avant*, at the
same time—
Lower the arms to the *fifth* position *en bas*.
When the body faces 5 for the last time—
Lower the *left* foot to the *fifth* position *front* and
demi-pliez on the *left* foot, at the same time—
Raise the *right* foot *sur le cou de pied en avant*.

20. Straighten the *left* knee, at the same time—
Slide the *right* foot to the *fourth* position *front*,
pointe tendue, to 1.
Raise the arms *en attitude*, *left* arm up.
Incline the head and body—from the waist—
towards 2.
The direction of the body is *effacé*.

Exercise of the Left Foot in Première et Seconde Arabesque.

Stand erect in the centre of the room and face 1, with
the head inclined to 4, the knees straight, the feet in the
fifth position, left foot in *front*, and the arms in the *fifth*
position *en bas*.

The direction of the body is *encroisé*.

Repeat the whole of the last exercise, reading *left* for
right, and *vice versa* ; while, owing to the reverse direction
of the body's turns, the wall numbers stated above will
now correspond to those directly opposite—that is : 8—6,
3—4, 4—3, 6—8, 1—2, 7—5, 5—7, 2—1.

---

[1] The body moves from 2-5-1-8-4-7-3-6-2-5.

Adagio

DEUX TOURS EN DEHORS DE PIROUETTE SUR LE COU-DE-PIED, JETÉ, ASSEMBLÉ, ET ENTRECHAT[1] QUATRE.

Stand erect in the centre of the room and face 5, with the head upright, the feet in the **fifth** position, **right foot in** *front*, and the arms in the *fifth* position *en bas*.

The direction of the body is *en face*.

1. *Demi-pliez* on both feet and rise *sur les demi-pointes*.

2. Lower the *left* heel to the ground, **at the same time—** Open the *right* foot to the *second* position and carry it out a little further so that the toe is raised six inches above the ground.
   Raise the arms to the *second* position.

3. Rise on the *left demi-pointe*, **at the same time—**

4. Lower the *left* heel to the ground.
   Lower the *right* foot to the *second* position.
   (Immediately the feet come to the ground, *demi-pliez* on both feet.)
   Carry the *right* arm to the *fourth* position *en avant*.

5. Execute *deux tours en dehors de pirouette sur le cou de pied*, as follows :—
   (*a*) Turn on the *left demi-pointe* to the **right**.
   Exactly at the commencement of the *pirouette*— Bring the *right* foot *sur le cou de pied en avant*, **at the same time—**
   Lower the arms to the *fifth* position *en bas*.
   Finish with the *right* foot in the same position, **and** the body facing 5.
   (*b*) Lower the *left* heel to the ground, **at the same time—**
   Demi-pliez on the *left* foot.

6. Execute a *Jeté à la seconde*,[2] as follows :—
   Open the *right* foot to the *second* position and **sweep** it to the *second* position, *en l'air* (*demi-position*), **at the same time—**
   Open the arms to the *demi-seconde* position.
   As the foot rises to the *second* position *en l'air* (*demi-position*)—

---

1 **Entrechat** is derived from the Italian *intrecciare*, to weave or to braid.

2 In the execution of *Jetés* and *Assemblés* slide the foot well along the ground before it is opened to the *second* position, *en l'air* (*demi-position*).

Spring lightly upward into the air on the *left* foot.
Come to the ground on the *right* foot—allowing the
knee to bend—in the place vacated by the *left* foot,
at the same time—
Bring the *left* foot *sur le cou de pied en arrière*.

7. Execute a **petit Assemblé de coté**[1] with the *left*
   foot, as follows:—
   (*a*) Open the *left* foot to the *second* position, *en l'air*
   (*demi-position*), **at the same time**—
   Open the arms to the *demi-seconde* position.
   (*b*) Spring lightly upward into the air on the *right*
   foot. While the body is in the air, quickly press
   together the flat of the toes of both feet, and come
   to the ground with the feet in the *fifth* position,
   left foot in *front*.

8. Execute an **Entrechat quatre**,[2] as follows :—
   Spring upward into the air on both feet. While
   the body is in the air, bend the knees and simultaneously interchange the feet (that is, as the *right*
   foot passes in front of the *left* foot, the *left* foot passes
   behind the *right* foot). At the same time beat the
   feet [3] one against the other.
   At the moment of alighting, again simultaneously
   interchange the feet and beat them one against the
   other, and come to the ground—allowing the knees
   to bend, to sustain the shock—with the feet in the
   fifth position, *left* foot in *front*.
   Bring the body erect.

REPEAT this exercise on the *left* foot, reading *left* for
right, and *vice versa*.

---

[1] In the execution of *Jeté* and *Assemblés* slide the foot well along the
ground before it is opened to the *second* position, *en l'air* (*demi-position*).

[2] *Entrechat quatre* corresponds to two *changements* executed successively, except that the feet beat one against the other in passing.

[3] In the execution of *entrechats* the **whole** of each foot **from the toe
to the calf** must beat one against the other **and not simply the heels alone**—
this is a common and serious fault.

Adagio

GRAND ROND DE JAMBE EN L'AIR EN TOURNANT AVEC LES JETÉS.

Stand erect in the centre of the room and face 2, with the head inclined to 3, the feet in the **fifth** position, **right** foot in *front*, and the arms in the *fifth* position *en bas*.

The direction of the body is *encroisé*.

1. *Pliez* on both feet.
   As the heels rise from the ground, carry the *left* hand outward so that it is held about six inches from the knee.
2. Turn on the *left demi-pointe* to the **right** until the body passes 5, and continue in the same direction until it faces 5 again.
   During the execution of the *tour*—
   (*a*) Gradually straighten the *left* knee and rise *sur la demi-pointe*, **at the same time**—
   Bring the *right* foot *sur le cou de pied en avant*, and raise the foot as high as possible—keeping the toe pointed well downwards—until the toe is in a line with the *left* knee and the thigh raised to the *second* position, *en l'air*.
   Bring the arms to the *fifth* position *en bas*.
   (*b*) When the body faces 5 for the last time—
   Lower the *left* heel to the ground, **at the same time**—
   Extend the *right* foot to the *fourth* position *front*.
   Raise the arms to the *fifth* position *en avant*.
3. Execute a *grand rond de jambe en l'air en dehors*.
   As the foot passes from the *fourth* position *front*, *en l'air*, to the *second* position, *en l'air*, open the arms to the *second* position.
   Keep the arms extended as the foot moves from the *second* position, *en l'air* to the *fourth* position *back*, *en l'air*.
   Having completed the *rond de jambe*, in continuation of the movement—
4. Execute a *Developpé à la seconde, en l'air, en tournant en dehors*. That is :
   (*a*) Turn to the **right** until the body faces 5 again, **at the same time**—
   Bend the *right* knee so that the thigh moves gradually to the *second* position, *en l'air*, and the *right* toe is in a line with the *left* knee.
   Lower the arms to the *fifth* position *en bas*.
   (*b*) When the body faces 5—

Extend the *right* foot to the *second* position, *en l'air*, at the same time—
Open the arms to the *second* position.

5. *Demi-pliez* on the *left* foot.
6. Execute a **Jeté de coté.** That is :—
    Spring sideways on the *right demi-pointe*.
    As the foot touches the ground—
    Raise the *left* foot to the *second* position, *en l'air*, at the same time—
    Lower the *right* heel to the ground.
    The arms remain in the *second* position.
7. *Demi-pliez* on the *right demi-pointe*.
8. Execute a *Jeté de coté.* That is :—
    Spring sideways on the *left demi-pointe*.
    As the foot touches the ground—
    Raise the *right* foot to the *second* position, *en l'air*, at the same time—
    Lower the *left* heel to the ground.
    The arms remain in the *second* position.
9. Lower the *left* arm to the *first* position, pass it to the *fifth* position and raise it to the *fourth* position *en avant*.
    The arms are in the *fourth* position *en avant*. **At the same time—**
    Slightly turn the body to the *right* so that it faces 1, and incline the head and body—from the waist—toward 2.
    Allow the *right* foot to turn on the pivot of the hip so that it is extended to the *fourth* position *front, en l'air*, pointing to 1.
    The direction of the body is *à la quatrième position* (*effacée*).
10. (*a*) Lower the *right* foot to the *fourth* position *front*, keeping it *sur la pointe tendue*.
    (*b*) Slide the *right* foot to the *first* position, execute a *plié* in the *first* position, then slide the *right* foot to *fourth* position *back, pointe tendue* (*encroisé*), **at the same time—**
    Lower the arms to the *fifth* position *en bas*, and raise them to the *fifth* position *en avant*.
11. Execute a *grand Jeté à l'attitude*. That is :—
    Spring upward on the *left* foot into the air, turning the body to the **left** so that it faces 2. Come to the ground on the *right demi-pointe*, and at the moment of alighting—

Adagio

Raise the *left* foot *à l'attitude*, **at the same time—**
Raise the arms *en attitude* (*left* arm up).
The pose is *en attitude* (*encroisée*).
Without stopping, pass to the next movement—

12. Lower the *right* heel to the ground and *demi-pliez* on the *right* foot, **at the same time—**
Slide the *left* foot backwards towards 4, keeping it *pointe tendue*.
Lower the *left* arm and extend it in a line with and at right angles to the shoulder.
Sweep the *right* arm in a semi-circle outward and backward until it is extended in a line parallel to the *left* calf.
The pose is *en quatrième arabesque* (*encroisée*).

13. Slide the *left* foot to the *fifth* position *back*, **at the same time—**
Lower the arms to the *fifth* position *en bas*.
Bring the body erect and rise *sur les demi-pointes*.

14. Lower the heels to the ground, **at the same time—**
Demi-pliez on both feet.
Incline the head towards 3.

15. Execute **one** *grand changement* and finish with the feet in the *fifth* position, *left* foot in *front*, facing 1.
While the body is in the air, bring the head erect.
When the feet come to the ground, incline the head to 4.

Exercise of the Left Foot in Grand Rond de Jambe en Tournant avec les Jetés.

Stand erect in the centre of the room and face 1, with the head inclined to 4, the knees straight, the feet in the **fifth** position, **left** foot in *front*, and the arms in the *fifth* position *en bas*.

The direction of the body is *encroisé*.

Repeat the whole of the last exercise, reading **left** for **right**, and *vice versa*; while, owing to the reverse direction of the body's turns, the wall numbers stated above will now correspond with those directly opposite—that is: 8—6, 3—4, 4—3, 6—8, 1—2, 7—5, 5—7, 2—1.

FOUETTÉ ET BALLOTTÉ.[1]

Stand erect in the centre of the room and face 2, with the head inclined to 3, the knees straight, the feet in the **fifth** position, **right** foot in *front*, and the arms in the *fifth* position *en bas*. The direction of the body is *encroisé*.

Part I.—*Fouetté et Ballotté en face.*

1. *Demi-pliez* on both feet, and rise *sur les demi-pointes*.
2. Raise the arms *en attitude, left* arm up.
3. Execute the *Second* Exercise on *port de bras*. That is:—
   (*a*) Move the *left* arm in a semi-circle outward and backward until it points to 4, **at the same time**—
   Move the *right* arm in a semi-circle forward and inward until it is extended in a line with and at right angles to the shoulder pointing to 2.
   Incline the head towards 1.
   (*b*) Lower the *left* arm to the *first* position, pass it to the *fifth* position, and raise it to the *fourth* position *en avant* so that the arms form the *fifth* position *en avant*. Bring the head erect.
   (*c*) Repeat No. 2.
4. Lower the *left* heel to the ground, **at the same time**—
   Raise the *right* foot *sur le cou de pied en avant*.
   Lower both arms to the *fifth* position *en bas*.
   Slightly turn to **right** so that the body faces 5.
5. Execute a *Developpé à la quatrième en avant, en l'air* (*effacé*). That is :—
   (*a*) Raise the *right* foot as high as possible—keeping the toe pointed well downwards—until the toe is in a line with the *left* knee and the thigh raised to the *second* position, *en l'air*, **at the same time**—
   Raise the arms to the *fifth* position *en avant*.
   (*b*) Extend the *right* foot to the *fourth* position front, *en l'air*, pointing to 1, **at the same time**—
   Open the *right* arm to the *second* position.
   Incline the head to 2.
6. *Demi-pliez* on the *left* foot.
7. In one sweeping movement—
   Turn slightly to the *left* so that the body faces 5, **at the same time**—
   Straighten the *left* knee and rise *sur la demi-pointe*.
   Move the *right* foot to the *second* position, *en l'air.*
   Raise *left* arm in semi-circular movement so that it passes above the head and then to the *second* position.

[1] From *ballotter*, to toss or shake about ; but movements in the **above** exercise more closely correspond to the rolling motion of a **ship.**

Raise the *right* arm above the head.
Bring the body erect, facing 5.
Lower the *left* heel to the ground.

8. Turn to the *left* on the flat of the *left* foot, so that
   the body faces 2.
   Pass the *right* foot *à l'attitude*, **at the same time**—
   Lower the *left* arm to the *demi-seconde* position.
   The pose is *en attitude* (*epaulée*).

9. (*a*) Lower the *left* arm to the *first* position, pass it
   to the *fifth* position, and raise it to the *fourth* position *en avant*, **at the same time**—
   Gradually lower the *right* arm so that the two arms
   form the *fifth* position *en avant*.
   (*b*) Raise the *left* arm above the head.
   Carry the *right* arm to the *demi-seconde* position.
   The arms are *en attitude* (*effacée*).

10. Extend the *left* arm in a line with and at right angles
    to the shoulder, pointing to 2, **at the same time**—
    Move the *right* arm backwards, pointing to 4.
    Extend the *right* foot to the *fourth* position *back*,
    en l'air, pointing to 4.
    Demi-pliez on the *left* foot.
    The pose is *en quatrième arabesque* (*effacée*).

11. Execute *Ballotté* (*position effacé*). That is :—
    (*a*) Lower the *right* foot to the *fourth* position *back*,
    pointe tendue.
    (*b*) Slide the *right* foot to the *fifth* position *back*,
    at the same time—
    Straighten the *left* knee, then—
    Rise *sur les demi-pointes*, **at the same time**—
    Lower the arms to the *fifth* position *en bas*.
    (*c*) Lower the *right* heel to the ground, **at the same
    time**—
    Raise the *left* foot *sur le cou de pied en avant*.
    (*d*) Raise the *left* foot as high as possible—keeping
    the toe pointed well downwards—until the toe is
    in a line with the *right* knee and the thigh raised to
    the *second* position, *en l'air*, **at the same time**—
    Raise the arms to the *fifth* position *en avant*.
    (*e*) Extend the *left* foot to the *fourth* position *front*,
    pointing to 2, **at the same time**—
    Open the arms to the *second* position.
    Slightly incline the head and body towards 1.
    (Position *effacé*.)

12. Execute *Ballotté* (*position epaulé*). That is :—
(*a*) *Demi-pliez* on the *right* foot, **at the same time**—
Lower the *left* foot to the *fourth* position *front*, keeping it *pointe tendue.*
(*b*) Slide the *left* foot to the *fifth* position *front*, **at the same time**—
Straighten the *right* knee, then—
Rise *sur les demi-pointes*, **at the same time**—
Lower the arms to the *fifth* position *en bas.*
(*c*) Lower the *left* heel to the ground, **at the same time**—
Raise the *right* foot *sur le cou de pied en arrière.*
(*d*) Raise the *right* foot as high as possible—keeping the toe pointed well downwards—until the toe is in a line with the *left* knee and the thigh raised to the *second* position, *en l'air*, **at the same time**—
Raise both arms to the *fifth* position *en avant*, then to the *fifth* position *en haut.*
(*e*) Raise the *right* foot *à l'attitude*, **at the same time**—
Turn the hands—palm downwards—at the same height (see Fig. 71).
(*f*) Extend the *right* foot to the *fourth* position *back*, *en l'air*, **at the same time**—
Demi-pliez on the *left* foot.
Extend the arms.
The pose is *en cinquième arabesque* (*epaulée*).

13. Execute *Ballotté* (*position effacé*).
(*a*) Lower the *right* foot to the *fourth* position *back, pointe tendue*, **at the same time**—
Bring the arms to *second* position (palms downwards).
(*b*) Slide the *right* foot to the *fifth* position *back*, **at the same time**—
Straighten the *left* knee, then—
Rise *sur les demi-pointes*, **at the same time**—
Lower the arms to the *fifth* position *en bas.*
(*c*) Lower the *right* heel to the ground, **at the same time**—
Raise the *left* foot *sur le cou de pied en avant.*

Repeat Nos. 5—13, reading *left* for *right*, and *vice versa* ; while, owing to the reverse direction of the body's turns, the wall numbers stated above will now correspond to those directly opposite—that is : 8—6, 3—4, 4—3, 6—8, 1—2, 7—5, 5—7, 2—1. Then turn slightly to the **left** so that the body faces 5.

Adagio

Part II.—*Fouetté et Ballotté en tournant.*

14. Execute a *Developpé à la quatrième en avant, en l'air.*
That is :—
(*a*) Raise the *right* foot as high as possible—keeping the toe pointed well downwards—until the toe is in a line with the side of the *left* knee and the thigh raised to the *second* position, *en l'air,* **at the same time**—
Raise the arms to the *fifth* position *en avant.*
(*b*) Extend the *right* foot to the *fourth* position *front, en l'air,* **at the same time**—
Open the *right* arm to the *second* position.

15. *Demi-pliez* on the *left* foot.

16. Straighten the *left* knee and rise *sur la demi-pointe,* **at the same time**—
Execute with the *right* foot a *demi-grand rond de jambe en l'air en dehors.* That is :—
Move the *right* foot from the *fourth* position *front, en l'air*—the *second* position, *en l'air,* **at the same time**—
Raise the *right* arm above the head.
Raise the *left* arm above the head and lower it to the *second* position.

17. Execute with the *right* foot a *demi-grand rond de jambe en l'air en dehors.* That is :—
Move the *right* foot from the *second* position, *en l'air*—the *fourth* position *back, en l'air.* Then pass the foot *à l'attitude.*

18. (*a*) Lower the *right* arm to the *fourth* position *en avant.*
(*b*) Extend the *right* foot to the *fourth* position *back, en l'air,* **at the same time**—
Extend the *right* arm so that it points to 5.
Move the *left* arm in a semi-circle outward and backward until it is in a line parallel to the *right* calf, pointing to 7.
The pose is *en deuxième arabesque.*

19. Execute a *Developpé à la quatrième en avant, en l'air (effacé) en tournant en dehors.*[1] That is :—
(*a*) Sweep the *right* arm between the *second* position and the *fourth* position *back,* **at the same time**—
Demi-pliez on the *left* foot.
(*b*) Straighten the *left* knee, rise *sur la demi-pointe* and turn to *right* until the body faces 1.

[1] The body moves from 5-1-8-4-7-3-6-2-5-1.

(*c*) As the body passes from 5—4—
Bend the *right* knee so that the thigh moves gradually to the *second* position, *en l'air*, and the *right* toe is in a line with the *left* knee, **at the same time**—
Bring the arms to the *fifth* position *en bas*.
Incline the head towards 2.

(*d*) As the body passes from 4—1—
Raise arms to *fifth* position *en avant*, **at the same time**—
Bring the head erect.

(*e*) When the body faces 1—
Extend *right* foot to *fourth* position *front*, *en l'air*, pointing to 1, **at the same time**—
Open the arms to the *second* position.
Incline the head to 2.

(*a*) is the preparation for the movement ; (*b*), (*c*) and (*d*) are to be executed during the tour.

20. (*a*) Rise on the *left demi-pointe*.
(*b*) Lower the *right* foot—with the leg well extended—to *fourth* position *front*, **at the same time**—
Bring the *left* arm to the *fourth* position *en avant*.
The pose is *à la quatrième position en avant* (*effacé*).

21. *Demi-pliez* in the *fourth* position, **at the same time**—
Bring the head erect.

22. Execute *un tour en dehors à l'attitude*. That is :—
Turn on the *right* foot to the **left** until the body faces 5.[1]
During the *tour*—
Rise on the *right demi-pointe*, straightening the *right* knee, **at the same time**—
Raise the *left* leg *à l'attitude*.
Raise the arms to the *fifth* position *en avant*, then raise the *left* arm above the head, **at the same time**—
Lower the *right* arm to the *demi-seconde* position.
When the body faces 5 for the last time—
Lower *right* heel to ground, **at the same time**—
Bring the arms to the *second* position, then—
Lower the *left* arm—turning the hand palm downwards—and gracefully pass it to the *first* position, to the *fifth* position, then raise it to the *fourth* position *en avant* and carry it near to the breast, **at the same time**—
Turn the *right* hand palm downwards and lower it to the *demi-seconde* position.

---

1 The body moves from 1-5-2-6-3-7-4-8-1-5.

Adagio

Both arms point to 8.

The pose is *en troisième arabesque.*

23. *Demi-pliez* on the *right* foot.

24. Execute a *Grand fouetté en tournant en dedans.* That is :—

    (*a*) Extend the *left* foot to the *fourth* position *back*, *en l'air.*

    (*b*) Spring backwards on the *left* foot, keeping it *sur la demi-pointe*, **at the same time**—

    Slide the *right* foot across the ground and execute a *grand battement à la quatrième en avant*, *en l'air*, so that the foot points to 7.

    Raise the arms to the *fifth* position *en avant.*

25. Continue to turn on the *left demi-pointe* to the **left** until the body faces 5.

    During this movement, keep the *right* foot **pointing to 7,** and allow it to turn on the pivot of **the hip.**

    When the body faces 5.

    Open the arms between the *fifth* position *en avant* and the *second* position, with the palms of the hands half turned upwards, **at the same time**—

    Lower the *left* heel to the ground and *demi-pliez* on the *left* foot.

26. **Lower** the *right* foot to the *fourth* position *back*, *pointe tendue,* and slide it to the *fifth* position *back*, allowing the knee to bend, then

    Bring the body erect and rise *sur les demi-pointes.*

    During this movement, gradually lower the arms to the *fifth* position *en bas.*

27. Lower the *right* heel to the ground, **at the same time**—

    Raise the *left* foot *sur le cou de pied en avant.*

Repeat Nos. 14—26, reading *left* for *right*, and *vice versa* ; while, owing to the reverse direction of the body's turns, the wall numbers stated above will now correspond to those directly opposite—that is : 8—6, 3—4, 4—3, 6—8, 1—2, 7—5, 5—7, 2—1.

TROISIÈME ET QUATRIÈME ARABESQUE.

Stand erect in the centre of the room and face 1, with the head upright, the knees straight, the feet in the *fifth* position, **right** foot in front, and the arms in the *fifth* position *en bas*.

The direction of the body is *effacé*.

1. (*a*) *Demi-pliez* on both feet and rise *sur les demi-pointes*.
   (*b*) Lower the *left* heel to ground, **at the same time—**
   Bring the *right* foot *sur le cou de pied en avant*.

2. Execute with the *right* foot a *Developpé à la quatrième en avant, en l'air—*
   (*a*) Raise the *right* foot as high as possible so that the toe—with the toe pointed well downwards—is in a line with the side of the *left* knee and the thigh raised to *second* position, *en l'air*, **at the same time—**
   Raise the arms to the *fifth* position *en avant*.
   (*b*) Extend the *right* foot to the *fourth* position *front en l'air*, pointing to 1, **at the same time—**
   Raise the arms *en attitude*, *right* arm up.

3. *Demi-pliez* on the *left* foot.

4. Execute a *Jeté en avant*. That is :—
   Spring forward on the *right demi-pointe* towards 1. As the foot touches the ground—
   Raise the *left* foot to the *fourth* position *back en l'air*, pointing to 3, **at the same time—**
   Extend the *left* arm to the *fourth* position *back*, pointing to 3.
   Extend the *right* arm to the *fourth* position *front*, pointing to 1.
   The pose is *en première arabesque*.

5. Bring the arms to the *second* position (palms downwards), lower them to the *first* position, pass them to the *fifth* position *en bas*, and raise them to the *fifth* position *en avant*, then—
   Bend the *right* arm at the elbow and turn the hand inwards so that the finger-tips touch the *right* jaw, at **the same time—**
   Bring the *left* arm—palm downwards—near the breast, so that the *right* elbow rests on the knuckles of the *left* hand.
   Turn the head towards 2 and incline it to 1.
   Position *epaulé* (see Fig. 72, but regard the limbs as if in reverse position).

Adagio

6. Return to the pose *en première arabesque.*
7. Execute a *Degagé developpé à la seconde en l'air.*
   That is :—
   Keep the *left* foot pointing to 6, and allowing it to turn on the pivot of the hip, turn the head and body—from the waist—to the *right* so that the body faces 5, **at the same time—**
   Incline the body towards 8.
8. Rise on the *right demi-pointe.*
   Gracefully lower the *left* hand so that the finger tips touch the lips.
9. Execute a *Jeté de coté.* That is :—
   Spring sideways on the *left demi-pointe* towards 2.
   As the foot touches the ground—
   Raise the *right* foot to the *fourth* position *back, en l'air,* **at the same time—**
   Lower the *left* heel to the ground and *demi-pliez* on the *left* foot.
   Extend the *left* hand—palm upwards—to the *fourth* position *front.*
   Without stopping, pass to the execution of the next movement—
10. Execute a *Pas de bourré en sussous.* That is :—
    (*a*) Straighten the *left* knee and rise *sur la demi-pointe,* **at the same time—**
    Lower the *right* foot to the *fifth* position *back,* and keep it *sur la demi-pointe.*
    Lower the arms to the *fifth* position *en bas.*
    (*b*) Open the *left* foot to the *second* position, keeping it *sur la demi-pointe.*
    (*c*) Lower the *left* heel to the ground, **at the same time—**
    Slide the *right* foot to the *first* position and **lower the** heel to the ground.
    (*d*) *Demi-pliez* on both feet, then slide the *right* foot to the *fifth* position *front,* then to *fourth* position *front (encroisé)* towards 2.
11. Straighten the *right* knee, **at the same time—**
    Raise the *left* foot to the *fourth* position *back, en l'air,* pointing to 4.
    Raise the arms to the *fifth* position *en avant,* and open them *en première arabesque, right* arm forward.
    The pose is *en première arabesque (encroisée).*
12. Execute *un tour en dedans renversé à la seconde en l'air.* That is :—

Turn to the **right** on the *right demi-pointe* so that the body faces 2.

At the commencement of the *tour*—

Move the arms—palms downwards—between the *second* and *fifth* positions *en avant*, **at the same time**—

Bend the *left* knee so that the toe is in a line with the side of the *right* knee and the thigh raised to the *second* position, *en l'air*.

Bring the body erect.

As the body passes from 2—1—

Bring the arms to the *fifth* position *en avant* and raise them to the *fifth* position *en hàut*, **at the same time**—

Incline the head and body—from the **waist**—**as** far as possible towards the *left* shoulder.

When the body faces 3—

Rise *sur les trois quarts de la pointe* and execute **a** *renversé*. That is :—

In one sweeping movement, simultaneously—

Quickly incline the head and body—from **the** waist—towards 1.

Open the *left* foot to the *second* position, *en l'air*, pointing to 3.

Bring the arms to the *second* position.

When the body faces 2—

Lower the *left* foot to the *fifth* position *front*, **at the same time**—

Bring the body erect.

Lower the arms to the *fifth* position *en bas*.

13. Rise *sur les demi-pointes*.

14. Execute a *Pas de bourré marché sur les demi-pointes*, That is :—

By a series of little close steps *sur les demi-pointes*, step to the *left* in a semi-circular direction so that the body passes 6—3—7—4—8—1—5—2, until you are in the centre of the room and the body faces 2.

15. Lower the *right* heel to the ground, **at the same time**— Raise the *left* foot *sur le cou de pied en avant*.

16. Execute with the *left* foot a *developpé à la quatrième en avant en l'air*.

(*a*) Raise the *left* foot as high as possible so that the toe is in a line with the *left* knee and the thigh raised to the *second* position, *en l'air*, **at the same time**— Raise the arms to the *fifth* position *en avant*.

(*b*) Extend the *left* foot to the *fourth* position *front*, *en l'air*, pointing to 2, **at the same time**—

Raise the arms *en attitude, left* arm up.

17. *Demi-pliez* on the *right* foot.

18. Execute a *Jeté en avant.* That is :—
Spring forward on the *left demi-pointe* towards 2.
As the foot touches the ground—
Raise the *right* foot to the *fourth* position *back, en l'air,*
pointing to 4, **at the same time**—
Extend the *right* arm to the *fourth* position *back,*
pointing to 4. ·
Extend the *left* arm to the *fourth* position *front,*
pointing to 2.
The pose is *en première arabesque.*

19. Bring the arms to the *second* position—palms downwards—lower them to the *first* position, pass them
to the *fifth* position *en bas,* and raise them to the
fifth position *en avant,* then—
Bring the hands together, and—allowing the elbows
to bend—carry the hands towards the *left* shoulder
—keeping them in the same closed position—so
that they touch the *left* jaw, **at the same time**—
Turn the head towards 1 and incline it to 2.
The pose is one of meditation (*position epaulé*) (**Fig. 73**)

20. Return to the pose *en première arabesque.*

21. (*a*) *Demi-pliez* on the *left* foot, straighten the
knee, and rise *sur la demi-pointe.*
(*b*) Lower the *left* heel to the ground.

22. Keep the same pose and turn on the flat of the
left foot until the body again faces 2.

23. Execute with the *right* foot a *grand rond de jambe
en l'air en dedans.*
As the foot moves from the *fourth* position *back, en
l'air*—the *second* position, *en l'air*—
Bring the arms to the *second* position.
As the foot moves from the *second* position, *en l'air*—
the *fourth* position *front, en l'air (encroisé),* pointing
to 2—
Bring the arms to the *fifth* position *en avant,* **at the
same time**—
Incline the head to 1.

24. Lower the *right* foot—with the leg extended—to the
ground, keeping it *pointe tendue,* **at the same time**—
Incline the head to the *left.*
Lower the arms—palms downwards—so that the
right hand falls over the *left.*

PAS DE L'ALLIANCE.[1]

Stand erect in the centre of the room and face 2, with the head inclined to 3, the knees straight, the feet in the *fifth* position, **right** foot in *front*, and the arms in the *fifth* position *en bas*. The direction of the body is *encroisé*.

1. (*a*) *Demi-pliez* on both feet.
   (*b*) Slide the *right* foot to the *fourth* position *front*, at the same time—
   Raise the *left* foot, *pointe tendue*, so that the weight of the body falls on the *right* foot.
   Open the arms to the *demi-seconde* position.
   Incline the head and body—from the waist—towards 3.

2. (*a*) *Pliez* on both feet, at the same time—
   Raise the arms to the *second* position and lower them to the *fifth* position *en bas* so that they touch the ground.
   (*b*) Straighten the knees, then—
   Raise the *right* foot *pointe tendue*, so that the weight of the body falls on the *left* foot, at the same time—
   Incline the head to the *right*.
   Open the arms between the *second* position and the *fifth* position *en avant*.

3. Lower the *right* heel to the ground and *demi-pliez* on both feet, at the same time—
   Lower the arms to the *fifth* position *en bas*, and with the *left* foot execute a *Glissade*. That is :—
   (*a*) Slide the *left* foot to the *third* position and then to the *second* position, *pointe tendue*, at the same time—
   Raise the arms to the *demi-seconde* position.
   (*b*) Lower the *left* heel to the ground, at the same time—
   Raise the *right* foot and place it in front of the *left* so that it falls in the *fifth* position *front*.
   Lower the arms to the *fifth* position *en bas*.

4. Execute a *Grand jeté à la seconde en l'air*. That is:—
   Raise the arms to the *second* position, at the same time—
   Open the *left* foot to the *second* position, *en l'air* and jump forward—slightly turning in the air to the

[1] This exercise is entitled *Pas de l'Alliance* because it was composed by the *Maestro Cecchetti* at the conclusion of the Great War, on the occasion of the signing of peace between the Allies and Germany.

right—and come to the ground—allowing the **knee** to bend—so that the body faces 1.

As the foot touches the ground—

Raise the *right* foot to the *fourth* position *back, en l'air*, pointing to 3, **at the same time**—

Keep the *left* arm extended and move it to the *fourth* position *front*, pointing to 1.

Keep the *right* arm extended and move it to the *fourth* position *back*, pointing to 3.

The pose is *en quatrième arabesque* (*encroisée*).

Without stopping, pass to the execution of the next movement—

5. Execute *deux tours en dedans de pirouette à l'attitude*, turning to the *right*. That is :—

(*a*) Execute a *Grand jeté en arrière*. That is :—

Leap backwards on the *right demi-pointe* towards 3.

As the foot touches the ground—

Raise the *left* foot *à l'attitude*, **at the same time**—

Raise the arms *en attitude, left* arm up.

Turn to the *right* so that the body faces 1.

(*b*) Continue in the same pose and direction until the body faces 2, **at the same time**—

Gradually raise the *right* arm so that when the body faces 2 the arms are in the *fifth* position *en haut*.

(*c*) When the body faces 2—

Lower the *right* heel to the ground, **at the same time**—

Incline the head and body—from the waist—as far as possible towards 1.

(The body should be well curved and the head thrown backwards.)

6. Execute a *Developpé à la seconde en l'air*. That is :—

(*a*) Bend the *left* knee so that the thigh moves gradually to the *second* position, *en l'air*, **at the same time**—

Bring the arms to the *second* position and lower them to the *fifth* position *en bas*.

Bring the head and body erect.

(*b*) Extend the *left* foot to the *second* position, *en l'air*, **at the same time**—

Open the arms to the *second* position.

7. Keep the same pose and turn to the *left* until the body faces 5.

8. Execute a *Fouetté à terre à la quatrième en arrière en l'air* (*encroisé*). That is :—
Sweep the *left* foot across the ground and behind the *right* leg until it is raised *à l'attitude*, **at the same time—**
Demi-pliez on the *right* foot.
Extend the *left* arm to the *fourth* position *front.*
Extend the *right* arm to the *fourth* position *back.*
Incline the head and body—from the waist—until it is almost in a horizontal line with the *left* knee, facing 2.
The pose is *en quatrième arabesque* (*encroisée*).

9. Execute a *Developpé degagé à la quatrième en avant en l'air* (*encroisé*), *en tournant en dehors.* That is :—
Turn on the *right* foot until the body faces 1.
At the commencement of the *tour—*
Gradually extend the *left* foot to the *fourth* position *back, en l'air,* **at the same time—**
Raise the *left* arm above the head.
Bring the body erect.
When the body faces 7—
Keep the *left* foot pointing to 5 and allow it to turn on the pivot of the hip.
When the body faces 8—
The *left* leg is extended in the *fourth* position *front, en l'air.*
As the body passes from 8—1—
Gradually raise the *right* arm above the head.
Correspondingly lower the *left* arm, so that when the body faces 1 the arms are *en attitude, right* arm up, **at the same time—**
Incline the head and body—from the waist—to 2.
The pose is *à la quatrième en avant, en l'air* (*encroisé*).

10. Execute a *Jeté en avant.* That is :—
(*a*) Rise on the *right demi-pointe.*
(*b*) Spring forward on the *left demi-pointe* towards 1.
When the foot comes to the ground—
Raise the *right* foot to the *fourth* position *back, en l'air,* **at the same time—**
Lower the *right* arm to the *fourth* position *en avant.*

11. Execute a *Grand jeté en arrière,* followed by *deux tours en dedans à l'attitude.* That is :—
Leap backwards on the *right demi-pointe* towards 3.
As the foot touches the ground—

Raise the *left* foot *à l'attitude*, **at the same time**—
Raise the arms *en attitude*, *left* arm up.
Keep the same pose and execute *deux tours en dedans à l'attitude*.

12. Lower the *right* heel to the ground and *demi-pliez* on the *right* foot, **at the same time**—
Extend the *left* foot to the *fourth* position *back, en l'air* (*epaulé*), pointing to 3.
Bring the arms to the *second* position, palms downwards.

13. Execute a *Pas de bourré en sussous*. That is :—
(*a*) Straighten the *right* knee and rise *sur la demi-pointe*, **at the same time**—
Lower the *left* foot to the *fifth* position *back*, and keep it *sur la demi-pointe*.
The arms remain in the *second* position.
(*b*) Open the *right* foot to the *second* position, keeping it *sur la demi-pointe*.
(*c*) Lower the *right* heel to the ground, **at the same time**—
Bring the *left* foot to the *fifth* position *front*.
Lower the arms to the *fifth* position *en bas*.

14. Execute *Grand preparation pour pirouette en dehors*.

15. Execute *deux tours en dehors de pirouette developpé à l'attitude*. That is :—
Pirouette to the **left** on the *right demi-pointe* until the body passes 5 and faces 5 again.
At the commencement of the *pirouette*—
Bring the *left* foot *sur le cou de pied en avant*.
During the *pirouette*—
Gradually raise the *left* foot as high as possible—keeping the toe pointed well downwards—until the toe is in a line with the *right* knee and the thigh raised to the *second* position, *en l'air*, **at the same time**—
Gradually raise the arms to the *fifth* position *en avant*.
When the body faces 5 for the last time—
Pass the *left* foot *à l'attitude*, **at the same time**—
Raise the arms *en attitude*, *left* arm up.
Raise the *right* foot *sur les trois quarts de la pointe*.

16. Execute a *Pas de bourré renversé en tournant en dehors*. That is :—
(*a*) Lower the *right* heel to the ground and *demi-pliez* on the *right* foot, **at the same time**—

Sweep the *left* arm above the head and lower it so that the two arms form the *fifth* position *en avant*.

(*b*)   Lower the *left* foot to the *fifth* position *back*, and keep it *sur la demi-pointe*, at the same time—
Turn the body to the *left* so that it faces 3—
Bring the body erect.
Straighten the *right* knee and rise *sur la demi-pointe*.

(*c*)   Turn to the left on the *left demi-pointe* so that the body faces 8, at the same time—
Open the *right* foot to the *second* position, keeping it *sur la demi-pointe*.
Open the arms to the *demi-seconde* position.

(*d*)   Lower the *right* heel to the ground, and *demi-pliez* on the *right* foot, at the same time—
Slide the *left* foot to the *fifth* position *front*, allowing the knee to bend, towards 1.
Lower the arms to the *fifth* position *en bas*.

17.   Slide the *left* foot to the *fourth* position *front*, straightening the knee, at the same time—
Raise the *right* foot *pointe tendue*, so that the weight of the body falls on the *left* foot.
Raise the arms to the *demi-seconde* position.
Incline the head and body—from the waist—to 4.

Repeat Nos. 2—17, reading *left* for *right*, and *vice versa*; while, owing to the reverse direction of the body's turns, the wall numbers stated above will now correspond to those directly opposite—that is : 8—6, 3—4, 4—3, 6—8, 1—2, 7—5, 5—7, 2—1.

Adagio

PIROUETTE EN DEHORS À LA SECONDE.

Stand erect in the centre of the room and face 5, with the head upright, the knees straight, the feet in the *fifth* position, **right** foot in *front*, and the arms in the *fifth* position *en bas*. The direction of the body is *en face*.

1. Execute with the *right* foot *Grand preparation pour pirouette en dehors.* That is :—

   (*a*) Rise *sur les demi-pointes*, **at the same time**— Bring the arms to the *fifth* position *en avant.*

   (*b*) Lower the *left* heel to the ground, **at the same time**— Open the *right* foot to the *second* position and carry it a little further, so that the toe is raised about four inches from the ground. The movement is exactly similar to that of *battement degagé.* **At the same time**— Open the arms to the *second* position.

   (*c*) Rise on the *left demi-pointe.*

   (*d*) Lower the *left* heel to the ground, **at the same time**— Lower the *right* foot to the *second* position. (Immediately the feet come to the ground, *demi-pliez* on both feet.) Carry the *right* arm to the *fourth* position *en avant.*

2. Execute *un tour en dehors de pirouette à la seconde.* That is :— Straighten the *left* knee and rise *sur la demi-pointe*, **at the same time**— Raise the *right* foot to the *second* position, *en l'air.* Sweep the *right* arm to the *second* position, and **immediately**— *Pirouette* to the *right* so that the body returns facing 5. When the body faces 5— Lower the *left* heel to the ground.

3. (*a*) Rise on the *left demi-pointe.*

   (*b*) Lower the *left* heel to the ground, **at the same time**— Lower the *right* foot to the *second* position. (Immediately the feet come to the ground, *demi-pliez* on both feet.) Carry the *right* arm to the *fourth* position *en avant*, and **immediately**—

4. Execute *deux tours en dehors de pirouette à la seconde*. That is :—
   Straighten the *left* knee and rise *sur la demi-pointe*, **at the same time**—
   Raise the *right* foot to the *second* position, *en l'air*.
   Sweep the *right* arm to the *second* position, **and immediately**—
   Pirouette to the **right** so that the body passes 5 and returns facing 5.
   When the body faces 5 for the *second* time—
   Lower the *left* heel to the ground.

5. Execute *trois tours en dehors de pirouette à la seconde*.

6. Execute *quatre tours en dehors de pirouette à la seconde*.

Repeat the whole exercise with the *left* foot, reading *left* for *right*, and *vice versa*.

Adagio

PIROUETTES EN DEHORS À LA SECONDE ET EN ATTITUDE.

Stand erect in the centre of the room and face 5, with the head upright, the knees straight, the feet in the *fifth* position, **right** foot in *front*, and the arms in the *fifth* position *en bas*. The direction of the body is *en face*.

1. Execute with the *right* foot Grand *preparation pour pirouette en dehors.*

2. Execute *un tour en dehors de pirouette en attitude.*
   That is :—
   (*a*) Straighten the *left* knee and rise *sur la demi-pointe*, **at the same time**—
   Raise the *right* foot to the *second* position, *en l'air*, and **immediately**—
   Pirouette to the **right** so that the body returns facing 5.
   When the body faces 5—
   Lower the *left* heel to the ground and *demi-pliez* on the *left* foot, **immediately**—
   (*b*) Straighten the *left* knee and rise *sur la demi-pointe*, **at the same time**—
   Execute with the *right* foot a *demi-grand rond de jambe en l'air en dehors*, **at the same time**—
   Raise the *right* arm above the head.
   Pirouette to the **right** so that the body returns facing 5.
   When the body faces 5—
   Lower the *left* heel to the ground.

3. Execute a *Developpé à la seconde en l'air*. That is :—
   (*a*) Bend the *right* knee so that the toe is in a line with the *left* knee and the thigh raised to the *second* position, *en l'air*, **at the same time**—
   Bring the arms to the *first* position, and pass them to *fifth* position *en bas.*
   (*b*) Extend the *right* foot to the *second* position, *en l'air*, **at the same time**—
   Open the arms to the *second* position.

4. Rise on the *left demi-pointe* and—
   Lower both feet to the ground in the *second* position, allowing the knees to bend, **at the same time**—
   Bring the *right* arm to the *fourth* position *en avant.*

5. Execute *un tour en dehors de pirouette à la seconde,* followed by *deux tours en dehors de pirouette en attitude.*

6. Execute *un tour en dehors de pirouette à la seconde,* followed by *trois tours en dehors de pirouette en attitude.*

7. Execute *un tour en dehors de pirouette à la seconde,* followed by *quatre tours en dehors de pirouette en attitude.*

Repeat the whole exercise with the *left* foot, reading *left* for *right,* and *vice versa.*

Adagio

PIROUETTES EN DEHORS À LA SECONDE ET EN ARABESQUE.

Stand erect in the centre of the room and face 5, with the head upright, the knees straight, the feet in the *fifth* position, **right** foot in *front*, and the arms in the *fifth* position *en bas*. The direction of the body is *en face*.

1. Execute with the *right* foot *Grand preparation pour pirouette en dehors*.

2. Execute *un tour en dehors de pirouette à la seconde*, followed by *un tour en dehors de pirouette en arabesque*. That is :—
   (*a*) Straighten the *left* knee and rise *sur la demi-pointe*, **at the same time**—
   Raise the *right* foot to the *second* position, *en l'air*.
   Sweep the *right* arm to the *second* position, and **immediately**—
   Pirouette to the **right** so that the body returns facing 5.
   Lower the *left* heel to the ground, *demi-pliez* on the *left* foot, straighten the knee, and rise *sur la demi-pointe*.
   The arms remain in the *second* position, and **immediately**—
   (*b*) Quickly turn the body to the **left** so that it faces 6, **at the same time**—
   Turn the hands palm downwards.
   (The pose is *en première arabesque*) and **immediately**—
   (*c*) *Pirouette* in the same pose to the **right** so that the body returns facing 6.

3. Execute a *Developpé à la seconde en l'air*. That is :—
   (*a*) Bend the *right* knee so that the toe is in a line with the *left* knee and the thigh in the *second* position, *en l'air*, **at the same time**—
   Bring the arms to the *fifth* position *en bas*.
   Turn the body to the **right** so that it faces 5.
   (*b*) Extend the *right* foot to the *second* position, *en l'air*, **at the same time**—
   Open the arms to the *second* position.

4. Rise on the *left demi-pointe* and—
   Lower both feet to the ground in the *second* position, allowing the knees to bend, **at the same time**—
   Bring the *right* arm to the *fourth* position *en avant*.

5. Execute *un tour en dehors de pirouette à la seconde*, followed by *deux tours en dehors de pirouette en arabesque.*

6. Execute *un tour en dehors de pirouette à la seconde*, followed by *trois tours en dehors de pirouette en arabesque.*

7. Execute *un tour en dehors de pirouette à la seconde*, followed by *quatre tours en dehors de pirouette en arabesque.*

Repeat the whole exercise on the *left* foot, reading *left* for *right*, and *vice versa*.

Adagio

PIROUETTES EN DEHORS À LA SECONDE
ET SUR LE COU DE PIED.

Stand erect in the centre of the room and face 5, with the head upright, the knees straight, the feet in the *fifth* position, right foot in *front*, and the arms in the *fifth* position *en bas.* The direction of the body is *en face.*

1. Execute with the *right* foot *Grand preparation pour pirouette en dehors.*
2. Execute *un tour en dehors de pirouette à la seconde.*
   (*a*) When the body faces 5—
   Lower the *left* heel to the ground, *demi-pliez* on the *left* foot, straighten the knee, and rise *sur la demi-pointe* As the *left* foot rises *sur la demi-pointe*—
   (*b*) Bring the *right* foot *sur le cou de pied en avant,* at the same time—
   Bring the arms to the *fifth* position *en bas,* and, without stopping—
   Pirouette in the same pose until the body returns to 5. When the body faces 5—
   Lower the *left* heel to the ground.
3. Open the *right* foot to *second* position and carry it a little further so that the toe is raised about four inches from the ground. The movement is exactly similar to that of *battement degagé.* At the same time— Open the arms to the *second* position.
4. Rise on the *left demi-pointe.*
5. Lower the *left* heel to the ground, at the same time— Lower the *right* foot to the *second* position.
   (Immediately the feet come to the ground, *demi-pliez* on both feet.)
   Carry the *right* arm to the *fourth* position *en avant.*
6. Execute *un tour en dehors de pirouette à la seconde,* followed by *deux tours en dehors de pirouette sur le cou de pied.*
7. Execute *un tour en dehors de pirouette à la seconde,* followed by *trois tours en dehors de pirouette sur le cou de pied.*
8. Execute *un tour en dehors de pirouette à la seconde,* followed by *quatre tours en dehors de pirouette sur le cou de pied.*
9. Execute an *Echappé à la quatrième position, left* foot back.

Repeat the whole exercise on the *left* foot, reading *left* for *right,* and *vice versa.*

PIROUETTES EN DEHORS SUR LE COU DE PIED.[1]

Stand erect in the centre of the room and face 5, with the head upright, the knees straight, the feet in the *fifth* position, **right** foot in *front*, and the arms in the *fifth* position *en bas*. The direction of the body is *en face*.

1. Execute with the *right* foot *Grand preparation pour pirouette en dehors*.

2. Execute *un tour en dehors de pirouette sur le cou de pied en avant*. That is :—
   (*a*) Straighten the *left* knee and rise *sur la demi-pointe*, **at the same time**—
   Bring the *right* foot *sur le cou de pied en avant*.
   Bring the arms to the *fifth* position *en bas*, and **immediately**—
   Pirouette to the *right* until the body returns facing 5.
   (*b*) When the body faces 5—
   Lower the *left* heel to the ground, **at the same time**—
   Open the *right* foot to the *second* position and carry it a little further so that it rises about four inches above the ground. The movement is exactly similar to that of *battement degagé*.
   Open the arms to the *second* position.
   (*c*) Rise on the *left demi-pointe*, and—
   Lower both feet to the ground in the *second* position, allowing the knees to bend, **at the same time**—
   Bring the *right* arm to the *fourth* position *en avant*.

3. Execute *deux tours en dehors de pirouette sur le cou de pied en avant*.

4. Execute *trois tours en dehors de pirouette sur le cou de pied en avant*.

5. Execute *quatre tours en dehors de pirouette sur le ·cou de pied en avant*.

Repeat the whole of the exercise on the *left* foot, reading *left* for *right*, and *vice versa*.

---

[1] This exercise is designed to enable the pupil to acquire the knowledge of how much force is required for the execution respectively of one, two, three, four, or more *tours de pirouettes*.

Adagio

PIROUETTES EN DEHORS SUR LE COU DE PIED EN AVANT.[1]

Stand erect in the centre of the room and face 5, with the head upright, the knees straight, the feet in the *fifth* position, **right** foot in *front*, and the arms in the *fifth* position *en bas*. The direction of the body is *en face*.

1. Execute *Grand preparation pour pirouette en dehors*.

2. Execute *un tour en dehors de pirouette sur le cou de pied en avant*. That is :—
   Straighten the *left* knee and rise *sur la demi-pointe*, **at the same time**—
   Bring the *right* foot *sur le cou de pied en avant*.
   Bring the arms to the *fifth* position *en bas*, and **immediately**—
   Pirouette to the **right** until the body returns facing 5. When the body faces 5—
   Execute a *petit echappé à la quatrième position, right* foot *back*.

3. Slide the *right* foot to the *fifth* position *back*, **at the same time**—
   Lower the arms to the *fifth* position *en bas*.

Repeat the whole of the exercise on the *left* foot reading *left* for *right*, and *vice versa*.

---

1 This exercise is designed to preserve the equilibrium. On no account should the exercise be performed with only one foot, for, owing to the continued turn in the same direction, the body tends to lean towards that side. Consequently, in a short time the equilibrium will be lost, and it will be found impossible to execute a *pirouette* at all.

A Manual of Classical Dancing

OBSERVATIONS ON PIROUETTES.

Pirouettes require considerable exercise and study. The essential qualities for their execution demand that the pupil should be slender, his limbs soft and pliable, and his legs formed naturally close together. You have seen that the body is supported entirely on the *demi-pointe* of one foot. Consider how slight is the base upon which the whole body turns. For this reason you must press strongly against the ground all the toes of the supporting foot, so that by their expansion you will increase the size of the base and thereby materially assist the equilibrium of the body. Unless these precautions are taken your body will sway and rock on the naturally convex surface of the sole, the equilibrium will be lost and the pirouette rendered impossible of execution. During the execution of a *pirouette*—(1) Take care that the supporting foot does not rise beyond *sur la demi-pointe* ; that is, *sur les trois quarts de la pointe*. (2) Do not jump on the supporting foot. (3) Take care that the head does not remain rigidly upright, but is *the last to move as the body turns away from the spectator*, and *the first to move as the body returns towards the spectator* (see Book I., Theory Section viii., *The Movement of the Head*). Finally, great care should be exercised in the force of momentum generated by the sweep across of the extended arm. Insufficient strength will cause the body to stop before the completion of the turn, similarly too much strength will cause the body to pass beyond the point desired.

Adagio

GRAND ROND DE JAMBE EN TOURNANT AVEC RELEVÉ.

Stand erect in the centre of the room and face 2, with the head inclined to 3, the feet in the **fifth** position, **right** foot in *front*, and the arms in the *fifth* position *en bas*. The direction of the body is *encroisé*.

1. *Pliez* on both feet.
   As the heels rise from the ground—
   Carry the *left* hand outwards so that it is about six inches from the *left* knee.

2. Execute *deux tours en dehors developpés à la quatrième en avant, en l'air*. That is :—
   Take strength with the *left* arm and turn on the *left demi-pointe* to the **right** so that the body passes 5, and continue in the same direction until it faces 5 again.[1]
   During the execution of the *tour*—
   (*a*) Gradually straighten the *left* knee and rise *sur la demi-pointe*, **at the same time**—
   Bring the *right* foot *sur le cou de pied en avant*, and raise the foot as high as possible—keeping the toe pointed well downwards—until the toe is in a line with the *left* knee and the thigh raised to the *second* position, *en l'air*.
   Bring the arms to the *fifth* position *en bas*.
   (*b*) When the body faces 5 for the last time—
   Lower the *left* heel to the ground, **at the same time**—
   Extend the *right* foot to the *fourth* position *front, en l'air*.
   Raise the arms to the *fifth* position *en avant*.

3. Execute a *Grand rond de jambe en l'air en dehors*.
   As the foot passes from the *fourth* position *front, en l'air*, to the *second* position, *en l'air*—
   Open the arms to the *second* position and keep them extended as the foot moves from the *second* position, *en l'air* to the *fourth* position *back, en l'air*.
   Without stopping, pass to the next movement.

4. Execute a *Developpé à la seconde en l'air*.

5. Execute a *Developpé à la quatrième en avant en l'air*.
   (*a*) Bend the *right* knee so that the toe of the *right* foot is in a line with the *left* knee and the thigh raised to the *second* position, *en l'air*.
   Lower the arms to the *fifth* position *en bas*.

---

1 The body moves from 2-5-1-8-4-7-3-6-2-5

(*b*)   Extend the *right* foot to the *fourth* position *front*, *en l'air*, **at the same time—**
Raise the arms to the *fifth* position *en avant*.
Demi-pliez on the *left* foot.

6.   Execute a *Relevé à la seconde en l'air*.   That is :—
Straighten the *left* knee and rise *sur la demi-pointe*.
Execute a *Demi-grand rond de jambe en l'air en dehors*.   That is :—
Move the *right* foot from the *fourth* position *front*, *en l'air*, to the *second* position, *en l'air*, **at the same time—**
Open the arms to the *second* position.

7.   Execute a *Developpé à la quatrième en arrière, en l'air*.   That is :—
(*a*)   Bend the *right* knee so that the toe of the *right* foot is in a line with the *left* knee and the thigh raised to the *second* position, *en l'air*.
Lower the arms to the *fifth* position *en bas*.
(*b*)   Extend the *right* foot to the *fourth* position *back, en l'air*, **at the same time—**
Raise the arms to the *fifth* position *en avant*.
Demi-pliez on the *left* foot.

8.   Execute a *Relevé à la seconde en l'air*.   That is :—
Straighten the *left* knee and rise on the *left demi-pointe*, **at the same time—**
Execute a *Demi-grand rond de jambe en l'air en dedans*.   That is :—
Move the *right* foot from *fourth* position *back, en l'air*—the *second* position, *en l'air*, **at the same time—**
Open the arms to the *second* position.

9.   Execute with the *right* foot a *Developpé à la quatrième en avant, en l'air*.   That is :—
(*a*)   Bend the *right* knee so that the toe of the *right* foot is in a line with the *left* knee and the thigh is raised to the *second* position, *en l'air*, **at the same time—**
Lower the arms to the *fifth* position *en bas*.
(*b*)   Extend the *right* foot to the *fourth* position *front*, *en l'air*, **at the same time—**
Demi-pliez on the *left* foot.
Raise the arms to the *fifth* position *en avant*.

10.   Execute a *Relevé à la seconde en l'air*, followed by *un tour en dehors de pirouette à la seconde*, and **un**

Adagio

tour en dehors de pirouette en attitude.[1]   That is :—
(*a*)   Straighten the *left* knee and rise *sur la demi-pointe*, **at the same time**—
Execute a *Demi-grand rond de jambe en l'air en dehors.*   That is :—
Move the *right* foot from the *fourth* position *front, en l'air*—the *second* position, *en l'air*, **at the same time**—
Open the arms to the *second* position.
Pirouette to the *right* so that the body returns facing **5**.[2]
When the body faces 5—
Lower the *left* heel to the ground and *demi-pliez* on the *left* foot.
The arms remain in the *second* position.
Without stopping, pass to the execution of the next movement.
(*b*)   Straighten the *left* knee and rise *sur la demi-pointe*, **at the same time**—
Execute a *Demi-grand rond de jambe en l'air en dehors.*   That is :—
Move the *right* foot from the *second* position, *en l'air*— the *fourth* position *back, en l'air.*   Then pass the foot *à l'attitude*, **at the same time**—
Raise the arms *en attitude, right* arm up.
Without stopping, pass to the execution of the next movement.
(*c*)   *Pirouette* to the **right** on the *left demi-pointe* until the body passes 1, and continue in the same direction until it faces 1 again.
When the body faces 1 for the last time—
Lower the *left* heel to the ground and *demi-pliez* on the *left* foot, **at the same time**—
Lower the *right* arm and extend it in a line with and at right angles to the shoulder.
Move the *left* arm backwards so that it is extended in a line parallel to the *right* calf.
The pose is *en quatrième arabesque (encroisée).*

11.   Lower the *right* foot to the *fifth* position *back*, as if in execution of *grand battement*, **at the same time**—
Straighten the *left* knee.
Incline the head towards 4.
Lower the arms to the *fifth* position *en bas.*

1 These two *pirouettes* must follow each other in quick succession, **without stopping**.
2 The body moves 5-1-8-4-7-3-6-2-5.

165

Exercise of the Left Foot in Grand Rond de Jambe en Tournant avec Relevé.

Stand erect in the centre of the room and face 1, with the head inclined to 4, the knees straight, the feet in the *fifth* position, *left* foot in front, and the arms in the *fifth* position *en bas*.

Repeat the whole of the last exercise, reading **left** for **right**, and *vice versa* ; while, owing to the reverse direction of the body's turns, the wall numbers stated above will now correspond to those directly opposite—that is : 8—6, 3—4, 4—3, 6—8, 1—2, 7—5, 5—7, 2—1.

Adagio

GLISSADE, JETÉ, FOUETTÉ.

Stand erect in the centre of the room and face 2, with the head inclined to 3, the feet in the **fifth** position, **right** foot in *front*, and the arms in the *fifth* position *en bas*.

The direction of the body is *encroisé*.

1. Execute a *Glissade* with the *right* foot. That is :—
   (*a*) *Demi-pliez* on both feet and—
   Slide the *right* foot to the *second* position, keeping it *sur la pointe tendue*, towards 1, **at the same time**—
   Open the arms to the *demi-seconde* position.
   (*b*) Lower the *right* heel to the ground and *demi-pliez* on the *right* foot, **at the same time**—
   Bring the *left* foot to the *fifth* position *back* and *demi-pliez* on the *left* foot.
   Lower the arms to the *fifth* position *en bas*.

2. Execute a *Jeté à la seconde en arrière* (*bien elancé*). That is :—
   Raise the *right* foot to the *second* position, *en l'air*, and leap sideways on the *right* foot.
   Come to the ground on the *right* foot, allowing the knee to bend.
   As the foot touches the ground—
   Bring the *left* foot *sur le cou de pied en avant*, then—
   Straighten the *right* knee, **at the same time**—
   Bring the head erect, and turn the body facing 5.

3. Execute a *Developpé à la quatrième en avant, en l'air* (*encroisé*). That is :—
   (*a*) Raise the *left* foot as high as possible so that the toe is in a line with the *right* knee and the thigh raised to the *second* position, *en l'air*, **at the same time**—
   Raise the arms to the *fifth* position *en avant*.
   (*b*) Extend the *left* foot to the *fourth* position *front*, *en l'air*, **at the same time**—
   Slightly turn to the **right** on the flat of the **right** foot so that the body faces 1.
   Raise the arms *en attitude* (*right* arm up).
   Incline the body **from the waist** towards 2.
   The direction of the body is *à la quatrième en avant* (*encroisé*).

4. Execute a *Developpé degagé à l'attitude en tournant en dedans*. That is :—
   Slowly turn to the **right** on the flat of the *right* foot until the body faces 2.

As the body passes from 1 to 8—
Gradually lower the *right* arm to the *second* position.
As the body faces 4—
Keep the *left* leg pointing to 4, and continue in the same direction, allowing the leg to turn on the pivot of the hip.
As the body passes from 4 to 3—
Lower the *right* arm to the *demi-seconde* position, **at the same time—**
Gradually raise the *left* arm above the head so that the arms are *en attitude* (*left* arm up).
The *left* leg—owing to the new position of **the body**— is now in the *second* position, *en l'air*.
Allow the body to turn **from the waist only** (the *left* foot continuing to point to 4), so that when the body faces 2 the *left* foot becomes in the *fourth* position *back*, *en l'air* (*encroisée*).

5. (*a*) Bring the *right* arm to the *first* position, pass it to the *fifth* position, and raise it to the *fourth* position *en avant*.
   (*b*) Gradually turn outward the *right* wrist and extend the arm in a line with but a little higher than at right angles to the shoulder, **at the same time—**
   Extend the *left* arm outwards.
   The pose is *en troisième arabesque* (*encroisée*).

6. Carry the *left* arm to the *fourth* position *en haut*, **at the same time—**
   Bring the *right* arm to the *fourth* position *en avant*.
   Pass the *left* foot *à l'attitude*.

7. Keep the same pose and incline the head and body— from the waist—as far as possible towards 1 (see Fig. 75).
   The body should be well curved and the head thrown backwards.

8. Execute a *Developpé à la seconde, en l'air*. That is :
   (*a*) Bend the *left* knee so that the thigh moves gradually to the *second* position, *en l'air*, **at the same time—**
   Bring the head and body erect, facing 5.
   Bring the arms to the *fifth* position *en avant*, and open them to the *second* position.
   (*b*) Extend the *left* foot to the *second* position, *en l'air*, pointing to 6, **at the same time—**
   Open the arms to the *second* position.

Adagio

9. Execute with the *left* foot a *double rond de jambe en l'air en dedans.*
The arms remain in the *second* position.

10. Execute a *Fouetté à terre en tournant en dedans.* That is :—
Without bending the *left* knee, sweep the *left* foot across the ground and bring it *sur le cou de pied en avant,* then quickly pass it *sur le cou de pied en arrière.* The movement is exactly similar to that of *petit battement sur le cou de pied.* **At the same time—**
Lower the arms to the *fifth* position *en bas.*
During the movement—
Pirouette on the *right* foot to the **right** until the body returns facing 5.

11. Execute a *Developpé à la seconde en l'air.* That is :—
(*a*) Raise the *left* foot as high as possible—keeping the toe pointed well downwards—until the toe is in a line with the *right* knee and the thigh raised to the *second* position, *en l'air,* **at the same time—**
Raise the arms to the *fifth* position *en avant.*
(*b*) Extend the *left* foot to the *second* position, *en l'air,* **at the same time—**
Open the arms to the *second* position.

12. Execute a *Fouetté en face en arrière.* That is :—
Without bending the *left* knee, sweep the *left* foot across the ground and bring it *sur le cou de pied en arrière,* **at the same time—**
Lower the arms to the *fifth* position *en bas.*
Slightly turn to the *left* so that the body faces 2.

13. Execute a *Developpé à la première arabesque—*
(*a*) Raise the *left* foot as high as possible—keeping the toe pointed well downwards—so that the toe is in a line with the *right* knee and the thigh raised to the *second* position, *en l'air,* **at the same time—**
Raise the arms to the *fifth* position *en avant.*
(*b*) Extend the *left* foot to the *fourth* position *back, en l'air,* pointing to 4, **at the same time—**
Extend the *right* arm to the *fourth* position *front,* pointing to 2.
Extend the *left* arm to the *fourth* position *back,* pointing to 4.
The pose is *en première arabesque (encroisée).*

14. Execute *un tour en dedans renversé à la seconde en l'air*. That is :—
  Pirouette on the *right demi-pointe* to the *right* until the body faces 2.
  As the body passes from 2—1 —
  Incline the arms, head and body—from the waist—to the *left*.
  Continue to turn until the body faces 2, **at the same time—**
  Gradually bring the head and body erect.
  The arms pass to the *fifth* position *en haut*.
  When the body faces 2—
  In one very quick movement, simultaneously—
  Open the arms to the *demi-seconde* position.
  Incline the head and body—from the waist—as far as possible to 1.
  Open the *left* foot to the *second* position, *en l'air*, pointing to 3.

15. Execute a *Pas de Bourré en sussous*—
  (*a*) Lower the *left* foot to the *fifth* position *back*, keeping it *sur la demi-pointe*, **at the same time—**
  Bring the arms to the *fifth* position *en bas*.
  (*b*) Open the *right* foot to the *second* position, keeping it *sur la demi-pointe*.
  (*c*) Bring the *left* foot to the *fifth* position *front* and lower both heels to the ground.
  The body faces 5.

Exercise of the Left Foot in Glissade, Jeté, Fouetté.

Stand erect in the centre of the room and face 1, with the head inclined to 4, the knees straight, the feet in the **fifth** position, **left** foot in *front*, and the arms in the *fifth* position *en bas*. The direction of the body is *encroisé*.

Repeat the whole of the last exercise, reading **left** for **right**, and *vice versa*; while, owing to the reverse direction of the body's turns, the wall numbers stated above will now correspond to those directly opposite—that is : 8—6, 3—4, 4—3, 6—8, 1—2, 7—5, 5—7, 2—1.

Adagio

GLISSADE CECCHETTI.

Stand erect in the centre of the room and face 2, with the head inclined to 3, the feet in the fifth position, **right** foot in *front*, and the arms in the *fifth* position *en bas*. The direction of the body is *encroisé*.

1. Execute a **Glissade** with the *right* foot, that is ;—
   (a) *Demi-pliez* on both feet and slide the *right* foot—straightening the knee—to the *second* position, *pointe tendue*, towards 1, **at the same time**—
   Raise the *left* foot to the *demi-seconde* position.
   Open the arms to the *demi-seconde* position.
   (b) Lower the *right* heel to the ground, and *demi-pliez* on the *right* foot, **at the same time**—
   Bring the *left* foot to the *fifth* position *back*, and *demi-pliez* on the *left* foot.
   Lower the arms to the *fifth* position *en bas*.
2. Execute a *Petit jeté de coté*. That is :—
   Spring sidewards on the *right demi-pointe* towards 1.
   As the foot touches the ground—
   Raise the *left* foot to the *fourth* position *back, en l'air*, **at the same time**—
   Raise the arms to the *fifth* position *en avant*.
3. Execute *deux tours en dedans de pirouette en arabesque*. That is :—
   Turn to the **right** until the body faces 3.
   Leave the *left* arm pointing to 3, and continue to turn until the body faces 1, when the pose is *en première arabesque*.
   Turn to the **right** on the *right demi-pointe* until the body faces 1 again.
4. (a) Move the *right* arm to the *second* position, **at the same time**—
   Raise the *left* arm to the *second* position.
   (b) Lower the arms to the *first* position, and raise them to the *fifth* position *en avant*, then—
   Bend *right* arm at elbow and turn hand inwards so that the finger-tips touch the *right* jaw, **at same time**—
   Bring the *left* arm—palm downwards—near the breast so that the *right* elbow rests on the knuckles of the *left* hand (see Fig. 72, but regard the limbs as if in reverse position).
   Turn the head towards 2 and incline it to 1.
5. Return to the pose *en première arabesque*.
6. Execute a *Developpé à la quatrième en avant en l'air (encroisé)*.

(*a*) Bend the *left* knee so that the toe is in a line with the *right* knee and the thigh raised to the *second* position, *en l'air*, at the same time—
Lower the arms to the *fifth* position *en bas*.
(*b*) Extend the *left* foot to the *fourth* position *front, en l'air*, pointing to 1.
Raise the arms *en attitude* (*right* arm up).

7. *Demi-pliez* on the *right* foot, at the same time—
Bring the *right* arm to the *fourth* position *en avant*.

8. Execute a *Fouetté degagé en l'air à la quatrième en arrière en l'air*. That is :—
(*a*) Straighten the *right* knee.
(*b*) Turn to the **right** on the *right demi-pointe*.
As the body passes from 1—4—
Sweep the *right* arm above the head and lower it to the *second* position, at the same time—
Gradually raise the *left* arm above the head.
The arms are *en attitude*.
(*c*) Continue to turn in the same pose and direction until the body faces 2.
As the body passes 4—2—
Keep the *left* foot pointing to 4, and, allowing the foot to turn on the pivot of the hip, turn the body—from the waist only—until it faces 2.
Now lower the *right* arm to the *first* position, pass it to the *fifth* position, raise it to the *fourth* position *en avant* and extend both arms outward.
The pose is *en troisième arabesque* (*encroisée*).

9. Bring both arms to the *fifth* position *en avant*, then—
Extend the *right* arm in a line with and at right angles to the shoulder, pointing to 2, at the same time—
Sweep the *left* arm in a semi-circle outward and backward until it is extended in a line parallel to the *left* calf, pointing to 4.

10. Execute a *Developpé degagé à la quatrième en avant en l'air* (*encroisé*).
(*a*) *Demi-pliez* on the *right* foot, rise *sur la demi-pointe*, and turn to the left so that the body faces 3 and the *left* foot points to 1.
(*b*) Leave the *left* foot pointing to 1, and, allowing the leg to turn on the pivot of the hip, turn to the *left* until the body faces 1.
During the *tour*—
Raise the *right* arm above the head.
The arms are *en attitude, right* arm up.

11. **Rise** on the *right demi-pointe*, **at the same time—**
    Incline the head and body—from the waist—to 4.
    Lower the *right* arm to the *demi-seconde* position.
    Bend the *left* elbow and gracefully touch the lips
    with the finger-tips of the *left* hand (see Fig. 74, but
    regard the limbs as if in reverse position).

12. Execute a *Jeté de coté*. That is :—
    Spring sideways on the *left demi-pointe* towards 2.
    As the foot touches the ground—
    Raise the *right* foot to the *fourth* position *back, en
    l'air*, **at the same time—**
    Extend the *left* arm—palm upwards—to the *fourth*
    position *front*, pointing to 2.
    The pose is *en quatrième arabesque* (*effacée*).

13. Execute a *Pas de bourré en sussous*. That is :—
    (*a*) Straighten the *left* knee and rise *sur la demi-
    pointe*, **at the same time—**
    Lower the *right* foot to the *fifth* position *back*, and
    keep it *sur la demi-pointe*.
    Lower the arms to the *demi-seconde* position.
    (*b*) Open the *left* foot to the *second* position, keeping
    it *sur la demi-pointe*.
    (*c*) Lower the *left* heel to the ground, **at the same
    time—**
    Bring the *right* foot to the *fifth* position *front*.
    Lower the arms to the *fifth* position *en bas*.
    The body faces 5.

14. Execute *Grand preparation pour pirouette en dehors*.

15. Execute *deux tours en dehors de pirouette sur le cou
    de pied en avant*.
    When the body faces 5—
    Execute an *Echappé à la quatrième position, right*
    foot *back*.

Exercise of the Left Foot in Glissade Cecchetti.

Stand erect in the centre of the room and face **1, with**
the head inclined to 4, the knees straight, the feet in the
fifth position, **left** foot in *front*, and the arms in the *fifth*
position *en bas*. The direction of the body is *encroisé*.

Repeat the whole of the last exercise, reading **left** for
right, and *vice versa* ; while, owing to the reverse direction of
the body's turns, the wall numbers stated above will now
correspond to those directly opposite—that is : 8—**6, 3—4,**
4—3, 6—8, 1—2, 7—5, 5—7, 2—1.

GLISSADE ARABESQUE ET PAS DE BOURRÉ RENVERSÉ.

Stand erect in the far end of the room near 3, and face 2, with the head upright, the feet in the *fifth* position, **right** foot in *front*, and the arms in the *fifth* position *en bas.*

The direction of the body is *encroisé.*

1. Execute a *Glissade* with the *right* foot. That is :—
   (*a*) *Demi-pliez* on both feet and slide the *right* foot—straightening the knee—to the *second* position, *pointe tendue*, towards 1, at the same time—
   Raise the *left* foot to the *second* position, *en l'air, demi-position.*
   Open the arms to the *demi-seconde* position.
   (*b*) Lower the *right* heel to the ground and *demi-pliez* on the *right* foot, at the same time—
   Bring the *left* foot to the *fifth* position *back* and *demi-pliez* on the *left* foot.
   Lower the arms to the *fifth* position *en bas.*

2. Execute a *Petit jeté de coté.* That is :—
   Straighten the *right* knee and spring sideways on the *right demi-pointe.*
   As the foot touches the ground—
   Raise the *left* foot to the *fourth* position *back, en l'air*, at the same time—
   Raise the arms to the *fifth* position *en avant.*

3. Execute *deux tours en dedans à l'arabesque.* That is :—
   Turn to the **right** until the body faces 3.
   Leave the *left* arm pointing to 3, and continue to turn until the body faces 1, when the pose is *en première arabesque.*
   Continue to turn in the same pose and direction until the body returns facing 1.

4. *Pliez* on *right* foot until *left* foot touches the ground.

5. Execute a *Pas de bourré en sussous en tournant en dedans.* That is :—
   (*a*) Execute a *Grand rond de jambe à terre en dedans*, and withdraw the *left* foot close to the *right* foot, as if to the *fifth* position *front*, gradually raising it *sur la demi-pointe* and immediately—
   Slightly raise the *right* foot off the ground.
   As the foot passes from the *fourth* position *back*—the *second* position—
   Bring the arms to the *second* position.

As the foot passes from the *second* position—*fourth*
position *front*—
Lower the arms to the *fifth* position *en bas*.
(*b*) Turn on the *left demi-pointe* to the **right** until
the body faces 6, **at the same time**—
Gradually lower the *right* foot to the *fourth* position
front, pointing to 6, keeping it *sur la demi-pointe*.
Raise the arms to the *second* position.
(*c*) Turn on the *right demi-pointe* until the body
faces 2, then—
Place the *left* foot to the *fifth* position *back* and *demi-
pliez* on the *left* foot, **at the same time**—
Raise the *right* foot to the *fourth* position *front, en
l'air* (*encroisé*), *demi-position*, pointing to 2.
Bring the arms to the *fifth* position *en avant*.

6.   Execute a *Pas de bourré renversé en dehors*. That
is :—

(*a*) Execute with the *right* foot a *Grand rond de
jambe en l'air en dehors*, and then pass the foot *à
l'attitude*.
As the foot moves from the *fourth* position *front, en
l'air*—*second* position, *en l'air*—
Open the arms to the *second* position.
As the foot passes *à l'attitude*—
Raise the arms *en attitude, right* arm up.
(*b*) Straighten the *left* knee, rise on the *left demi-
pointe* and turn to **right** so that the body faces 1.
The pose is *en attitude encroisée*.
(*c*) Lower the *left* heel to the ground and *demi-pliez*
on the *left* foot, **at the same time**—
Lower the *right* arm to the *fourth* position *en avant*,
so that the two arms meet in the *fifth* position *en
avant*.
Extend the *right* foot to the *fourth* position *back,
en l'air*, pointing to 3.
The pose is *en cinquième arabesque* (*encroisée*).
(*c*) Straighten the *left* knee and rise *sur la demi-
pointe*, **at the same time**—
Lower the *right* foot to the *fifth* position *back*,
keeping it *sur la demi-pointe*.
Open the arms to the *second* position.
During the execution of these movements, turn **the**
body to the **right** until it faces 4.
(*d*) Step on the *left demi-pointe* towards **3**.
(Note that the feet are in the *second* position.)

(*e*) Lower both heels to the ground and *demi-pliez* on both feet, **at the same time—**
Bring the *right* foot to the *fifth* position *front.*
Lower the arms to the *fifth* position *en bas.*
(*f*) Slide the *right* foot to the *fourth* position *front* (*encroisé*), straightening the knee, **at the same time—**
Straighten the *left* knee and raise the foot, *pointe tendue,* so that the weight of the body falls on the *right* foot.
Raise the arms between the *second* position and the *fifth* position *en avant,* palms half-turned upwards. Slightly incline the head and body—from the waist—towards 6.
(*g*) Slide the *left* foot to the *fifth* position *back,* **at the same time—**
Lower the arms to the *fifth* position *en bas.*

Repeat the whole exercise *ad libitum.*

Exercise of the Left Foot in Glissade Arabesque et Pas de Bourré Renversé.

Stand erect in the far end of the room near 4, and face 1, with the head upright, the feet in the *fifth* position, **left** foot in front, and the arms in the *fifth* position *en bas.*

The direction of the body is *encroisé.*

Repeat the whole of the last exercise *ad libitum,* reading *left* for *right,* and *vice versa*; while, owing to the reverse direction of the body's turns, the wall numbers stated above will now correspond to those directly opposite—that is : 8—6, 3—4, 4—3, 6—8, 1—2, 7—5, 5—7, 2—1.

Adagio

GLISSADE DE MAMI.[1]

Stand erect in the centre of the room and face 2, with the head inclined to 3, the feet in the *fifth* position, **right** foot in *front*, and the arms in the *fifth* position *en bas*.

The direction of the body is *encroisé*.

1. Execute a *Glissade* with the *right* foot. That is :—
   (a) *Demi-pliez* on both feet and slide the *right* foot—straightening the knee—to the *second* position, *pointe tendue*, towards 1, **at the same time**—
   Raise the *left* foot to the *second* position, *en l'air* (*demi-position*).
   Open the arms to the *demi-seconde* position.
   (b) Lower the *right* heel to the ground and *demi-pliez* on the *right* foot, **at the same time**—
   Bring the *left* foot to the *fifth* position *back*, and *demi-pliez* on the *left* foot.
   Lower the arms to the *fifth* position *en bas*.

2. Execute a *Petit jeté de coté*. That is :—
   Straighten the *right* knee and spring sideways on the *right demi-pointe*.
   As the foot touches the ground.
   Raise the *left* foot to the *fourth* position *back*, *en l'air*, **at the same time**—
   Raise the arms to the *fifth* position *en avant*.

3. Execute *deux tours en dedans à l'arabesque*. That is :
   Turn to the **right** until the body faces 3.
   Leave the *left* arm pointing to 3 and continue to turn until the body faces 1, when the pose is *en première arabesque*.
   Continue to turn in the same pose and direction until the body faces 8.

4. Execute a *Fouetté developpé en tournant en dedans*. That is :—
   (a) Rise on the *right demi-pointe*, **at the same time**—
   Bend the *left* knee so that the toe is in a line with the side of the *right* knee and the thigh raised to the *second* position, *en l'air*.
   Bring the arms to the *fifth* position *en bas*.
   (b) Lower the *right* heel to the ground and *demi-pliez* on the *right* foot, **at the same time**—
   Extend the *left* foot to the *fourth* position *front*, *en l'air*, pointing to 8.

[1] The uncommon title of *Mami* may give rise to so much speculation as to its origin that it must be explained. The exercise is named after the pet cat attached to *Maestro Cecchetti's Academie de Danse*.

Raise the arms to the *fifth* position *en avant*.

Incline head and body—from the waist—towards 2.

(*c*) Straighten the *right* knee, rise *sur la demi-pointe*, and turn to the *right* until the body faces 6.

When the body faces 6—

Leave the *left* arm pointing to 6.

Leave the *left* foot pointing to 6 and continue to turn in the same direction until the body faces 5.

During the turn, raise the *right* arm above the head.

When the body faces 5—

The arms are in the *fourth* position *en haut*, while the *left* foot, owing to the new position of the body, becomes in the *second* position, *en l'air*.

Keep the *left* arm and *left* foot pointing to 6, and continue to turn in the same direction until the body faces 8.

When the body faces 8—

Extend the *right* arm—palm downwards—to the *fourth* position *front*, pointing to 8.

The pose is *en première arabesque*.

5. Execute with the *right* foot a *Grand fouetté sauté en tournant en dedans*. That is :—

Leap upwards into the air on the *right* foot and turn round in the air to the **right**. Come to the ground on the *right* foot, allowing the knee to bend, facing 8.

Simultaneously with the leap upward on *right* foot—

Sweep the *left* foot across the ground and to the *fourth* position *front*, *en l'air*, pointing to 8.

Raise the arms to the *fifth* position *en avant*.

When the body—while turning in the air—faces 6—

Leave the *left* arm and foot pointing to 6.

Continue to turn to the **right** until the body faces 8, allowing the *left* leg to turn on the pivot of the hip.

Simultaneously as the *right* foot comes to the ground, Extend the *right* arm in the *fourth* position *front*, pointing to 8.

The pose is *en première arabesque*.

6. Execute a *Pas de bourré en sussous*. That is :—

(*a*) Straighten the *right* knee and rise *sur la demi-pointe*, at the same time—

Lower the *left* foot to the *fifth* position *back*, and keep it *sur la demi-pointe*.

Lower the arms to the *fifth* position *en bas*.

(*b*) Open the *right* foot to the *second* position,

keeping it *sur la demi-pointe*, **at the same time**—
Open the arms to the *second* position.

(*c*) Lower *right* heel to ground, **at the same time**—
Slide the *left* foot to the *first* position and lower the heel to the ground.

(*d*) *Demi-pliez* on both feet, then slide the *left* foot to the *fifth* position *front*, then to the *fourth* position *front* (*encroisé*) to 1, **at the same time**—
Raise the *right* foot to the *fourth* position *back*, *en l'air* (*demi-position*), pointing to 3.
Extend the *left* arm in the *fourth* position *front* to 1.
Extend the *right* arm in the *fourth* position *back* to 3.
Incline the head to 2.

7. Execute a *Developpé degagé en tournant en dehors.* That is :—
Straighten the *left* knee, rise *sur la demi-pointe*, and turn to the **right** until the body faces 2.
Now leave the *right* foot pointing to 2, and, allowing the leg to turn on the pivot of the hip, continue to turn the body until it faces 3.
Retain same pose, turn to **right** until body faces 2.
When the body faces 2—
Lower the *left* heel to the ground, **at the same time**—
Raise the *left* arm above the head.
Incline the head and body—from the waist—towards 1, and bend the body well backwards.
The pose is *à la quatrième en avant en l'air* (*encroisé*).

8. Execute a *Jeté de coté* with the *right* foot. That is :—
(*a*) Rise on the *left demi-pointe*, **at the same time**—
Gracefully lower the *right* hand so that the finger-tips touch the lips.
Incline the head and body—from the waist—to 3.
(*b*) Spring on the *right demi-pointe*, allowing the knee to bend, towards 1.
As the foot touches the ground—
Raise the *left* foot to the *fourth* position *back*, *en l'air*, **at the same time**—
Extend the *right* arm—palm upwards—towards 1.
The pose is *en quatrième arabesque* (*effacée*).

9. Execute a *Pas de bourré en sussous.* That is :—
(*a*) Straighten the *right* knee and rise *sur la demi-pointe*, **at the same time**—
Lower the *left* foot to the *fifth* position *back* and keep it *sur la demi-pointe*.
Lower the arms to the *fifth* position *en bas*.

(*b*) Open the *right* foot to the *second* position, keeping it *sur la demi-pointe*, **at the same time**—
Open the arms to the *second* position.

(*c*) Lower the *right* heel to the ground, **at the same time**—
Slide the *left* foot to the *fifth* position *front*.
Lower the arms to the *fifth* position *en bas*.

10. Execute *Grand preparation pour pirouette en dehors*.

11. Execute *deux tours en dehors de pirouette sur le cou de pied developpé à l'attitude*. That is :—
Pirouette to the **left** on the *right demi-pointe* until the body passes 5 and faces 5 again.
At the commencement of the *pirouette*—
Bring the *left* foot *sur le cou de pied en avant*.
During the *pirouette*—
Gradually raise the *left* foot as high as possible until the toe is in a line with the *right* knee and the thigh raised to the *second* position, *en l'air*, **at the same time**—
Gradually raise the arms to the *fifth* position *en avant*.
When the body faces 5 for the last time—
Pass the *left* foot *à l'attitude*, **at the same time**—
Raise the arms *en attitude*, *left* arm up.
Raise the *right* foot *sur les trois quarts de la pointe*.

12. Execute a *Pas de bourré renversé en tournant en dehors*. That is :—
(*a*) Lower the *right* heel to the ground and *demi-pliez* on the *right* foot, **at the same time**—
Sweep the *left* arm above the head and lower it so that the two arms meet in the *fifth* position *en avant*.
(*b*) Lower the *left* foot to the *fifth* position *back* and keep it *sur la demi-pointe*, **at the same time**—
Turn the body to the *left* so that it faces 3.
Bring the body erect.
Straighten the *right* knee and rise *sur la demi-pointe*.
(*c*) Turn to the *left* on the *left demi-pointe* so that the body faces 8, **at the same time**—
Open the *right* foot to the *second* position, keeping it *sur la demi-pointe*.
Open the arms to the *second* position.
(*d*) Lower the *right* heel to the ground and *demi-pliez* on the *right* foot, **at the same time**—
Slide the *left* foot to the *fifth* position *front*, allowing the knee to bend.
Lower the arms to the *fifth* position *en bas*.

Adagio

13. Slide the *left* foot to the *fourth* position *front*, straightening the knee, at the same time—
    Raise the *right* foot *sur la pointe tendue*, so that the weight of the body falls on the *left* foot.
    Open the arms between the *second* position and the *fifth* position *en bas*, palms half-turned upwards.
    Incline the body to 8.

Exercise of the Left Foot in Glissade de Mami.

Stand erect in the centre of the room and face 1, with the head inclined to 4, the feet in the *fifth* position, left foot in front, and the arms in the *fifth* position *en bas*. The direction of the body is *encroisé*.

Repeat the whole of the last exercise, reading *left* for *right*, and *vice versa* ; while, owing to the reverse direction of the body's turns, the wall numbers stated above will now correspond to those directly opposite—that is : 8—6, 3—4, 4—3, 6—8, 1—2, 7—5, 5—7, 2—1.

GLISSADE SUR LES POINTES.[1]

Stand erect in the centre of the room and face 5, with the head upright, the feet in the *fifth* position, **right** foot in *front*, and the arms in the *fifth* position *en bas*.

The direction of the body is *en face*.

Part I.—*Glissade sur les pointes, en face.*

1. Execute a *Glissade* with the *right* foot.   That is :—
   (*a*)   *Demi-pliez* on both feet and slide the *right* foot —straightening the knee—to the *second* position, *pointe tendue*, **at the same time—**
   Raise the *left* foot to the *second* position *en l'air* (*demi-position*).
   Open the arms to the *demi-seconde* position.
   (*b*)   Bring the *left* foot *sur le cou de pied en avant*.
   Lower the arms to the *fifth* position *en bas*.
   (*c*)   Lower the *left* foot to the *fifth* position *front*, **at the same time—**
   Lower the *right* heel to the ground and *demi-pliez* on both feet.
   Consequently,[2] incline the head towards the *left* shoulder.

2. Repeat 1, but instead of bringing the *left* foot *sur le cou de pied en avant*, bring it *sur le cou de pied en arrière*, and incline the head towards the *right* shoulder.

3. Repeat 1.

4. Execute *deux petits changements*.
   First time, finish with the *right* foot in *front*.
   Second time, finish with the *left* foot in *front*.

Repeat Nos. 1—4, with the *left* foot, reading *left* for *right*, and *vice versa*.

Part II.—*Glissade sur les pointes, en tournant.*

Stand erect in the centre of the room and face 5, with the head upright, the feet in the *fifth* position, **right foot** in *front*, and the arms in the *fifth* position *en bas*.

The direction of the body is *en face*.

5. Execute a *Glissade* with the *left* foot, sliding the foot towards 5, so that at the conclusion of the movement the body faces 8.

---

[1] This exercise is designed more especially for female pupils.   It can, however, be executed by male pupils, in which case they will **rise** *sur les demi-pointes* instead of *sur les pointes*.

[2] See Book 1, Theory, Section VIII, *The Movement of the Head.*

Adagio

[1] Consequently, incline the head towards the *left* shoulder, since the *right* foot passes **behind** the *left* foot.

6. Repeat 2, but slide the *left* foot towards 7, so that at the conclusion of the movement the body faces 6.

   [1] Consequently, incline the head towards the *right* shoulder, since the *right* foot passes in **front of** the *left* foot.

7. Repeat 5, but slide the *left* foot towards 6, so that at the conclusion of the movement the body faces 5.

   [1] Consequently, incline the head towards the *left* shoulder, since the *right* foot passes **behind** the *left* foot.

8. Execute *deux petits changements.*
   First time, finish with the *right* foot in *front.*
   Second time, finish with the *left* foot in *front.*

Repeat Nos. 5—8, with the *right* foot, reading *right* for *left,* and *vice versa;* while, owing to the reverse direction of the body's turns, the wall numbers stated above will now correspond to those directly opposite—that is: 8—6, 3—4, 4—3, 6—8, 1—2, 7—5, 5—7, 2—1.

---

[1] See Book 1, Theory, Section VIII, *The Movement of the Head.*

HUIT RELEVÉS.

Stand erect in the centre of the room and face 2, with the head inclined to 3, the feet in the *fifth* position, **right** foot in *front*, and the arms in the *fifth* position *en bas*.

The direction of the body is *encroisé*.

1. *Pliez* on both feet in the *fifth* position, then straighten both knees.

2. *Demi-pliez* on both feet and rise *sur les demi-pointes*.

3. Lower the *left* heel to the ground, **at the same time**— Raise the *right* foot *sur le cou de pied en avant*.

4. Execute a *Developpé à la quatrième en avant, en l'air (encroisé)*.
   (*a*) Raise the *right* foot as high as possible—keeping the toe pointed well downwards—until the toe is in a line with the side of the *left* knee and the thigh raised to the *second* position, **en l'air**, **at the same time** – Gradually raise the arms to the *fifth* position *en avant*.
   (*b*) Extend the *right* foot to the *fourth* position *front, en l'air*, pointing to 2, **at the same time**— Raise the *left* arm above the head.
   Open the *right* arm to the *demi-seconde* position.
   (The arms are *en attitude, left* arm up.)
   Incline the head towards 1.
   The direction of the body is **encroisé en avant** (see Fig. 41).

5. Rise on the *left demi-pointe* to preserve the equilibrium.

6. Lower the *left* heel to the ground, **at the same time**— Without bending the knee, lower the *right* foot to the *fourth* position *front, pointe tendue*.
   The arms remain in the same position.

7. Withdraw the *right* foot *sur le cou de pied en avant,* **at the same time**— Rise on the *left demi-pointe* and turn slightly to the **right** so that the body faces 5.
   Lower the arms to the *fifth* position *en bas*.
   When the body faces 5, lower the *left* heel to the ground.

8. Execute a *Developpé à la quatrième en avant, en l'air (en face)*.
   (*a*) Raise the *right* foot as high as possible— keeping the toe pointed well downwards—until the toe is in a line with the side of the *left* knee and the

thigh raised to the *second* position, *en l'air*, **at the same time—**
Gradually raise the arms to the *fifth* position *en avant*.

(*b*) Extend the *right* foot to the *fourth* position *front, en l'air* (*en face*), pointing to 5, **at the same time—**
Gradually raise the arms to the *second* position.
The direction of the body is **à la quatrième en avant** (*en face*) (see Fig. 42).

9. Rise on the *left demi-pointe* to preserve the equilibrium.

10. Lower the *left* heel to the ground, **at the same time—**
Without bending the knee, lower the *right* foot to the *fourth* position *front, pointe tendue*.

11. Withdraw the *right* foot *sur le cou de pied en avant*, **at the same time—**
Rise on the *left demi-pointe* and slightly turn to the **left**, so that the body faces 2.
Lower the arms to the *fifth* position *en bas*.
When the body faces 2, lower the *left* heel to the ground.

12. Execute a *Developpé à la seconde en l'air*.
(*a*) Raise the *right* foot as high as possible—keeping the toe pointed well downwards—until the toe is in a line with the side of the *left* knee, and the thigh raised to the *second* position, *en l'air*, **at the same time—**
Raise the arms to the *fifth* position *en avant*.
(*b*) Extend the *right* foot to the *second* position, *en l'air*, pointing to 1, **at the same time—**
Raise the arms *en attitude, right* arm up, and, continuing the movement, lower the *right* arm to the *second* position, pointing to 1.
The *left* arm points to 3.
Turn the head towards 1.
The direction of the body is **ecarté** (see Fig. 43).

13. Rise on the *left demi-pointe* to preserve the equilibrium.

14. Lower the *left* heel to the ground, **at the same time—**
Lower the *right* foot—without bending the knee—to the *second* position, *pointe tendue*.
The arms remain in the same position.

15. Withdraw the *right* foot *sur le cou de pied en avant*, **at the same time—**

Rise on the *left demi-pointe* and slightly turn to the right so that the body faces 1.

Lower the arms to the *fifth* position *en bas*.

When the body faces 1, lower the *left* heel to the ground.

16. Execute a *Developpé à la quatrième en avant, en l'air (effacé)*.

    (*a*) Raise the *right* foot as high as possible—keeping the toe pointed well downwards—until the toe is in a line with the side of the *left* knee, and the thigh raised to the *second* position, *en l'air*, at the same time—

    Raise the arms to the *fifth* position *en avant*.

    (*b*) Extend the *right* foot to the *fourth* position *front*, *en l'air*, pointing to 1, at the same time—

    Raise the arms *en attitude*, *left* arm up.

    Look towards the *left* hand.

    The direction of the body is effacé (see Fig. 44).

17. Rise on the *left demi-pointe* to preserve the equilibrium.

18. Lower the *left* heel to the ground, at the same time—

    Lower the *right* foot—without bending the knee—to the *fourth* position *front, pointe tendue.*

    The arms remain in the same position.

19. Withdraw the *right* foot *sur le cou de pied en avant*, at the same time—

    Rise on the *left demi-pointe* and slightly turn to the left so that the body faces 5.

    Lower the arms to the *fifth* position *en bas*.

    When the body faces 5, lower the *left* heel to the ground.

20. Execute a *Developpé à la seconde, en l'air*.

    (*a*) Raise the *right* foot as high as possible—keeping the toe pointed well downwards—until the toe is in a line with the side of the *left* knee and the thigh raised to the *second* position, *en l'air*, at the same time—

    Raise the arms to the *fifth* position *en avant*.

    (*b*) Extend the *right* foot to the *second* position *en l'air*, pointing to 8, at the same time—

    Open the arms to the *second* position.

    The direction of the body is à la seconde (*en face*) (see Fig. 45).

21. Rise on the *left demi-pointe* to preserve the equilibrium.

22. Lower the *left* heel to the ground, **at the same time**—
Without bending the knee, lower the *right* foot to the *second* position, *pointe tendue*.
The arms remain in the same position.

23. Withdraw the *right* foot *sur le cou de pied en arrière*, **at the same time**—
Rise on the *left demi-pointe* and slightly turn to the **left** so that the body faces 2.
Lower the arms to the *fifth* position *en bas*.
When the body faces 2, lower the *left* heel to the ground.

24. Execute a *Developpé à la quatrième en arrière, en l'air (epaulé)*.
(*a*) Raise the *right* foot as high as possible—keeping the toe pointed well downwards—until the toe is in a line with the side of the *left* knee and the thigh raised to the *second* position, *en l'air*, **at the same time**—
Raise the arms to the *fifth* position *en avant*.
(*b*) Extend the *right* foot to the *fourth* position *back, en l'air*, pointing to 4, **at the same time**—
Extend the *right* arm in the *fourth* position *front*, pointing to 2.
Extend the *left* arm in the *fourth* position *back*, pointing to 4.
The pose is *en deuxième arabesque*.
The direction of the body is **epaulé** (see Fig. 46).

25. Rise on the *left demi-pointe* to preserve the equilibrium.

26. Lower the *left* heel to the ground, **at the same time**—
Without bending the knee, lower the *right* foot to the *fourth* position *back, pointe tendue*.
The arms remain in the same position.

27. Withdraw the *right* foot *sur le cou de pied en arrière*, **at the same time**—
Rise on the *left demi-pointe* and slightly turn to the **right** so that the body faces 5.
Lower the arms to the *fifth* position *en bas*.
When the body faces 5, lower the *left* heel to the ground.

28. Execute a *Developpé à la quatrième en arrière, en l'air (en face)*.
(*a*) Raise the *right* foot as high as possible—keeping the toe pointed well downwards—until the

toe is in a line with the side of the *left* knee and the thigh raised to the *second* position, *en l'air*, **at the same time—**

Raise the arms to the *fifth* position *en avant*.

(*b*) Extend the *right* foot to the *fourth* position *back, en l'air*, pointing to 7, **at the same time—**

Open the arms to the *second* position.

The direction of the body is **à la** quatrième **en arrière** (*en face*) (see Fig. 47).

29. Rise on the *left demi-pointe* to preserve the equilibrium.

30. Lower the *left* heel to the ground, **at the same time—**
Without bending the knee, lower the *right* foot to the *fourth* position *back, pointe tendue*.
The arms remain in the same position.

31. Withdraw the *right* foot *sur le cou de pied en arrière*, **at the same time—**
Rise on the *left demi-pointe* and slightly turn to the **right** so that the body faces 1.
Lower the arms to the *fifth* position *en bas*.
When the body faces 1, lower the *left* heel **to the** ground.

32. Execute a *Developpé à la quatrième en arrière, en l'air* (*encroisé*).
(*a*) Raise the *right* foot as high as possible—keeping the toe pointed well downwards—until the toe is in a line with the side of the *left* knee and the thigh raised to the *second* position, *en l'air*, **at the same time—**
Raise the arms to the *fifth* position *en avant*.
(*b*) Pass the *right* foot *à l'attitude*, pointing **to 3, at the same time—**
Raise the arms *en attitude, left* arm up.
The pose is *en attitude* (*encroisée*).
The direction of the body is **encroisé en arrière** (see Fig. 48).

33. Gradually raise the *right* arm above the head, **at the same time—**
Lower the *left* arm to the *second* position, to the *first* position, pass it to the *fifth* position, **and raise** it to the *fourth* position *en avant*.
Keep the *left* knee straight and bend the head and body—from the waist—as far as possible towards 2 (see Fig. 75).

As the body is inclined towards 2—
Gradually bring the *right* foot as near as possible towards the head.

34. Bring the body erect, facing 1, **at the same time**—
Lower the *right* foot to the *fifth* position *back.*
Lower the arms to the *fifth* position *en bas.*

Exercise of the Left Foot in Huit Relevés.

Stand erect in the centre of the room and face 1, with the head inclined to 4, the feet in the *fifth* position, *left* foot in *front,* and the arms in the *fifth* position *en bas.*

The direction of the body is *encroisé.*

Repeat the whole of the last exercise, reading *left* for *right,* and *vice versa* ; while, owing to the reverse direction of the body's turns, the wall numbers stated above will now correspond to those directly opposite—that is : 8—6, 3—4, 4—3, 6—8, 1—2, 7—5, 5—7, 2—1.

DEUX GRANDS RONDS DE JAMBE EN L'AIR AVEC ARABESQUE.

Stand erect in the centre of the room and face 2, with the head inclined to 3, the feet in the *fifth* position, **right** foot in *front*, and the arms in the *fifth* position *en bas*.

The direction of the body is *encroisé*.

1. *Pliez* in the *fifth* position and straighten both knees.
2. *Demi-pliez* on both feet and rise *sur les demi-pointes*.
3. Lower the *left* heel to the ground, **at the same time—**
   Raise the *right* foot *sur le cou de pied en avant*.
   Slightly turn to the **right** so that the body faces **5**. When the body faces 5, lower the *left* heel to the ground.
4. Execute a *Developpé à la quatrième en avant, en l'air*.
   (*a*) Raise the *right* foot as high as possible—keeping the toe pointed well downwards—until the toe is in a line with the side of the *left* knee and the thigh raised to the *second* position, *en l'air*, **at the same time—**
   Raise the arms to the *fifth* position *en avant*.
   (*b*) Extend the *right* foot to the *fourth* position *front, en l'air*, pointing to 5.
   The arms remain in the *fifth* position *en avant*.
5. Execute with the *right* foot a *Grand rond de jambe en l'air en dehors*.
   As the foot moves from the *fourth* position *front, en l'air—second* position, *en l'air—*
   Open the arms to the *second* position.
   Keep the arms extended as the foot moves from *second* position, *en l'air—fourth* position *back, en l'air*.
6. Execute a *Developpé à la quatrième en avant, en l'air*.
   (*a*) Bend the *right* knee so that the toe is in a line with the side of the *left* knee and the thigh raised to the *second* position, *en l'air*, **at the same time—**
   Lower the arms to the *fifth* position *en bas*.
   (*b*) Extend the *right* foot to the *fourth* position *front, en l'air*, **at the same time—**
   Raise the arms to the *fifth* position *en avant*.
7. Execute a *grand rond de jambe en l'air en dehors*.
8. Execute a *Developpé à la seconde, en l'air*.
   (*a*) Bend the *right* knee so that the toe is in a line

with the side of the *left* knee and the **thigh raised**
to the *second* position, *en l'air*, **at the same time—**
Lower the arms to the *fifth* position *en bas*.

(*b*) Extend the *right* foot to the *second* **position,**
en l'air, pointing to 8, **at the same time—**
Raise the arms to the *fifth* position *en avant* and
open them to the *second* position.

9. Rise on the *left demi-pointe* **to find the equilibrium.**[1]

10. Keep the *right* arm and foot pointing to 8, and the
left arm pointing to 6, and **quickly turn the body
to the left** so that it faces 6, **at the same time—**
Turn the hands—palms downwards—and slightly
raise the *left* arm and consequently lower the *right*
arm.
The pose is *en première arabesque*.

11. Retain the pose for an instant, then—
Lower the *right* foot to the *fifth* position *back*, **at the
same time—**
Lower the *left* heel to the ground.
Lower the arms to the *fifth* position *en bas*.

*Exercise of the Left Foot in Deux Grands Ronds de Jambe
en l' Air avec Arabesque.*

Stand erect in the centre of the room and face 1, **with**
the head inclined to 4, the feet in the *fifth* position, *left* foot
in *front*, and the arms in the *fifth* position *en bas*.

The direction of the body is *encroisé*.

Repeat the whole of the last exercise, reading *left* for
right, and *vice versa*; while, owing to the reverse direction
of the body's turns, the wall numbers stated above will
now correspond to those directly opposite—that is: 8—6,
3—4, 4—3, 6—8, 1—2, 7—5, 5—7, 2—1.

---

1 Take great care in finding the equilibrium, because the quick movement to the left must be accomplished **without lowering the heel to the
ground.**

PART V.

ALLEGRO.

There are an infinite number of steps, such as *Assemblés, Ballonnés, Brisés, Cabrioles, Coupés, Echappés, Emboités, Entrechats, Fouettés, Gargouillades, Jetés, Pas de Basque, Pas de Bourré, Pas de Chat, Pas de Cheval, Pas de Poisson, Pas Fleurets, Petits Battements, Ronds de Jambe, Sissonnes, Saut de Flêche, Temps de Cuisse, Temps Levés, etc.,* grouped under *Allegro* which would thus require a very large volume in order to detail their manner of execution. We have, therefore, merely described a few of those movements in frequent use, so as to acquaint the pupil with some idea of their construction. Perhaps, in the future, we shall issue another volume entirely devoted to these brilliant steps.

LES ASSEMBLÉS.

An *Assemblé* is simply a *grand battement, sauté* (see Fig. 76, *a, b, c, d, e, f*).

GRAND ASSEMBLÉ SOUTENU EN AVANT.

Stand erect in the centre of the room and face 5, with the head upright, the feet in the *fifth* position, **right** foot in *front*, and the arms in the *fifth* position *en bas*.

The direction of the body is *en face*.

1. *Demi-pliez* on both feet and slide the *left* foot to the *second* position, *pointe tendue* ; then to the *second* position, *en l'air*, **at the same time—**
Open the arms to the *demi-seconde* position.
Incline the head towards 6.
Exactly as the *left* foot rises to the *second* position, *en l'air—*
Leap upwards into the air on the *right* foot.
While the body is in the air—
Bend both knees (a *plié à quart*), and bring together the flat of the toes of both feet, **at the same time—**
Lower the arms to the *fifth* position *en bas*.
Come to the ground—allowing the knees to bend— with the feet in the *fifth* position, *left* foot in *front*, and lower the heels to the ground, then—
Straighten both knees, **at the same time—**
Bring the head erect.

Note.—This *pas* can be executed *en avant* and *en arrière.*

Allegro

GRAND ASSEMBLÉ DE SUITE.

This *pas* is executed in the same manner as *Grand Assemblé soutenu en avant*, except that the *assemblé* is performed successively and alternately with the *left* foot and *right* foot, or *vice versa*.

LES JETÉS.

A *Jeté* is a similar *pas* to the *Grand Assemblé*, except that instead of coming to the ground with both feet in the *fifth* position, you come to the ground on *one* foot with the other raised *sur le cou de pied* (see Fig. 77a, b, c, d, e, f).

GRAND JETÉ À LA SECONDE EN AVANT.

Stand erect in the centre of the room and face 5, with the head inclined to 6, the feet in the *fifth* position, right foot in *front*, and the arms in the *fifth* position *en bas*.
The direction of the body is *en face.*

1. *Demi-pliez* on both feet and slide the *left* foot to the *second* position, *pointe tendue*; then to the *second* position, *en l'air*, at the same time—
   Open the arms to the *demi-seconde* position.
   Leap upwards into the air on the *right* foot.
   While the body is in the air—
   Bend both knees (a *plié à quart*) and bring together the flat of the toes of both feet.
   Come to the ground—allowing the knee to bend—on the *left demi-pointe*, in the position vacated by the *right* foot, and quickly lower the *left* heel to the ground.
   Exactly as the *left* foot comes to the ground—
   Bring the *right* foot *sur le cou de pied en arrière*, at the same time—
   Bring the arms to the *fifth* position *en bas*.

NOTE.—To recommence, *pliez* on the *left* foot, so that the *pointe* of the *right* foot touches the ground, then repeat 1, reading *left* for *right*, and *vice versa*. This *pas* is executed *en avant* and *en arrière*.

When the *pas* is executed *en arrière*, slide the foot in front to the *second* position, *pointe tendue*, while at the conclusion of the movement the rear foot comes *sur le cou de pied en avant*.

GRAND JETÉ À L'ATTITUDE.

Stand erect in the centre of the room and face 5, with the head inclined to 6, the feet in the *fourth* position, left

193

foot *back* and raised *pointe tendue,* and the arms in the *fifth* position *en bas.* The direction of the body is *en face.*

1. *Demi-pliez* on the *right* foot, **at the same time—**
   Raise the *left* foot *à l'attitude* (*demi-position*).
   The arms remain in the *fifth* position *en bas.*

2. Spring upward into the air on the **right** foot—keeping the knee bent—so that the two feet are parallel.
   Come to the ground—allowing the knee to bend—on the *left* foot.
   The *right* foot remains *à l'attitude* (*demi-position*).
   The arms remain in the *fifth* position *en bas.*

NOTE.—In the execution of a series of this *pas,* it is permissible to raise the arms to the *fifth* position *en avant* or *en haut,* according to the number performed.

PAS DE BASQUE EN FACE.

The *Pas de Basque* is composed of three movements ; a *jeté,* a sliding movement, and a *coupé.*

Stand erect in the centre of the room and face 2, with the head inclined to 3, the feet in the *fifth* position, *right* foot in front, and the arms in the *fifth* position *en bas.*

The direction of the body is *encroisé.*

1. (*a*) Open the *right* foot to the *fourth* position *front, pointe tendue.*
   (*b*) Raise the *right* foot and spring on it towards 1, **at the same time—**
   Dégagez the *left* foot.
   Open the arms to the *demi-seconde* position.
   Incline the head towards the *right* shoulder.

2. *Demi-pliez* on the *right* foot, **at the same time—**
   Slide the *left* foot across to the *fifth* position *front,* allowing the knee to bend, then to the *fourth* position *front* (*encroisé*), pointing to 1.
   Slightly turn the body to the *right* so that it faces 1.
   Lower the arms to the *fifth* position *en bas.*
   As the *left* foot comes to the *fourth* position *front* (*encroisé*)—
   Straighten the *right* knee and raise the foot *pointe tendue.*

3. Bring the *right* foot to the *fifth* position *back,* **at the same time—**
   Raise the *left* foot *sur le cou de pied en avant.*

NOTE.—This *pas* can be executed *en avant, en arrière, sauté,* and *en tournant.*

Allegro

BALLONNÉ SIMPLE.

A *Ballonné* is simply a *battement frappé sur le cou de pied, sauté.*

Stand erect in the centre of the room and face 5, with the head upright, the feet in the *fifth* position, **right** foot in front, and the arms in the *fifth* position *en bas.*

The direction of the body is *en face.*

1. Bring the *right* foot *sur le cou de pied en avant*, **at the same time—**
   Demi-pliez on the *left* foot.

2. Spring upwards into the air on the *left* foot, **at the same time—**
   Open the *right* foot to the *second* position, *en l'air* (*demi-position*).
   Open the arms to the *demi-seconde* position.
   Come to the ground on the *left* foot—allowing the knee to bend.
   As the foot touches the ground—
   Bring the *right* foot *sur le cou de pied en avant*, at the same time—
   Lower the arms to the *fifth* position *en bas.*

NOTE.—This *pas* can be executed in all the directions of the body.

BALLONNÉ À TROIS TEMPS.

Stand erect in the centre of the room and face 5, with the head upright, the feet in the *fifth* position, **right** foot in *front*, and the arms in the *fifth* position *en bas.*

The direction of the body is *en face.*

This *ballonné* is composed of *three* movements : (*a*) *Temps levé* ; (*b*) *Glissade* ; (*c*) *Coupé.*

1. Bring the *right* foot *sur le cou de pied en avant* and execute a *battement frappé sur le cou de pied*, **at the same time—**
   Leap upward into the air on the *left* foot.
   Come to the ground—allowing the knee to bend—on the *left* foot.
   Leap upward into the air on the *left* foot, **at the same time—**
   Open the *right* foot to the *second* position, *en l'air* (*demi-position*).
   Raise the arms *en attitude*, *right* arm up.
   Come to the ground—allowing the knee to bend—on the *left* foot, **at the same time—**

Bring the *right* foot *sur le cou de pied en avant*.

2. Slide the *right* foot to the *second* position, *pointe tendue*.

3. Bring the *left* foot to the *fifth* position *back*, **at the same time—**
Bring the arms to the *fifth* position *en bas*.

NOTE.—This *pas* can be executed in all the directions of the body.

TEMPS DE CUISSE.

A *Temps de Cuisse* is simply a *battement degagé* and *battement fondu, sauté*.

Stand erect in the centre of the room and face 5, with the head upright, the feet in the *fifth* position, **right** foot in *front*, and the arms in the *fifth* position *en bas*.

The direction of the body is *en face*.

1. Execute with the *left* foot a *battement dégagé à la seconde en l'air*, **at the same time—**
Open the arms to the *demi-seconde* position, **and immediately—**

2. Execute with the *left* foot a *battement fondu* to the *fifth* position *front*, and *demi-pliez* on both feet, **at the same time—**
Lower the arms to the *fifth* position *en bas*.

3. Lightly spring upwards into the air on the *right* foot, **at the same time—**
Execute with the *left* foot a *battement dégagé à la seconde, en l'air*.
Come to the ground on the *right* foot—allowing the knee to bend.
Slide the *left* foot to the *fifth* position *front*, **at the same time—**
Lower the arms to the *fifth* position *en bas*.

NOTE.—This *pas* can be executed *en arrière* and in all the directions of the body.

TEMPS LEVÉ.

Stand erect in the centre of the room and face 5, with the head upright, the feet in the *fifth* position, right foot in front, and the arms in the *fifth* position *en bas*.

The direction of the body is *en face*.

1. (*a*) *Demi-pliez* on both feet.
(*b*) Spring upward into the air on the *left* foot, **at the same time—**

Allegro

Raise the *right* foot *sur le cou de pied en avant.*
Come to the ground, allowing the knee to bend, on the *left* foot.

Note.—This *pas* can be executed *en avant, en arrière, en attitude, en arabesque,* or *en tournant.*

PAS DE CHAT.

This *pas* is composed of *three* movements, generally executed *en diagonale.*

Stand erect in the centre of the room and face 5, with the head inclined to 2, the feet in the *fifth* position, right foot in front, and the arms in the *fifth* position *en bas.*

The direction of the body is *en face.*

1. Bring the *left* foot *sur le cou de pied en arrière,* at the same time—
Raise the *left* arm to the *fourth* position *en avant,* and carry it near the breast.
Extend the *right* arm to the *fourth* position *back (demi-position)*—palm downwards—pointing to 4.
Incline the head so that it regards the raised foot.
2. Spring *en diagonale* on the *left* foot—allowing the knee to bend—towards 2, at the same time—
Bring the *right* foot *sur le cou de pied en avant.*
3. Lower the *right* foot to the *fifth* position *front,* allowing the knee to bend.

Note.—Throughout the execution of this *pas* the arms remain *en troisième arabesque (encroisée).*

ECHAPPÉ SAUTÉ À LA SECONDE.

Stand erect in the centre of the room and face 5, with the head upright, the feet in the *fifth* position, right foot in front, and the arms in the *fifth* position *en bas.*

The direction of the body is *en face.*

1. *Demi-pliez* on both feet and spring upward into the air.
Exactly as the feet leave the ground, instantaneousl open the feet to the *second* position, keeping the knees well bent.
2. Come to the ground in the same position—allowing the knees to bend—and immediately again spring upwards into the air.
3. Come to the ground with the feet in the *fifth* position, *right* foot in *front.*

Note.—This exercise can be repeated on the same for

or executed successively and alternately with the *left* foot and *right* foot, or *vice versa*. This *pas* can be executed *en arrière* and *à la quatrième position* in all the directions of the body.

ECHAPPÉ SUR LES POINTES.

Stand erect in the centre of the room and face 5, with the head upright, the feet in the *fifth* position, **right** foot in *front*, and the arms in the *fifth* position *en bas*.

The direction of the body is *en face*.

1. *Demi-pliez* on both feet, and *with a little spring*,[1] **instantaneously** open the feet *sur les pointes* in the *second* position (see Fig. 78*a*). *Note that both feet move*. **At the same time—** Open the arms to the *demi-seconde* position.

2. Return to the *fifth* position, *with a little spring*, **without changing the feet, at the same time—** Lower the arms to the *fifth* position *en bas*.

[1] In raising the feet from a position *à terre* to a position *sur les pointes*, always employ a slight "spring." Similarly in bringing the feet from a position *sur les pointes* to a position *à terre*, always employ a slight "spring." Fig. 78*b* shows the incorrect execution of an *Echappé sur les pointes*.

CONCLUSION.

Observe with attention and dissect all your movements. Lose no opportunity of adding to your knowledge of your art. Do not disdain to learn from an inferior. From a mediocre dancer you will learn the effect produced by the faulty execution of a movement. On the other hand, there are few dancers who do not possess some good point in their work from which you may derive profit.

Do not be afraid of asking questions of your professor ; by this means you will discover those minute details of execution which are the distinguishing marks of a good dancer. A mediocre dancer contents himself with the main outlines and neglects those degrees of light and shade which give his work relief and distinction.

Do not be afraid of criticism, neither ignore it. If your work is criticised to your detriment and you feel in your heart that such remarks are justified, strive immediately to correct your faults.

In your study of technique, never depart from the true principles of your art, so that technique degenerates into acrobatics. Do not be led into a false self-appreciation of your talent by counterfeit applause. There is that involuntary, unrestrained, uplifting, genuine applause which comes from the heart and which is the true approbation of the faultless execution of a dance. There is also that other applause produced by certain members of the audience who noisily clap their hands and loudly shout 'Brava,' not because they appreciate the talent of the executant, but merely because they desire to draw attention to themselves, so that they may derive a certain distinction from being considered the friends of such a dancer.

Examine well the style of dancing best suited to yourself. Nothing looks more ridiculous than the spectacle of a tall, majestic dancer who undertakes the *rôle* of a woodland elf. Similarly, nothing can be more ludicrous than the appearance of a short, slightly-built dancer who assumes the *rôle* of some mighty prince of noble renown. A well-proportioned dancer of average height, so that he is neither too tall nor too short, may, by dint of practice and study, make himself proficient in many diverse *rôles*. On the stage, stature is very deceptive. The dancer's height is qualified by many factors ; comparison with the other members of the company, his costume, and the proportions of the scenery. In general, on the stage a person tends to appear slightly taller than he really is.

Try to invest your dancing with style. Suppose that in one ballet you dance an eighteenth century *minuet*, and in another a *pas de villageois*. These two dances must differ in something more than the arrangement of steps, manner of make-up and costume—and that is, **style**. For your *minuet*, study the paintings and engravings of the period. Try to invest your dancing with something of the decorum, delicacy, and charm of manner; grace and stateliness of deportment; which are the characteristics of the period. Similarly, in your *pas de villageois* there must be something of the abandon, vigour, easy manners, and vivacious temperament typical of those who live a great part of their life in the open air.

Study music, for in the explanation of the theme of a ballet, music is all important. It inspires the dancer with the expression necessary to the spirit of the piece. It serves as a preparation for a phase of comedy or drama. It serves as a signal for the commencement and conclusion of a dance, and the speed at which it must be executed.

Finally, aim at ease and softness in your performance of a dance. Endeavour that all shall be harmonious, flowing and rhythmic. However hard you work at your lessons or at rehearsal, let none of this labour be visible in your performance. There must be no sign of concentration, exertion, or tension. All must be free and natural, for the true art is that which conceals the labour that produced it.

TABLE OF DAILY EXERCISES FOR THE WEEK.

MONDAY.	TEMPS D'ADAGE.

Trois Relevés.
Grand Rond de Jambe en Dehors et en Dedans.
Grand Fouetté.
Coupé et Fouetté, en Avant et en Arrière.
Quatre Pirouettes en Dedans.

TEMPS D'ALLEGRE.

Des Assemblés.

TUESDAY.	TEMPS D'ADAGE.

Rond de Jambe Developpé.
Developpé Cecchetti.
Developpé Fouetté Cecchetti.
Pas de Chaconne Cecchetti.
Renversés.
Temps de Courante.

TEMPS D' ALLEGRE.

Des Petits Battements.

WEDNESDAY.	TEMPS D'ADAGE.

Cinq Relevés.
Pas de la Mascotte.
Pas de Chaconne.
Première et Seconde Arabesque.
Deux Tours en Dehors de Pirouette sur le cou de pied, Jeté, Assemblé et Entrechat Quatre.

TEMPS D' ALLEGRE.

Des Ronds de Jambe.

THURSDAY.	TEMPS D'ADAGE.

Grand Rond de Jambe en l'air en tournant avec les Jetés.
Fouetté et Ballotté.
Première, Seconde, Troisième et Quatrième Arabesque.
Pas de l'Alliance.
Liaison des Pirouettes.

TEMPS D'ALLEGRE.

Des Jetés.

FRIDAY.	TEMPS D'ADAGE.

Grand Rond de Jambe en tournant avec Relevé.
Glissade, Jeté, Fouetté.
Glissade Cecchetti.
Glissade Arabesque et Pas de Bourré Renversé.
Glissade de Mami.
Glissade sur les Pointes.

TEMPS D'ALLEGRE.

Des Temps de Pointe, Temps de Batterie et Temps en Tournant.

SATURDAY.	TEMPS D'ADAGE.

Huit Relevés.
Deux Grands Ronds de Jambe en l'Air avec Arabesque.
Grand Fouetté.
Coupé et Fouetté, en Avant et en Arrière.
Quatre Pirouettes en Dedans.

TEMPS D'ALLEGRE.

Des Grands Fouettés Sautés.

Plate XI.

Plate XI.

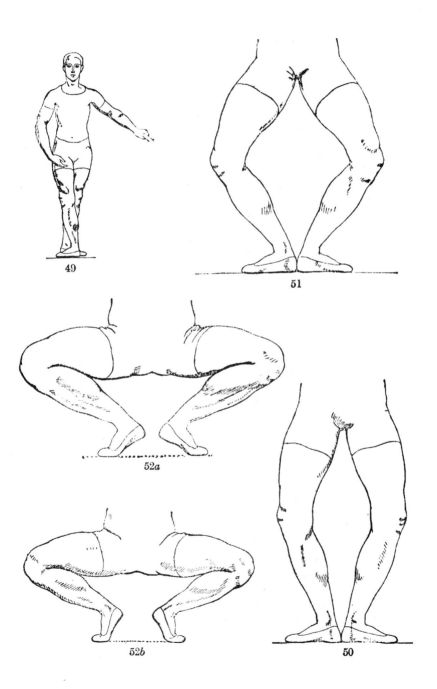

49

51

52a

52b

50

PLATE XII.

Fig. **53a**   Diagram to illustrate the execution of *rond de jambe à terre en dehors.*

The dotted line from 4—1 indicates the active—in this case the **right**—foot passing from *first* position to *fourth* position *front, pointe tendue.*

The dotted curve from 1—2 indicates the active foot passing from *fourth* position *front. pointe tendue,* to *second* position, *pointe tendue.*

The dotted curve from 2—3 indicates the active foot passing from *second* position, *pointe tendue,* to *fourth position back, pointe tendue.*

The dotted line from 3—4 indicates the active foot passing from *fourth* position *back, pointe tendue,* to *first* position.

„ **53b**   Diagram to illustrate the execution of *rond de jambe à terre en dedans.*

The dotted line from 4—1 indicates the active—in this case the **right**—foot passing from *first* position to *fourth* position *back, pointe tendue.*

The dotted curve from 1—2 indicates the active foot passing from *fourth* position *back, pointe tendue,* to *second* position, *pointe tendue.*

The dotted curve from 2—3 indicates the active foot passing from *second* position, *pointe tendue,* to *fourth* position *front, pointe tendue.*

The dotted line from 3—4 indicates the active foot passing from *fourth* position *front, pointe tendue,* to *first* position.

„ **54a**   Preparatory position for the execution of *battements frappés sur le cou de pied* and *petits battements sur le cou de pied.* The **right** foot is placed *sur le cou de pied en avant.*

„ **54b**   Diagram to illustrate the execution of *battements frappés sur le cou de pied.* The arrow indicates the accent of the beat and the point of contact of the active foot when passing from *sur le cou de pied* to *degagé* position.

Plate XII.

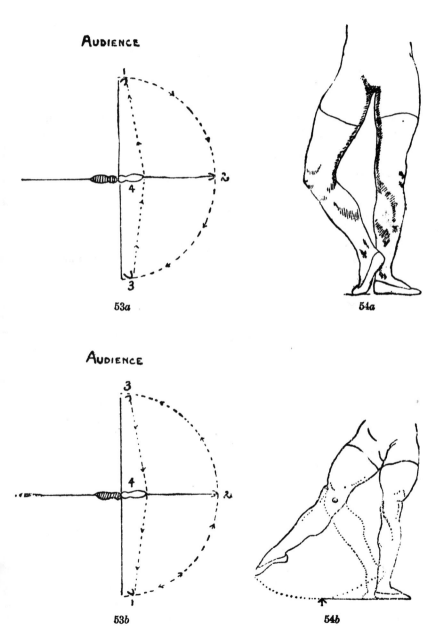

AUDIENCE

53a

54a

AUDIENCE

53b

54b

Plate XIII.

Plate XIII.

AUDIENCE

55

56

57

58

PLATE XIV.

Plate XIV.

59

60

61

Plate XV.

Plate XV.

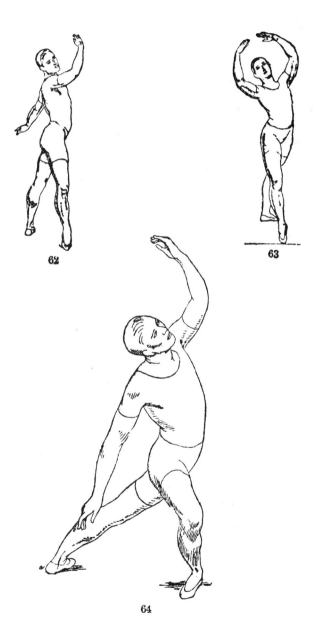

62

63

64

Plate XVI.

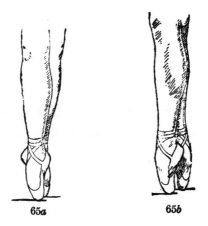

65a 65b

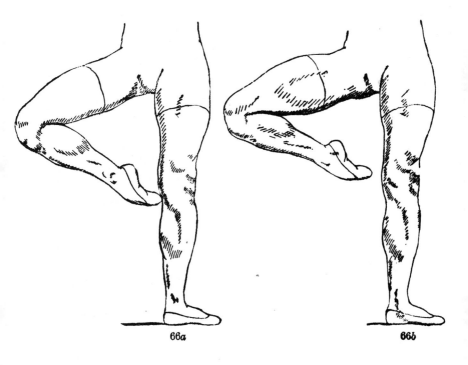

66a 66b

Plate XVII.

Plate XVII.

67

68

69

70

PLATE XVIII.

Fig. 71   Pose from No. 12 Adagio Exercise *Fouetté et Ballotté.*

Note.—This diagram is to be consulted for the position of the head and arms only.

,,   72   Pose from No. 5 Adagio Exercise *Troisième et Quatrième Arabesque.*[1]

,,   78   Pose from No. 19 Adagio Exercise *Troisième et Quatrième Arabesque.*

,,   74   Pose from No. 11 Adagio Exercise *Glissade Cecchetti.*[1]

[1] If the exercise is commenced with the feet in the *fifth* position, **right** foot in front, regard the illustrations as if the limbs were in the reverse position. If the exercise is begun with the feet in the *fifth* position, **left** foot in front, regard the illustration as shown.

Plate XVIII.

71

74

72

73

PLATE XIX.

Fig. 75 Pose from No. 7 Adagio Exercise *Glissade, Jeté, Fouetté.*

Pose from **No. 33** Adagio Exercise *Huit Relevés.*

„ 78*a* Feet in the *second* position, *sur les pointes.*

„ 78*b* Incorrect execution of 78*a*, caused by raising the heels from a position *à terre* to the *second* position *sur les pointes*, without employing a slight " spring."

Note.—In raising the feet from a position *à terre* to a position *sur les pointes, always employ a slight ' spring.'* Similarly in bringing the feet from a position *sur les pointes* to a position *à terre,* **always employ a slight spring.**

Plate XIX.

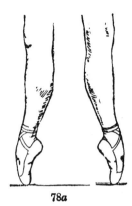

78a

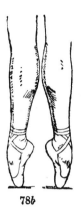

78b

75

PLATE XX.

Fig. 76 Diagram to illustrate sequence of movements of the feet in the execution of an *Assemblé*.

    a Shows preparation with the feet in the *fifth* position, **right** foot in front.

    b A *demi-plié* in the *fifth* position.

    c The *left* foot executing a *grand battement à la seconde en l'air*, while the *right* foot rises *sur la demi-pointe*.

    d A *plié à quart* in the air in order to bring together the flat of the toes of both feet.

    e The feet *sur les demi-pointes* at the moment of alighting.

    f The feet in the *fifth* position, *left* foot in front.

Plate XX.

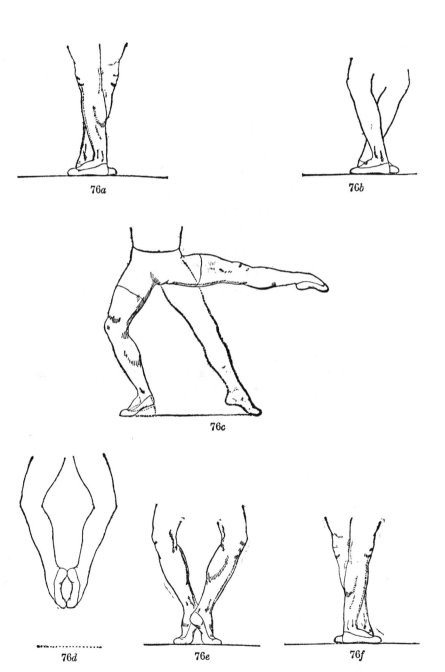

76a

76b

76c

76d

76e

76f

PLATE XXI.

Fig. 77   Diagram to illustrate sequence of movements of the feet in the execution of a *Jeté*.

a   Shows preparation with the feet in the fifth position, *right* foot in front.

b   A *demi-plié* in the *fifth* position.

c   The *left* foot executing a *grand battement à la seconde en l'air,* while the right foot rises sur la demi-pointe.

d   A *plié à quart* in the air in order to bring together the flat of the toes of the feet.

e   The feet at the moment of alighting, with the *left* foot *sur la demi-pointe* and the *right* foot raised *sur le cou de pied en arrière.*

Plate XXI.

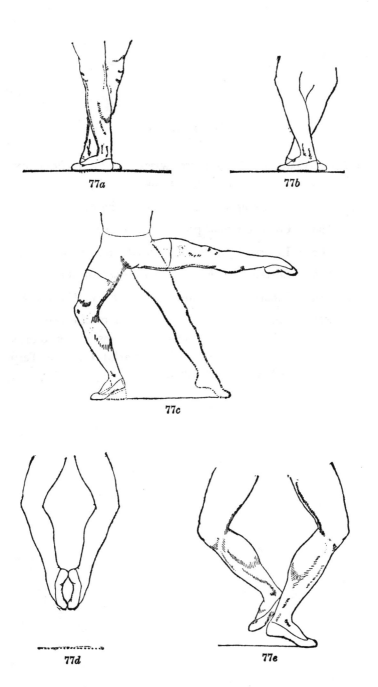

77a

77b

77c

77d

77e

Plate XXII.

A Comparison of Incorrect with Correct Positions of the Arms.

Fig. 79*a*   Incorrect *second* position of the arms.

,,   79*b*   Correct *second* position of the arms.

,,   80*a*   Incorrect *fourth* position *en haut* of the arms.

,,   80*b*   Correct *fourth* position *en haut* of the arms.

,,   81*a*   Incorrect *fifth* position *en haut* of the arms.

,,   81*b*   Correct *fifth* position *en haut* of the arms.

The false positions of the arms are reproduced from Plate III., Blasis (Carlo) Code de Terpsichore.   *Bull,* 1830.

Plate XXII.

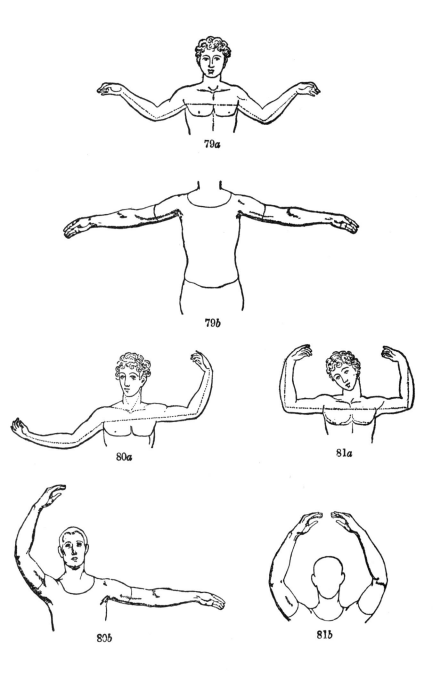

79a

79b

80a

81a

80b

81b

INDEX.

The titles of exercises are printed in italics.

Index (continued).

Index (continued).

Index (continued).

A CATALOGUE OF SELECTED DOVER BOOKS
IN ALL FIELDS OF INTEREST

A CATALOGUE OF SELECTED DOVER BOOKS
IN ALL FIELDS OF INTEREST

AMERICA'S OLD MASTERS, James T. Flexner. Four men emerged unexpectedly from provincial 18th century America to leadership in European art: Benjamin West, J. S. Copley, C. R. Peale, Gilbert Stuart. Brilliant coverage of lives and contributions. Revised, 1967 edition. 69 plates. 365pp. of text.
21806-6 Paperbound $3.00

FIRST FLOWERS OF OUR WILDERNESS: AMERICAN PAINTING, THE COLONIAL PERIOD, James T. Flexner. Painters, and regional painting traditions from earliest Colonial times up to the emergence of Copley, West and Peale Sr., Foster, Gustavus Hesselius, Feke, John Smibert and many anonymous painters in the primitive manner. Engaging presentation, with 162 illustrations. xxii + 368pp.
22180-6 Paperbound $3.50

THE LIGHT OF DISTANT SKIES: AMERICAN PAINTING, 1760-1835, James T. Flexner. The great generation of early American painters goes to Europe to learn and to teach: West, Copley, Gilbert Stuart and others. Allston, Trumbull, Morse; also contemporary American painters—primitives, derivatives, academics—who remained in America. 102 illustrations. xiii + 306pp.
22179-2 Paperbound $3.50

A HISTORY OF THE RISE AND PROGRESS OF THE ARTS OF DESIGN IN THE UNITED STATES, William Dunlap. Much the richest mine of information on early American painters, sculptors, architects, engravers, miniaturists, etc. The only source of information for scores of artists, the major primary source for many others. Unabridged reprint of rare original 1834 edition, with new introduction by James T. Flexner, and 394 new illustrations. Edited by Rita Weiss. 6⅝ x 9⅝.
21695-0, 21696-9, 21697-7 Three volumes, Paperbound $15.00

EPOCHS OF CHINESE AND JAPANESE ART, Ernest F. Fenollosa. From primitive Chinese art to the 20th century, thorough history, explanation of every important art period and form, including Japanese woodcuts; main stress on China and Japan, but Tibet, Korea also included. Still unexcelled for its detailed, rich coverage of cultural background, aesthetic elements, diffusion studies, particularly of the historical period. 2nd, 1913 edition. 242 illustrations. lii + 439pp. of text.
20364-6, 20365-4 Two volumes, Paperbound $6.00

THE GENTLE ART OF MAKING ENEMIES, James A. M. Whistler. Greatest wit of his day deflates Oscar Wilde, Ruskin, Swinburne; strikes back at inane critics, exhibitions, art journalism; aesthetics of impressionist revolution in most striking form. Highly readable classic by great painter. Reproduction of edition designed by Whistler. Introduction by Alfred Werner. xxxvi + 334pp.
21875-9 Paperbound $3.00

VISUAL ILLUSIONS: THEIR CAUSES, CHARACTERISTICS, AND APPLICATIONS, Matthew Luckiesh. Thorough description and discussion of optical illusion, geometric and perspective, particularly; size and shape distortions, illusions of color, of motion; natural illusions; use of illusion in art and magic, industry, etc. Most useful today with op art, also for classical art. Scores of effects illustrated. Introduction by William H. Ittleson. 100 illustrations. xxi + 252pp.

21530-X Paperbound $2.00

A HANDBOOK OF ANATOMY FOR ART STUDENTS, Arthur Thomson. Thorough, virtually exhaustive coverage of skeletal structure, musculature, etc. Full text, supplemented by anatomical diagrams and drawings and by photographs of undraped figures. Unique in its comparison of male and female forms, pointing out differences of contour, texture, form. 211 figures, 40 drawings, 86 photographs. xx + 459pp. 5⅜ x 8⅜.

21163-0 Paperbound $3.50

150 MASTERPIECES OF DRAWING, Selected by Anthony Toney. Full page reproductions of drawings from the early 16th to the end of the 18th century, all beautifully reproduced: Rembrandt, Michelangelo, Dürer, Fragonard, Urs, Graf, Wouwerman, many others. First-rate browsing book, model book for artists. xviii + 150pp. 8⅜ x 11¼.

21032-4 Paperbound $3.50

THE LATER WORK OF AUBREY BEARDSLEY, Aubrey Beardsley. Exotic, erotic, ironic masterpieces in full maturity: Comedy Ballet, Venus and Tannhauser, Pierrot, Lysistrata, Rape of the Lock, Savoy material, Ali Baba, Volpone, etc. This material revolutionized the art world, and is still powerful, fresh, brilliant. With *The Early Work*, all Beardsley's finest work. 174 plates, 2 in color. xiv + 176pp. 8⅛ x 11.

21817-1 Paperbound $3.75

DRAWINGS OF REMBRANDT, Rembrandt van Rijn. Complete reproduction of fabulously rare edition by Lippmann and Hofstede de Groot, completely reedited, updated, improved by Prof. Seymour Slive, Fogg Museum. Portraits, Biblical sketches, landscapes, Oriental types, nudes, episodes from classical mythology—All Rembrandt's fertile genius. Also selection of drawings by his pupils and followers. "Stunning volumes," *Saturday Review*. 550 illustrations. lxxviii + 552pp. 9⅛ x 12¼.

21485-0, 21486-9 Two volumes, Paperbound $10.00

THE DISASTERS OF WAR, Francisco Goya. One of the masterpieces of Western civilization—83 etchings that record Goya's shattering, bitter reaction to the Napoleonic war that swept through Spain after the insurrection of 1808 and to war in general. Reprint of the first edition, with three additional plates from Boston's Museum of Fine Arts. All plates facsimile size. Introduction by Philip Hofer, Fogg Museum. v + 97pp. 9⅜ x 8¼.

21872-4 Paperbound $2.50

GRAPHIC WORKS OF ODILON REDON. Largest collection of Redon's graphic works ever assembled: 172 lithographs, 28 etchings and engravings, 9 drawings. These include some of his most famous works. All the plates from *Odilon Redon: oeuvre graphique complet,* plus additional plates. New introduction and caption translations by Alfred Werner. 209 illustrations. xxvii + 209pp. 9⅛ x 12¼.

21966-8 Paperbound $5.00

DESIGN BY ACCIDENT; A BOOK OF "ACCIDENTAL EFFECTS" FOR ARTISTS AND DESIGNERS, James F. O'Brien. Create your own unique, striking, imaginative effects by "controlled accident" interaction of materials: paints and lacquers, oil and water based paints, splatter, crackling materials, shatter, similar items. Everything you do will be different; first book on this limitless art, so useful to both fine artist and commercial artist. Full instructions. 192 plates showing "accidents," 8 in color. viii + 215pp. 8⅜ x 11¼. 21942-9 Paperbound $3.75

THE BOOK OF SIGNS, Rudolf Koch. Famed German type designer draws 493 beautiful symbols: religious, mystical, alchemical, imperial, property marks, runes, etc. Remarkable fusion of traditional and modern. Good for suggestions of timelessness, smartness, modernity. Text. vi + 104pp. 6⅛ x 9¼.
20162-7 Paperbound $1.25

HISTORY OF INDIAN AND INDONESIAN ART, Ananda K. Coomaraswamy. An unabridged republication of one of the finest books by a great scholar in Eastern art. Rich in descriptive material, history, social backgrounds; Sunga reliefs, Rajput paintings, Gupta temples, Burmese frescoes, textiles, jewelry, sculpture, etc. 400 photos. viii + 423pp. 6⅜ x 9¾. 21436-2 Paperbound $5.00

PRIMITIVE ART, Franz Boas. America's foremost anthropologist surveys textiles, ceramics, woodcarving, basketry, metalwork, etc.; patterns, technology, creation of symbols, style origins. All areas of world, but very full on Northwest Coast Indians. More than 350 illustrations of baskets, boxes, totem poles, weapons, etc. 378 pp.
20025-6 Paperbound $3.00

THE GENTLEMAN AND CABINET MAKER'S DIRECTOR, Thomas Chippendale. Full reprint (third edition, 1762) of most influential furniture book of all time, by master cabinetmaker. 200 plates, illustrating chairs, sofas, mirrors, tables, cabinets, plus 24 photographs of surviving pieces. Biographical introduction by N. Bienenstock. vi + 249pp. 9⅞ x 12¾. 21601-2 Paperbound $4.00

AMERICAN ANTIQUE FURNITURE, Edgar G. Miller, Jr. The basic coverage of all American furniture before 1840. Individual chapters cover type of furniture—clocks, tables, sideboards, etc.—chronologically, with inexhaustible wealth of data. More than 2100 photographs, all identified, commented on. Essential to all early American collectors. Introduction by H. E. Keyes. vi + 1106pp. 7⅞ x 10¾.
21599-7, 21600-4 Two volumes, Paperbound $11.00

PENNSYLVANIA DUTCH AMERICAN FOLK ART, Henry J. Kauffman. 279 photos, 28 drawings of tulipware, Fraktur script, painted tinware, toys, flowered furniture, quilts, samplers, hex signs, house interiors, etc. Full descriptive text. Excellent for tourist, rewarding for designer, collector. Map. 146pp. 7⅞ x 10¾.
21205-X Paperbound $2.50

EARLY NEW ENGLAND GRAVESTONE RUBBINGS, Edmund V. Gillon, Jr. 43 photographs, 226 carefully reproduced rubbings show heavily symbolic, sometimes macabre early gravestones, up to early 19th century. Remarkable early American primitive art, occasionally strikingly beautiful; always powerful. Text. xxvi + 207pp. 8⅜ x 11¼. 21380-3 Paperbound $3.50

ALPHABETS AND ORNAMENTS, Ernst Lehner. Well-known pictorial source for decorative alphabets, script examples, cartouches, frames, decorative title pages, calligraphic initials, borders, similar material. 14th to 19th century, mostly European. Useful in almost any graphic arts designing, varied styles. 750 illustrations. 256pp. 7 x 10.   21905-4 Paperbound $4.00

PAINTING: A CREATIVE APPROACH, Norman Colquhoun. For the beginner simple guide provides an instructive approach to painting: major stumbling blocks for beginner; overcoming them, technical points; paints and pigments; oil painting; watercolor and other media and color. New section on "plastic" paints. Glossary. Formerly *Paint Your Own Pictures*. 221pp.   22000-1 Paperbound $1.75

THE ENJOYMENT AND USE OF COLOR, Walter Sargent. Explanation of the relations between colors themselves and between colors in nature and art, including hundreds of little-known facts about color values, intensities, effects of high and low illumination, complementary colors. Many practical hints for painters, references to great masters. 7 color plates, 29 illustrations. x + 274pp.
20944-X Paperbound $2.75

THE NOTEBOOKS OF LEONARDO DA VINCI, compiled and edited by Jean Paul Richter. 1566 extracts from original manuscripts reveal the full range of Leonardo's versatile genius: all his writings on painting, sculpture, architecture, anatomy, astronomy, geography, topography, physiology, mining, music, etc., in both Italian and English, with 186 plates of manuscript pages and more than 500 additional drawings. Includes studies for the Last Supper, the lost Sforza monument, and other works. Total of xlvii + 866pp. 7⅞ x 10¾.
22572-0, 22573-9 Two volumes, Paperbound $11.00

MONTGOMERY WARD CATALOGUE OF 1895. Tea gowns, yards of flannel and pillow-case lace, stereoscopes, books of gospel hymns, the New Improved Singer Sewing Machine, side saddles, milk skimmers, straight-edged razors, high-button shoes, spittoons, and on and on . . . listing some 25,000 items, practically all illustrated. Essential to the shoppers of the 1890's, it is our truest record of the spirit of the period. Unaltered reprint of Issue No. 57, Spring and Summer 1895. Introduction by Boris Emmet. Innumerable illustrations. xiii + 624pp. 8½ x 11⅝.
22377-9 Paperbound $6.95

THE CRYSTAL PALACE EXHIBITION ILLUSTRATED CATALOGUE (LONDON, 1851). One of the wonders of the modern world—the Crystal Palace Exhibition in which all the nations of the civilized world exhibited their achievements in the arts and sciences—presented in an equally important illustrated catalogue. More than 1700 items pictured with accompanying text—ceramics, textiles, cast-iron work, carpets, pianos, sleds, razors, wall-papers, billiard tables, beehives, silverware and hundreds of other artifacts—represent the focal point of Victorian culture in the Western World. Probably the largest collection of Victorian decorative art ever assembled— indispensable for antiquarians and designers. Unabridged republication of the Art-Journal Catalogue of the Great Exhibition of 1851, with all terminal essays. New introduction by John Gloag, F.S.A. xxxiv + 426pp. 9 x 12.
22503-8 Paperbound $5.00

A HISTORY OF COSTUME, Carl Köhler. Definitive history, based on surviving pieces of clothing primarily, and paintings, statues, etc. secondarily. Highly readable text, supplemented by 594 illustrations of costumes of the ancient Mediterranean peoples, Greece and Rome, the Teutonic prehistoric period; costumes of the Middle Ages, Renaissance, Baroque, 18th and 19th centuries. Clear, measured patterns are provided for many clothing articles. Approach is practical throughout. Enlarged by Emma von Sichart. 464pp.   21030-8 Paperbound $3.50.

ORIENTAL RUGS, ANTIQUE AND MODERN, Walter A. Hawley. A complete and authoritative treatise on the Oriental rug—where they are made, by whom and how, designs and symbols, characteristics in detail of the six major groups, how to distinguish them and how to buy them. Detailed technical data is provided on periods, weaves, warps, wefts, textures, sides, ends and knots, although no technical background is required for an understanding. 11 color plates, 80 halftones, 4 maps. vi + 320pp. 6⅛ x 9⅛.   22366-3 Paperbound $5.00

TEN BOOKS ON ARCHITECTURE, Vitruvius. By any standards the most important book on architecture ever written. Early Roman discussion of aesthetics of building, construction methods, orders, sites, and every other aspect of architecture has inspired, instructed architecture for about 2,000 years. Stands behind Palladio, Michelangelo, Bramante, Wren, countless others. Definitive Morris H. Morgan translation. 68 illustrations. xii + 331pp.   20645-9 Paperbound $3.00

THE FOUR BOOKS OF ARCHITECTURE, Andrea Palladio. Translated into every major Western European language in the two centuries following its publication in 1570, this has been one of the most influential books in the history of architecture. Complete reprint of the 1738 Isaac Ware edition. New introduction by Adolf Placzek, Columbia Univ. 216 plates. xxii + 110pp. of text. 9½ x 12¾.
21308-0 Clothbound $12.50

STICKS AND STONES: A STUDY OF AMERICAN ARCHITECTURE AND CIVILIZATION, Lewis Mumford. One of the great classics of American cultural history. American architecture from the medieval-inspired earliest forms to the early 20th century; evolution of structure and style, and reciprocal influences on environment. 21 photographic illustrations. 238pp.   20202-X Paperbound $2.00

THE AMERICAN BUILDER'S COMPANION, Asher Benjamin. The most widely used early 19th century architectural style and source book, for colonial up into Greek Revival periods. Extensive development of geometry of carpentering, construction of sashes, frames, doors, stairs; plans and elevations of domestic and other buildings. Hundreds of thousands of houses were built according to this book, now invaluable to historians, architects, restorers, etc. 1827 edition. 59 plates. 114pp. 7⅞ x 10¾.
22236-5 Paperbound $3.50

DUTCH HOUSES IN THE HUDSON VALLEY BEFORE 1776, Helen Wilkinson Reynolds. The standard survey of the Dutch colonial house and outbuildings, with constructional features, decoration, and local history associated with individual homesteads. Introduction by Franklin D. Roosevelt. Map. 150 illustrations. 469pp. 6⅝ x 9¼.   21469-9 Paperbound $5.00

THE ARCHITECTURE OF COUNTRY HOUSES, Andrew J. Downing. Together with Vaux's *Villas and Cottages* this is the basic book for Hudson River Gothic architecture of the middle Victorian period. Full, sound discussions of general aspects of housing, architecture, style, decoration, furnishing, together with scores of detailed house plans, illustrations of specific buildings, accompanied by full text. Perhaps the most influential single American architectural book. 1850 edition. Introduction by J. Stewart Johnson. 321 figures, 34 architectural designs. xvi + 560pp.

22003-6 Paperbound $4.00

LOST EXAMPLES OF COLONIAL ARCHITECTURE, John Mead Howells. Full-page photographs of buildings that have disappeared or been so altered as to be denatured, including many designed by major early American architects. 245 plates. xvii + 248pp. 7⅞ x 10¾.

21143-6 Paperbound $3.50

DOMESTIC ARCHITECTURE OF THE AMERICAN COLONIES AND OF THE EARLY REPUBLIC, Fiske Kimball. Foremost architect and restorer of Williamsburg and Monticello covers nearly 200 homes between 1620-1825. Architectural details, construction, style features, special fixtures, floor plans, etc. Generally considered finest work in its area. 219 illustrations of houses, doorways, windows, capital mantels. xx + 314pp. 7⅞ x 10¾.

21743-4 Paperbound $4.00

EARLY AMERICAN ROOMS: 1650-1858, edited by Russell Hawes Kettell. Tour of 12 rooms, each representative of a different era in American history and each furnished, decorated, designed and occupied in the style of the era. 72 plans and elevations, 8-page color section, etc., show fabrics, wall papers, arrangements, etc. Full descriptive text. xvii + 200pp. of text. 8⅜ x 11¼.

21633-0 Paperbound $5.00

THE FITZWILLIAM VIRGINAL BOOK, edited by J. Fuller Maitland and W. B. Squire. Full modern printing of famous early 17th-century ms. volume of 300 works by Morley, Byrd, Bull, Gibbons, etc. For piano or other modern keyboard instrument; easy to read format. xxxvi + 938pp. 8⅜ x 11.

21068-5, 21069-3 Two volumes, Paperbound $10.00

KEYBOARD MUSIC, Johann Sebastian Bach. Bach Gesellschaft edition. A rich selection of Bach's masterpieces for the harpsichord: the six English Suites, six French Suites, the six Partitas (Clavierübung part I), the Goldberg Variations (Clavierübung part IV), the fifteen Two-Part Inventions and the fifteen Three-Part Sinfonias. Clearly reproduced on large sheets with ample margins; eminently playable. vi + 312pp. 8⅛ x 11.

22360-4 Paperbound $5.00

THE MUSIC OF BACH: AN INTRODUCTION, Charles Sanford Terry. A fine, nontechnical introduction to Bach's music, both instrumental and vocal. Covers organ music, chamber music, passion music, other types. Analyzes themes, developments, innovations. x + 114pp.

21075-8 Paperbound $1.50

BEETHOVEN AND HIS NINE SYMPHONIES, Sir George Grove. Noted British musicologist provides best history, analysis, commentary on symphonies. Very thorough, rigorously accurate; necessary to both advanced student and amateur music lover. 436 musical passages. vii + 407 pp.

20334-4 Paperbound $2.75

JOHANN SEBASTIAN BACH, Philipp Spitta. One of the great classics of musicology, this definitive analysis of Bach's music (and life) has never been surpassed. Lucid, nontechnical analyses of hundreds of pieces (30 pages devoted to St. Matthew Passion, 26 to B Minor Mass). Also includes major analysis of 18th-century music. 450 musical examples. 40-page musical supplement. Total of xx + 1799pp.

(EUK) 22278-0, 22279-9 Two volumes, Clothbound $17.50

MOZART AND HIS PIANO CONCERTOS, Cuthbert Girdlestone. The only full-length study of an important area of Mozart's creativity. Provides detailed analyses of all 23 concertos, traces inspirational sources. 417 musical examples. Second edition. 509pp.

21271-8 Paperbound $3.50

THE PERFECT WAGNERITE: A COMMENTARY ON THE NIBLUNG'S RING, George Bernard Shaw. Brilliant and still relevant criticism in remarkable essays on Wagner's Ring cycle, Shaw's ideas on political and social ideology behind the plots, role of Leitmotifs, vocal requisites, etc. Prefaces. xxi + 136pp.

(USO) 21707-8 Paperbound $1.75

DON GIOVANNI, W. A. Mozart. Complete libretto, modern English translation; biographies of composer and librettist; accounts of early performances and critical reaction. Lavishly illustrated. All the material you need to understand and appreciate this great work. Dover Opera Guide and Libretto Series; translated and introduced by Ellen Bleiler. 92 illustrations. 209pp.

21134-7 Paperbound $2.00

BASIC ELECTRICITY, U. S. Bureau of Naval Personel. Originally a training course, best non-technical coverage of basic theory of electricity and its applications. Fundamental concepts, batteries, circuits, conductors and wiring techniques, AC and DC, inductance and capacitance, generators, motors, transformers, magnetic amplifiers, synchros, servomechanisms, etc. Also covers blue-prints, electrical diagrams, etc. Many questions, with answers. 349 illustrations. x + 448pp. 6½ x 9¼.

20973-3 Paperbound $3.50

REPRODUCTION OF SOUND, Edgar Villchur. Thorough coverage for laymen of high fidelity systems, reproducing systems in general, needles, amplifiers, preamps, loudspeakers, feedback, explaining physical background. "A rare talent for making technicalities vividly comprehensible," R. Darrell, *High Fidelity.* 69 figures. iv + 92pp.

21515-6 Paperbound $1.35

HEAR ME TALKIN' TO YA: THE STORY OF JAZZ AS TOLD BY THE MEN WHO MADE IT, Nat Shapiro and Nat Hentoff. Louis Armstrong, Fats Waller, Jo Jones, Clarence Williams, Billy Holiday, Duke Ellington, Jelly Roll Morton and dozens of other jazz greats tell how it was in Chicago's South Side, New Orleans, depression Harlem and the modern West Coast as jazz was born and grew. xvi + 429pp.

21726-4 Paperbound $3.00

FABLES OF AESOP, translated by Sir Roger L'Estrange. A reproduction of the very rare 1931 Paris edition; a selection of the most interesting fables, together with 50 imaginative drawings by Alexander Calder. v + 128pp. 6½x9¼.

21780-9 Paperbound $1.50

AGAINST THE GRAIN (A REBOURS), Joris K. Huysmans. Filled with weird images, evidences of a bizarre imagination, exotic experiments with hallucinatory drugs, rich tastes and smells and the diversions of its sybarite hero Duc Jean des Esseintes, this classic novel pushed 19th-century literary decadence to its limits. Full unabridged edition. Do not confuse this with abridged editions generally sold. Introduction by Havelock Ellis. xlix + 206pp. 22190-3 Paperbound $2.50

VARIORUM SHAKESPEARE: HAMLET. Edited by Horace H. Furness; a landmark of American scholarship. Exhaustive footnotes and appendices treat all doubtful words and phrases, as well as suggested critical emendations throughout the play's history. First volume contains editor's own text, collated with all Quartos and Folios. Second volume contains full first Quarto, translations of Shakespeare's sources (Belleforest, and Saxo Grammaticus), Der Bestrafte Brudermord, and many essays on critical and historical points of interest by major authorities of past and present. Includes details of staging and costuming over the years. By far the best edition available for serious students of Shakespeare. Total of xx + 905pp. 21004-9, 21005-7, 2 volumes, Paperbound $7.00

A LIFE OF WILLIAM SHAKESPEARE, Sir Sidney Lee. This is the standard life of Shakespeare, summarizing everything known about Shakespeare and his plays. Incredibly rich in material, broad in coverage, clear and judicious, it has served thousands as the best introduction to Shakespeare. 1931 edition. 9 plates. xxix + 792pp. 21967-4 Paperbound $4.50

MASTERS OF THE DRAMA, John Gassner. Most comprehensive history of the drama in print, covering every tradition from Greeks to modern Europe and America, including India, Far East, etc. Covers more than 800 dramatists, 2000 plays, with biographical material, plot summaries, theatre history, criticism, etc. "Best of its kind in English," *New Republic*. 77 illustrations. xxii + 890pp. 20100-7 Clothbound $10.00

THE EVOLUTION OF THE ENGLISH LANGUAGE, George McKnight. The growth of English, from the 14th century to the present. Unusual, non-technical account presents basic information in very interesting form: sound shifts, change in grammar and syntax, vocabulary growth, similar topics. Abundantly illustrated with quotations. Formerly *Modern English in the Making*. xii + 590pp. 21932-1 Paperbound $4.00

AN ETYMOLOGICAL DICTIONARY OF MODERN ENGLISH, Ernest Weekley. Fullest, richest work of its sort, by foremost British lexicographer. Detailed word histories, including many colloquial and archaic words; extensive quotations. Do not confuse this with the Concise Etymological Dictionary, which is much abridged. Total of xxvii + 830pp. 6½ x 9¼. 21873-2, 21874-0 Two volumes, Paperbound $7.90

FLATLAND: A ROMANCE OF MANY DIMENSIONS, E. A. Abbott. Classic of science-fiction explores ramifications of life in a two-dimensional world, and what happens when a three-dimensional being intrudes. Amusing reading, but also useful as introduction to thought about hyperspace. Introduction by Banesh Hoffmann. 16 illustrations. xx + 103pp. 20001-9 Paperbound $1.25

POEMS OF ANNE BRADSTREET, edited with an introduction by Robert Hutchinson. A new selection of poems by America's first poet and perhaps the first significant woman poet in the English language. 48 poems display her development in works of considerable variety—love poems, domestic poems, religious meditations, formal elegies, "quaternions," etc. Notes, bibliography. viii + 222pp.

22160-1 Paperbound $2.50

THREE GOTHIC NOVELS: THE CASTLE OF OTRANTO BY HORACE WALPOLE; VATHEK BY WILLIAM BECKFORD; THE VAMPYRE BY JOHN POLIDORI, WITH FRAGMENT OF A NOVEL BY LORD BYRON, edited by E. F. Bleiler. The first Gothic novel, by Walpole; the finest Oriental tale in English, by Beckford; powerful Romantic supernatural story in versions by Polidori and Byron. All extremely important in history of literature; all still exciting, packed with supernatural thrills, ghosts, haunted castles, magic, etc. xl + 291pp.

21232-7 Paperbound $2.50

THE BEST TALES OF HOFFMANN, E. T. A. Hoffmann. 10 of Hoffmann's most important stories, in modern re-editings of standard translations: Nutcracker and the King of Mice, Signor Formica, Automata, The Sandman, Rath Krespel, The Golden Flowerpot, Master Martin the Cooper, The Mines of Falun, The King's Betrothed, A New Year's Eve Adventure. 7 illustrations by Hoffmann. Edited by E. F. Bleiler. xxxix + 419pp.

21793-0 Paperbound $3.00

GHOST AND HORROR STORIES OF AMBROSE BIERCE, Ambrose Bierce. 23 strikingly modern stories of the horrors latent in the human mind: The Eyes of the Panther, The Damned Thing, An Occurrence at Owl Creek Bridge, An Inhabitant of Carcosa, etc., plus the dream-essay, Visions of the Night. Edited by E. F. Bleiler. xxii + 199pp.

20767-6 Paperbound $1.50

BEST GHOST STORIES OF J. S. LEFANU, J. Sheridan LeFanu. Finest stories by Victorian master often considered greatest supernatural writer of all. Carmilla, Green Tea, The Haunted Baronet, The Familiar, and 12 others. Most never before available in the U. S. A. Edited by E. F. Bleiler. 8 illustrations from Victorian publications. xvii + 467pp.

20415-4 Paperbound $3.00

MATHEMATICAL FOUNDATIONS OF INFORMATION THEORY, A. I. Khinchin. Comprehensive introduction to work of Shannon, McMillan, Feinstein and Khinchin, placing these investigations on a rigorous mathematical basis. Covers entropy concept in probability theory, uniqueness theorem, Shannon's inequality, ergodic sources, the E property, martingale concept, noise, Feinstein's fundamental lemma, Shanon's first and second theorems. Translated by R. A. Silverman and M. D. Friedman. iii + 120pp.

60434-9 Paperbound $2.00

SEVEN SCIENCE FICTION NOVELS, H. G. Wells. The standard collection of the great novels. Complete, unabridged. *First Men in the Moon, Island of Dr. Moreau, War of the Worlds, Food of the Gods, Invisible Man, Time Machine, In the Days of the Comet.* Not only science fiction fans, but every educated person owes it to himself to read these novels. 1015pp. (USO) 20264-X Clothbound $6.00

LAST AND FIRST MEN AND STAR MAKER, TWO SCIENCE FICTION NOVELS, Olaf Stapledon. Greatest future histories in science fiction. In the first, human intelligence is the "hero," through strange paths of evolution, interplanetary invasions, incredible technologies, near extinctions and reemergences. Star Maker describes the quest of a band of star rovers for intelligence itself, through time and space: weird inhuman civilizations, crustacean minds, symbiotic worlds, etc. Complete, unabridged. v + 438pp. (USO) 21962-3 Paperbound $2.50

THREE PROPHETIC NOVELS, H. G. WELLS. Stages of a consistently planned future for mankind. *When the Sleeper Wakes,* and *A Story of the Days to Come,* anticipate *Brave New World* and *1984,* in the 21st Century; *The Time Machine,* only complete version in print, shows farther future and the end of mankind. All show Wells's greatest gifts as storyteller and novelist. Edited by E. F. Bleiler. x + 335pp. (USO) 20605-X Paperbound $2.50

THE DEVIL'S DICTIONARY, Ambrose Bierce. America's own Oscar Wilde— Ambrose Bierce—offers his barbed iconoclastic wisdom in over 1,000 definitions hailed by H. L. Mencken as "some of the most gorgeous witticisms in the English language." 145pp. 20487-1 Paperbound $1.25

MAX AND MORITZ, Wilhelm Busch. Great children's classic, father of comic strip, of two bad boys, Max and Moritz. Also Ker and Plunk (Plisch und Plumm), Cat and Mouse, Deceitful Henry, Ice-Peter, The Boy and the Pipe, and five other pieces. Original German, with English translation. Edited by H. Arthur Klein; translations by various hands and H. Arthur Klein. vi + 216pp. 20181-3 Paperbound $2.00

PIGS IS PIGS AND OTHER FAVORITES, Ellis Parker Butler. The title story is one of the best humor short stories, as Mike Flannery obfuscates biology and English. Also included, That Pup of Murchison's, The Great American Pie Company, and Perkins of Portland. 14 illustrations. v + 109pp. 21532-6 Paperbound $1.25

THE PETERKIN PAPERS, Lucretia P. Hale. It takes genius to be as stupidly mad as the Peterkins, as they decide to become wise, celebrate the "Fourth," keep a cow, and otherwise strain the resources of the Lady from Philadelphia. Basic book of American humor. 153 illustrations. 219pp. 20794-3 Paperbound $2.00

PERRAULT'S FAIRY TALES, translated by A. E. Johnson and S. R. Littlewood, with 34 full-page illustrations by Gustave Doré. All the original Perrault stories— Cinderella, Sleeping Beauty, Bluebeard, Little Red Riding Hood, Puss in Boots, Tom Thumb, etc.—with their witty verse morals and the magnificent illustrations of Doré. One of the five or six great books of European fairy tales. viii + 117pp. 8⅛ x 11. 22311-6 Paperbound $2.00

OLD HUNGARIAN FAIRY TALES, Baroness Orczy. Favorites translated and adapted by author of the *Scarlet Pimpernel.* Eight fairy tales include "The Suitors of Princess Fire-Fly," "The Twin Hunchbacks," "Mr. Cuttlefish's Love Story," and "The Enchanted Cat." This little volume of magic and adventure will captivate children as it has for generations. 90 drawings by Montagu Barstow. 96pp. (USO) 22293-4 Paperbound $1.95

THE RED FAIRY BOOK, Andrew Lang. Lang's color fairy books have long been children's favorites. This volume includes Rapunzel, Jack and the Bean-stalk and 35 other stories, familiar and unfamiliar. 4 plates, 93 illustrations x + 367pp.
21673-X Paperbound $2.50

THE BLUE FAIRY BOOK, Andrew Lang. Lang's tales come from all countries and all times. Here are 37 tales from Grimm, the Arabian Nights, Greek Mythology, and other fascinating sources. 8 plates, 130 illustrations. xi + 390pp.
21437-0 Paperbound $2.75

HOUSEHOLD STORIES BY THE BROTHERS GRIMM. Classic English-language edition of the well-known tales — Rumpelstiltskin, Snow White, Hansel and Gretel, The Twelve Brothers, Faithful John, Rapunzel, Tom Thumb (52 stories in all). Translated into simple, straightforward English by Lucy Crane. Ornamented with headpieces, vignettes, elaborate decorative initials and a dozen full-page illustrations by Walter Crane. x + 269pp.
21080-4 Paperbound **$2.00**

THE MERRY ADVENTURES OF ROBIN HOOD, Howard Pyle. The finest modern versions of the traditional ballads and tales about the great English outlaw. Howard Pyle's complete prose version, with every word, every illustration of the first edition. Do not confuse this facsimile of the original (1883) with modern editions that change text or illustrations. 23 plates plus many page decorations. xxii + 296pp.
22043-5 Paperbound $2.75

THE STORY OF KING ARTHUR AND HIS KNIGHTS, Howard Pyle. The finest children's version of the life of King Arthur; brilliantly retold by Pyle, with 48 of his most imaginative illustrations. xviii + 313pp. 6⅛ x 9¼.
21445-1 Paperbound $2.50

THE WONDERFUL WIZARD OF OZ, L. Frank Baum. America's finest children's book in facsimile of first edition with all Denslow illustrations in full color. The edition a child should have. Introduction by Martin Gardner. 23 color plates, scores of drawings. iv + 267pp.
20691-2 Paperbound **$2.50**

THE MARVELOUS LAND OF OZ, L. Frank Baum. The second Oz book, every bit as imaginative as the Wizard. The hero is a boy named Tip, but the Scarecrow and the Tin Woodman are back, as is the Oz magic. 16 color plates, 120 drawings by John R. Neill. 287pp.
20692-0 Paperbound $2.50

THE MAGICAL MONARCH OF MO, L. Frank Baum. Remarkable adventures in a land even stranger than Oz. The best of Baum's books not in the Oz series. 15 color plates and dozens of drawings by Frank Verbeck. xviii + 237pp.
21892-9 Paperbound $2.25

THE BAD CHILD'S BOOK OF BEASTS, MORE BEASTS FOR WORSE CHILDREN, A MORAL ALPHABET, Hilaire Belloc. Three complete humor classics in one volume. Be kind to the frog, and do not call him names . . . and 28 other whimsical animals. Familiar favorites and some not so well known. Illustrated by Basil Blackwell. 156pp.
(USO) 20749-8 Paperbound $1.50

EAST O' THE SUN AND WEST O' THE MOON, George W. Dasent. Considered the best of all translations of these Norwegian folk tales, this collection has been enjoyed by generations of children (and folklorists too). Includes True and Untrue, Why the Sea is Salt, East O' the Sun and West O' the Moon, Why the Bear is Stumpy-Tailed, Boots and the Troll, The Cock and the Hen, Rich Peter the Pedlar, and 52 more. The only edition with all 59 tales. 77 illustrations by Erik Werenskiold and Theodor Kittelsen. xv + 418pp.   22521-6 Paperbound $3.50

GOOPS AND HOW TO BE THEM, Gelett Burgess. Classic of tongue-in-cheek humor, masquerading as etiquette book. 87 verses, twice as many cartoons, show mischievous Goops as they demonstrate to children virtues of table manners, neatness, courtesy, etc. Favorite for generations. viii + 88pp. 6½ x 9¼.
22233-0 Paperbound $1.50

ALICE'S ADVENTURES UNDER GROUND, Lewis Carroll. The first version, quite different from the final Alice in Wonderland, printed out by Carroll himself with his own illustrations. Complete facsimile of the "million dollar" manuscript Carroll gave to Alice Liddell in 1864. Introduction by Martin Gardner. viii + 96pp. Title and dedication pages in color.   21482-6 Paperbound $1.25

THE BROWNIES, THEIR BOOK, Palmer Cox. Small as mice, cunning as foxes, exuberant and full of mischief, the Brownies go to the zoo, toy shop, seashore, circus, etc., in 24 verse adventures and 266 illustrations. Long a favorite, since their first appearance in St. Nicholas Magazine. xi + 144pp. 6⅝ x 9¼.
21265-3 Paperbound $1.75

SONGS OF CHILDHOOD, Walter De La Mare. Published (under the pseudonym Walter Ramal) when De La Mare was only 29, this charming collection has long been a favorite children's book. A facsimile of the first edition in paper, the 47 poems capture the simplicity of the nursery rhyme and the ballad, including such lyrics as I Met Eve, Tartary, The Silver Penny. vii + 106pp. (USO) 21972-0 Paperbound
$2.00

THE COMPLETE NONSENSE OF EDWARD LEAR, Edward Lear. The finest 19th-century humorist-cartoonist in full: all nonsense limericks, zany alphabets, Owl and Pussycat, songs, nonsense botany, and more than 500 illustrations by Lear himself. Edited by Holbrook Jackson. xxix + 287pp.   (USO) 20167-8 Paperbound $2.00

BILLY WHISKERS: THE AUTOBIOGRAPHY OF A GOAT, Frances Trego Montgomery. A favorite of children since the early 20th century, here are the escapades of that rambunctious, irresistible and mischievous goat—Billy Whiskers. Much in the spirit of Peck's Bad Boy, this is a book that children never tire of reading or hearing. All the original familiar illustrations by W. H. Fry are included: 6 color plates, 18 black and white drawings. 159pp.   22345-0 Paperbound $2.00

MOTHER GOOSE MELODIES. Faithful republication of the fabulously rare Munroe and Francis "copyright 1833" Boston edition—the most important Mother Goose collection, usually referred to as the "original." Familiar rhymes plus many rare ones, with wonderful old woodcut illustrations. Edited by E. F. Bleiler. 128pp. 4½ x 6⅜.   22577-1 Paperbound $1.00

TWO LITTLE SAVAGES; BEING THE ADVENTURES OF TWO BOYS WHO LIVED AS INDIANS AND WHAT THEY LEARNED, Ernest Thompson Seton. Great classic of nature and boyhood provides a vast range of woodlore in most palatable form, a genuinely entertaining story. Two farm boys build a teepee in woods and live in it for a month, working out Indian solutions to living problems, star lore, birds and animals, plants, etc. 293 illustrations. vii + 286pp.

20985-7 Paperbound $2.50

PETER PIPER'S PRACTICAL PRINCIPLES OF PLAIN & PERFECT PRONUNCIATION. Alliterative jingles and tongue-twisters of surprising charm, that made their first appearance in America about 1830. Republished in full with the spirited woodcut illustrations from this earliest American edition. 32pp. 4½ x 6⅜.

22560-7 Paperbound $1.00

SCIENCE EXPERIMENTS AND AMUSEMENTS FOR CHILDREN, Charles Vivian. 73 easy experiments, requiring only materials found at home or easily available, such as candles, coins, steel wool, etc.; illustrate basic phenomena like vacuum, simple chemical reaction, etc. All safe. Modern, well-planned. Formerly *Science Games for Children*. 102 photos, numerous drawings. 96pp. 6⅛ x 9¼.

21856-2 Paperbound $1.25

AN INTRODUCTION TO CHESS MOVES AND TACTICS SIMPLY EXPLAINED, Leonard Barden. Informal intermediate introduction, quite strong in explaining reasons for moves. Covers basic material, tactics, important openings, traps, positional play in middle game, end game. Attempts to isolate patterns and recurrent configurations. Formerly *Chess*. 58 figures. 102pp. (USO) 21210-6 Paperbound $1.25

LASKER'S MANUAL OF CHESS, Dr. Emanuel Lasker. Lasker was not only one of the five great World Champions, he was also one of the ablest expositors, theorists, and analysts. In many ways, his Manual, permeated with his philosophy of battle, filled with keen insights, is one of the greatest works ever written on chess. Filled with analyzed games by the great players. A single-volume library that will profit almost any chess player, beginner or master. 308 diagrams. xli x 349pp.

20640-8 Paperbound $2.75

THE MASTER BOOK OF MATHEMATICAL RECREATIONS, Fred Schuh. In opinion of many the finest work ever prepared on mathematical puzzles, stunts, recreations; exhaustively thorough explanations of mathematics involved, analysis of effects, citation of puzzles and games. Mathematics involved is elementary. Translated by F. Göbel. 194 figures. xxiv + 430pp. 22134-2 Paperbound $3.50

MATHEMATICS, MAGIC AND MYSTERY, Martin Gardner. Puzzle editor for Scientific American explains mathematics behind various mystifying tricks: card tricks, stage "mind reading," coin and match tricks, counting out games, geometric dissections, etc. Probability sets, theory of numbers clearly explained. Also provides more than 400 tricks, guaranteed to work, that you can do. 135 illustrations. xii + 176pp.

20335-2 Paperbound $1.75

MATHEMATICAL PUZZLES FOR BEGINNERS AND ENTHUSIASTS, Geoffrey Mott-Smith. 189 puzzles from easy to difficult—involving arithmetic, logic, algebra, properties of digits, probability, etc.—for enjoyment and mental stimulus. Explanation of mathematical principles behind the puzzles. 135 illustrations. viii + 248pp.
20198-8 Paperbound $1.75

PAPER FOLDING FOR BEGINNERS, William D. Murray and Francis J. Rigney. Easiest book on the market, clearest instructions on making interesting, beautiful origami. Sail boats, cups, roosters, frogs that move legs, bonbon boxes, standing birds, etc. 40 projects; more than 275 diagrams and photographs. 94pp.
20713-7 Paperbound $1.00

TRICKS AND GAMES ON THE POOL TABLE, Fred Herrmann. 79 tricks and games— some solitaires, some for two or more players, some competitive games—to entertain you between formal games. Mystifying shots and throws, unusual caroms, tricks involving such props as cork, coins, a hat, etc. Formerly *Fun on the Pool Table*. 77 figures. 95pp.
21814-7 Paperbound $1.25

HAND SHADOWS TO BE THROWN UPON THE WALL: A SERIES OF NOVEL AND AMUSING FIGURES FORMED BY THE HAND, Henry Bursill. Delightful picturebook from great-grandfather's day shows how to make 18 different hand shadows: a bird that flies, duck that quacks, dog that wags his tail, camel, goose, deer, boy, turtle, etc. Only book of its sort. vi + 33pp. 6½ x 9¼.   21779-5 Paperbound $1.00

WHITTLING AND WOODCARVING, E. J. Tangerman. 18th printing of best book on market. "If you can cut a potato you can carve" toys and puzzles, chains, chessmen, caricatures, masks, frames, woodcut blocks, surface patterns, much more. Information on tools, woods, techniques. Also goes into serious wood sculpture from Middle Ages to present, East and West. 464 photos, figures. x + 293pp.
20965-2 Paperbound $2.00

HISTORY OF PHILOSOPHY, Julián Marías. Possibly the clearest, most easily followed, best planned, most useful one-volume history of philosophy on the market; neither skimpy nor overfull. Full details on system of every major philosopher and dozens of less important thinkers from pre-Socratics up to Existentialism and later. Strong on many European figures usually omitted. Has gone through dozens of editions in Europe. 1966 edition, translated by Stanley Appelbaum and Clarence Strowbridge. xviii + 505pp.
21739-6 Paperbound $3.50

YOGA: A SCIENTIFIC EVALUATION, Kovoor T. Behanan. Scientific but non-technical study of physiological results of yoga exercises; done under auspices of Yale U. Relations to Indian thought, to psychoanalysis, etc. 16 photos. xxiii + 270pp.
20505-3 Paperbound $2.50

Prices subject to change without notice.
Available at your book dealer or write for free catalogue to Dept. GI, Dover Publications, Inc., 180 Varick St., N. Y., N. Y. 10014. Dover publishes more than 150 books each year on science, elementary and advanced mathematics, biology, music, art, literary history, social sciences and other areas.